Good Housekeeping

NEW RECIPE BOOK

Good Housekeeping

NEW
RECIPE
BOOK

OVER 300 GREAT RECIPES FOR BUSY PEOPLE

Felicity Barnum-Bobb
The Good Housekeeping Cook

Frank Wieder
Special Photography

HarperCollins*Publishers*

First published in 2001 by
HarperCollinsPublishers
77–85 Fulham Palace Road
London W6 8JB

The HarperCollins website address is:
www.**fire**and**water**.com

05 04 03 02 01 00
9 8 7 6 5 4 3 2 1

Published in association with The National
Magazine Company Limited
Good Housekeeping is a registered trade
mark of
The National Magazine Company Limited

The Good Housekeeping website address is:
www.goodhousekeeping.com

A CIP catalogue record for this book is
available from the British Library

ISBN: 0 00711691 8

Colour reproduction by Saxon Photo Litho
Printed and bound in the Hong Kong by
Printing Express

This book is typeset in Gillsans, GillSans Light
and GillSans Bold.

contents

Foreword

There are so many cookery books to choose from, so many TV chefs offering advice; you might wonder why you would need this book. One good reason is that all the recipes (over 300) have been triple tested – that means after you've gone to all the effort of buying and preparing the food we can guarantee that the recipe will work and, most importantly, taste fantastic, thanks to our team of dedicated recipe testers in the GHI.

I recently visited Vermont and, wow, the Americans really know how to breakfast! I was so impressed that it inspired our opening chapter, Wake-up Calls. Why not treat yourselves to a long, lazy morning feast at the weekend? When you need a quick-fix bite to eat or have friends for tea try some of our wicked snacks, such as Sticky Ginger Ring, Ultimate Chocolate Brownie, or the savoury Hot Spiced Nuts or Mini Ham Pastry Croissants – everyone will appreciate the effort.

I'm a working mother with three small children so I know how important it is to have speedy, but satisfying midweek meals and there is lots of choice here. Need inspiration for packed lunches for children and for yourself at work? We've lots of great ideas in the Packed To Go chapter – Courgette and Parmesan Frittata is one of my favourites. Looking for an impressive dinner party dish? Turn to Main Events where you'll find imaginative combinations with practical advice on what to prepare ahead, so you can have fun with your guests and not be left slaving in the kitchen. Only have 30 minutes to make a scrumptious pud? No problem – why not try the easy Sticky Banoffee Pies or, for something more elaborate, the Caramelised Citrus Tart is bound to become a favourite.

There will be no need to make do with a simple gin and tonic again once you've pored over our final Liquid Refreshments chapter. Treat yourself to the best ever Bloody Mary and settle down with this book to decide what you're going to make first. Here are my tips on creating the ultimate eating experience that I hope you'll find helpful.

10 ways to make that special meal a success

1. Plan ahead – find out if anyone has any special dietary requirements.

2. Write down your menu and reflect on it overnight, to check if it still sounds good in the morning.

3. Make your shopping list – dividing it into sections for meat, vegetable's, etc.

4. Always use fresh herbs, buy meat from the butcher's if you can, check fish and vegetables are at their best. Gently squeeze fruit – it should 'give' a little when it's sufficiently ripe to guarantee a good flavour.

5. Prepare as much as possible in advance – so you remain perky enough to enjoy the meal, too.

6. Think about your table setting. I always use classic white china with crisp linen napkins.

7. Serve hot food on warm plates.

8. Chill your wine, and have plenty of bottled water in the fridge, too.

9. Don't be over ambitious – it's far better to serve one dish that tastes amazing and looks impressive, rather than lots of fiddly little bits that will look a muddle and where the flavours may clash.

10. Aim to have everything finished 20 minutes before everyone arrives so you can compose yourself.

Happy cooking!

Felicity

Felicity Barnum-Bobb
The Good Housekeeping Cook

Introduction

These few simple hints and tips, with advice on preparation, menu planning and a full explanation of some of the cooking equipment you may find useful, will help you to create the recipes with ease. There are also comprehensive conversion tables for weights, measurements and oven temperatures.

Kitchen equipment

Although a good cook needs very few tools, there are some basic utensils that will be needed for preparing recipes and that will make life easier in the kitchen.

To ensure success when cooking always try to use the correct amounts of ingredients; the following items are recommended:

Scales A good set of scales is necessary for measuring ingredients given in weights; we recommend flat digital display ones that give both metric and imperial weights for easy storage and flexible weighing options.

Measuring jugs are essential for liquid measurements; the best have metric and imperial markings.

Measuring spoons are crucial for consistent results, particularly when baking. You can buy them in sets of ¼ teaspoon (1.25ml), ½ teaspoon (2.5ml), 1 teaspoon (5ml) and 1 tablespoon (15ml).

Other than general cooking equipment including a good selection of wooden spoons, bakeware and ovenware, the following items are also useful:

Vegetable peeler There are several really good types available, the ones with swivel blades are particularly good and look for those with a pointed tip for coring.

Kitchen scissors Ideal for snipping and chopping herbs, they should be made of stainless steel for easy cleaning.

Cutting boards Keep several boards for different purposes, separate ones for raw meats, and strong-smelling foods such as garlic and onions.

Slotted spoons These are wide, flat spoons with holes, ideal for lifting and draining foods out of hot sauces, stocks, oil and other liquids.

Grater There's a whole variety of different graters – try to find one that is multi-purpose (Microplane are most efficient), for finely grating citrus rind and grating cheese and vegetables.

Fish slice You can buy metal or plastic ones for lifting delicate flat foods, with holes in to let cooking liquids and fats drain off.

Palette knife This has a thin blade and is flexible, with a rounded end. Use for turning pancakes and for spreading icing.

Lemon squeezer Glass, plastic and wooden hand-held juicers work well. Check that trendy stainless steel types are designed for lemons, not larger fruit.

Potato masher Choose a good strong masher with the smallest possible grid to mash carrots, potatoes and other root vegetables.

Pans Good pans need to be heavy enough to sit well on the oven top, but not too heavy to lift. The best have fireproof and heatproof handles. You will need various sizes of pans, as well as a good non-stick frying pan. Frying pans that are also ovenproof are a good investment, too. A wok is ideal for stir-frying.

Knives Every cook should have these basic knives: you'll need one small vegetable knife for peeling and segmenting; a large cook's knife for chopping; a small serrated blade for cutting and peeling soft fruits; a bread knife and a long, thin carving knife.

Casseroles These are essential items. Buy the largest one you can afford and check that it is flameproof for use on top of the stove as well as in the oven.

Machines A food processor is ideal for chopping, mincing and puréeing. You can also buy hand-held blenders – ideal for making purées, soups and dips. Freestanding mixers are best for whisking, whipping, cakes and breadmaking.

Preparation

The secret to success and enjoying your cooking is to plan ahead where possible. Read through the recipe fully before you start cooking to make sure that everything is at your fingertips when you need it. For stir-frying, for example, the vegetables will need to be prepared and cut to size so everything can be cooked in minutes, without the need to stop and fetch or chop something. Sometimes a dish may need to be marinated for a few hours or overnight. You may be able to make pastries and batters ahead of cooking a dish to save time on the actual day, especially if preparing for a dinner party. It's also worth building up a storecupboard of non-perishable essential items, such as soy sauce, olive and vegetable oils, some sauces, sea salt and black pepper and a good spice selection, cans of beans and lentils to cut down the time needed to soak and cook dried beans, and a selection of dried pastas. You could even make your own flavoured oils, to keep as a standby, by adding herbs, garlic or chillies to oils; these are ideal for salads and sauces. Garnishes and decoration are also a core part of any meal, as is the table setting and the choice of crockery and cutlery. Attention to the way the food is presented is all part and parcel of the enjoyment of a meal.

Menu planning

Try to create a balance when planning any menu, whether it's an informal supper, family gathering, or a celebratory dinner. Make sure the dishes complement one another and try to create contrasts of flavours and textures and even colours. You may want a light starter to accompany a heartier or rich main course, or you may want to plan your meal around a dessert. Some dishes may call for a good selection of vegetables served on the side, or a salad may be better after a one-pot dish that includes everything that is needed for a complete meal. You may need an accompaniment such as potatoes, rice or bread to soak up delicious juices or to give a dish more substance. It's always a good idea, too, to find out any likes and dislikes of guests when preparing for a dinner party and, of course, find out if there are any vegetarians.

Shopping

Go through your recipes carefully and ensure you have all the basic storecupboard ingredients – and that they are not out of date! Make a comprehensive shopping list and always buy the best quality ingredients as fresh as possible – it really makes a difference to the end result, especially to such things as salads, lightly cooked dishes and, of course, fish and meat dishes. However, you may have to buy ahead to make sure that fruit and vegetables are ripe enough for the recipe. You can always ask your fishmonger and butcher for help and advice on the best cuts and cooking times. Don't be shy either of asking your fishmonger to fillet, skin or descale the fish, or the butcher to bone, slice or cut the meat to whatever specifications you want – anything to make life easier.

Cooking times

The cooking times given are also approximate and vary according to different ovens, the size and thickness of a meat or fish and various other factors, so always check to see if a dish is cooked. For meat pierce with a knife in the thickest part of the flesh to see if it is done, or press it to see if it yields to pressure – the less it yields the more well done it is. For chicken always pierce with a knife in the thickest part of the joint or between the thigh and the body; if the juices run clear it is done. After cooking, cover meat with foil and let it rest for about 10 minutes before carving.

Conversion Tables

All the recipes in this book are given in both metric and imperial. When cooking always follow either metric or imperial measurements, never mix the two. The only exception is when specific packet sizes are given; these are in metric only as they are sold as such. All fruits and vegetables are medium-sized unless otherwise stated. Milk is full fat unless otherwise stated. All spoon measurements are level unless otherwise stated. Black Pepper is always freshly ground unless otherwise stated. All recipes have nutritional information. These analyses are approximate, based on average values, and give values per portion.

Weights

The metric conversions are approximate rather than precise, to make cooking and weighing out simpler. The actual metric conversion of 1oz is 28g. When references to teaspoon and tablespoon measurements are made, a teaspoon is equivalent to a 5ml measuring spoon and a tablespoon is equivalent to a 15ml measuring spoon.

15g	½oz	400g	14oz	850g	1lb 14oz
25g	1oz	425g	15oz	875g	1lb 15oz
40g	1½oz	450g	1lb	900g	2lb
50g	2oz	475g	1lb 1oz	1kg	2¼lb
75g	3oz	500g	1lb 2oz	1.1kg	2½lb
100g	3½oz	525g	1lb 3oz	1.25kg	2¾lb
125g	4oz	550g	1lb 4oz	1.4kg	3lb
150g	5oz	575g	1lb 5oz	1.5kg	3¼lb
175g	6oz	625g	1lb 6oz	1.6kg	3½lb
200g	7oz	650g	1lb 7oz	1.7kg	3¾lb
225g	8oz	700g	1½lb	1.8kg	4lb
250g	9oz	725g	1lb 9oz	2kg	4½lb
275g	10oz	750g	1lb 10oz	2.3kg	5lb
300g	11oz	775g	1lb 11oz	2.5kg	5½lb
350g	12oz	800g	1lb 12oz	2.7kg	6lb
375g	13oz	825g	1lb 13oz		

Volume

25ml	1fl oz	500ml	17fl oz
40ml	1½fl oz	525ml	18fl oz
50ml	2fl oz	550ml	19fl oz
65ml	2½fl oz	600ml	1pt
75ml	3fl oz	750ml	1¼pt
100ml	3½fl oz	900ml	1½pt
120ml	4fl oz	1ltr	1¾pt
150ml	5fl oz	1.1ltr	2pt
175ml	6fl oz	1.3ltr	2¼pt
200ml	7fl oz	1.4ltr	2½pt
225ml	8fl oz	1.7ltr	3pt
250ml	9fl oz	1.8ltr	3¼pt
300ml	10fl oz	2ltr	3½pt
325ml	11fl oz	2.1ltr	3¾pt
350ml	12fl oz	2.3ltr	4pt
375ml	13fl oz	2.6ltr	4½pt
400ml	14fl oz	2.8ltr	5pt
450ml	15fl oz	3.1ltr	5½pt
475ml	16fl oz	3.4ltr	6pt

15ml	1 tbsp
30ml	2 tbsp
30ml	3 tbsp
60ml	4 tbsp
75ml	5 tbsp
90ml	6 tbsp

Measurements

2.5cm	1in	15cm	6in
3cm	1¼in	16cm	6½in
4cm	1½in	18cm	7in
4.5cm	1¾in	19cm	7½in
5cm	2in	20cm	8in
6cm	2½in	23cm	9in
7.5cm	3in	24cm	9½in
9cm	3½in	25cm	10in
10cm	4in	28cm	11in
13cm	5in	30cm	12in

Oven Temperatures

All regular oven and fan oven temperatures shown are in Centigrade.

Gas Mark	Regular Oven	Fan Oven
¼	100	90
½	130	110
1	140	120
2	150	130
3	170	150
4	180	160
5	190	170
6	200	180
7	220	200
8	230	210
9	240	220

wake-up calls

Smoked Haddock and Bacon Bites

potatoes	350g (12oz), peeled
butter	40g (1½oz)
smoked haddock	450g (1lb)
smoked streaky bacon	4 rashers, about 125g (4oz) total weight, rind removed
chopped fresh chives	2 tbsp
large egg	1, beaten
fresh white breadcrumbs	75g (3oz)
oil	for deep frying
lemon slices and	
fresh flat-leaf parsley	to garnish
diced tomato, seasoned	
with black peppercorns	
and Tabasco	to accompany

1. Cook the potatoes in boiling salted water for 20 minutes or until tender. Drain, return to the pan and dry over a low heat for a few minutes, then mash them with the butter.

2. Meanwhile, put the haddock, skin-side up, in a pan with just enough water to cover. Bring to the boil and simmer gently for 10 minutes or until just cooked. Remove the fish from the pan and, when cool enough to handle, skin and flake the flesh. Grill the bacon for 5 minutes or until crisp. Cool and then crumble into small pieces.

3. In a bowl, mix the mashed potato, haddock, bacon and chives together until well combined. Season with pepper. Shape into 20 golf ball-sized pieces. Dip each in beaten egg, then roll in breadcrumbs to coat.

4. Heat the oil to 190°C (375°F) or until a cube of bread sizzles. Deep fry the haddock bites until golden and crisp, then drain on kitchen paper. Garnish with lemon and parsley and serve with the tomato.

Preparation time: 30 min   **Cooking time:** 35 min
Cals per serving: 580   **Serves:** 4

Kedgeree

butter	50g (2oz)
onions	700g (1½lb), sliced
garam masala	2 tsp
garlic clove	1, crushed
split green lentils	75g (3oz), soaked in 300ml (10fl oz) boiling water for 15 min, then drained
vegetable stock	750ml (1¼ pt)
basmati rice	225g (8oz)
green chilli	1, deseeded and finely chopped
salmon fillet	350g (12oz)
fresh coriander sprigs	to garnish

1. Melt the butter in a flameproof casserole. Add the onions and cook for 5 minutes or until soft. Remove one-third and put to one side. Increase the heat and cook the remaining onions for 10 minutes to caramelise. Remove and put to one side.

2. Return the first batch of onions to the casserole, add the garam masala and garlic and cook, stirring, for 1 minute. Add the drained lentils and stock, cover and cook for 15 minutes. Add the rice and chilli, season, bring to the boil, then cover and simmer for 5 minutes.

3. Put the salmon fillet on top of the rice, cover and continue to cook gently for 15 minutes, or until the rice is cooked, the stock is absorbed and the salmon opaque.

4. Lift the salmon and divide into flakes. Return the salmon to the casserole and fork through the rice. Garnish with the reserved caramelised onions and coriander and serve.

Preparation time: 15 min, plus 15 min soaking
Cooking time: 15 min   **Cals per serving:** 540   **Serves:** 4

Smoked Cod
Rarebit

milk	450ml (15fl oz)
bay leaf	1
parsley	2 tbsp
onion	1, sliced
lemon, preferably unwaxed	2 slices
undyed smoked cod loin	2, about 175g (6oz) each, skinned
crusty white bread	2 thick slices
mature cheddar	125g (4oz), grated
small egg	1, beaten
double cream	4 tbsp
Dijon mustard	1 tsp
Worcestershire sauce	1 tsp
butter	25g (1oz), softened

1. Preheat the grill to high. Heat the milk, bay leaf, parsley, onion and lemon together in a small deep-sided frying pan and add the fish. Poach for 6 to 8 minutes or until the fish is cooked through.

2. Remove the fish from the pan with a fish slice and discard the milk.

3. Toast the bread on both sides until golden, then place in a dish.

4. Mix together 75g (3oz) of the cheddar, the egg, cream, mustard, Worcestershire sauce, butter and a pinch of pepper in a bowl. Place the fish on the toast, top with the cheese mixture and sprinkle over the remaining cheese.

5. Place on the lower shelf of the grill and cook for 5 to 6 minutes, until the cheese topping is bubbling, golden and set. Serve straight away.

Preparation time: 15 min **Cooking time:** 15 min
Cals per serving: 738 **Serves:** 2

Bacon and
Tuna Hash

new potatoes	450g (1lb), cut into small chunks
butter	25g (1oz)
streaky bacon or lardons	125g (4oz), cut into 2.5cm (1in) strips
large onion	1, roughly chopped
pitted green or black olives	125g (4oz), chopped
tuna in oil	200g can, drained and flaked
fresh coriander sprigs	to garnish

1. Cook the potatoes in boiling salted water for 5 to 10 minutes or until beginning to soften. Drain and set aside.

2. Melt the butter in a non-stick frying pan, add the bacon and cook on a medium heat until beginning to brown, then add the onion. Cook for 5 minutes or until soft. Add the potatoes and olives. Turn down the heat and cook for 10 minutes.

3. Using a spatula, turn the hash over and continue to cook for a further 10 minutes, turning every now and again. Add the tuna and cook for a further 4 to 5 minutes or until the potatoes are done to the centre and the tuna is hot.

4. Season with salt and pepper and garnish with coriander sprigs.

Preparation time: 10 min **Cooking time:** 35 min
Cals per serving: 328 **Serves:** 4

Crab Cakes with Hazelnut Dressing

milk	150ml (5fl oz)
single cream	150ml (5fl oz)
onion	1 slice
carrot	1 slice
celery	1 slice
small bay leaf	1
black peppercorns	3
butter	25g (1oz), plus extra for cooling sauce
plain flour	25g (1oz)
ground white pepper	
medium eggs	2, beaten
parmesan	25g (1oz), grated
lemon	½, rind finely grated
white crabmeat	450g (1lb)
ciabatta loaf breadcrumbs	125g (4oz)
clarified butter	for frying (see below)
salad leaves and lime wedges	to accompany

For the hazelnut dressing

white wine vinegar	2 tbsp
runny honey	2 tsp
olive oil	4 tbsp
hazelnut oil	2 tbsp

1. Put the milk, cream, vegetable slices, bay leaf and peppercorns in a saucepan and slowly bring to the boil. Remove from the heat, cover and set aside to infuse for 30 minutes. Strain, reserving the milk. Melt the butter in a saucepan, stir in the flour and cook gently for 1 minute, stirring. Remove from the heat and gradually stir in the reserved milk. Bring to the boil and continue to cook, stirring, until the sauce thickens. Remove from the heat, season and smear the top with a little extra butter to prevent a skin forming. Allow to cool.

2. Mix the eggs, parmesan and lemon rind into the cold sauce until well combined. Very lightly mix in the chunks of crabmeat, taking care not to break them up. Chill for at least 1 hour.

3. Gently coat one large serving spoon of crabmeat mixture with the breadcrumbs. Scoop the breadcrumbs over and around the crabmeat to help shape the cake. Only mould it sufficiently to make the crumbs stick. Repeat the process with the remaining crabmeat mixture. Place on a baking sheet and chill uncovered, for 2 to 3 hours.

4. Heat the clarified butter in a frying pan. Add the crab cakes, and fry for 1 to 2 minutes on each side, until golden all over. Take care not to overcook the cakes.

5. To make the hazelnut dressing, shake all the ingredients together in a screw-topped jar. Accompany the crab cakes with salad leaves tossed in the dressing and lime wedges.

Clarified Butter: Melt some butter in a small pan and heat gently without allowing it to colour. Skim off the foam as it rises to the top, leaving the milk solids to sink to the bottom. Pour the clear butter into a bowl through a sieve lined with kitchen paper. Allow to settle for 10 minutes, then pour into another bowl, leaving any sediment behind. Cool, then store in a jar in the fridge for up to six months.

Preparation time: 25 min, plus 30 min standing and 3–4 hr chilling
Cooking time: 15 min   **Cals per serving:** 405   **Serves:** 6

Crab Cakes with
Hazelnut Dressing

A healthy hearty
breakfast: Lemon and
Blueberry Pancakes and
Golden Honey Fruits

Family Breakfast: A healthy, **hearty** breakfast will set you and **your family** up for the whole day. Mix **cooked breakfasts** with **fresh fruits and juices**. If you have time there is nothing like **freshly baked muffins** enjoyed after a **steaming bowl of kedgeree**. Even the laziest member of the family will be tempted out of bed by the thought of **Lemon and Blueberry Pancakes,** make the **batter** and the **blueberry syrup** the night before and **deliver them sizzling** to the table in seconds. It's got to be the most **delicious** start to the day. Serve **Golden Honey Fruits**, made from **colourful exotic fruits** drizzled with **plenty of honey** and then **grilled until caramelised**, on the side.

Hash Browns with Smoked Salmon
and Scrambled Eggs

potatoes	1.4kg (3lb), unpeeled, cut into 2.5cm (1in) chunks
butter	25g (1oz)
olive oil	2 tbsp
spring onions	1 bunch, finely sliced on the diagonal

For the scrambled eggs

butter	25g (1oz)
shallots	50g (2oz), chopped
large eggs	10, beaten
soured cream	4 tbsp
smoked salmon	450g (1lb), sliced to accompany
crushed black peppercorns and spring onion curls	to garnish

1. To make the hash browns, bring a large pan of salted water to the boil. Add the potatoes, bring back to the boil and cook for 3 minutes. Drain well and dry on kitchen paper. Heat the butter and oil in a large frying pan, add the potatoes and cook for 8 minutes, scraping the crispy bits from the bottom of the pan. Add the spring onions and seasoning and cook for a further 1 to 2 minutes or until the potatoes are golden and crisp. Cover with a lid or a piece of foil and keep warm.

2. To make the scrambled eggs, heat the butter in a large heavy-based frying pan, preferably non-stick, add the shallots and cook for 3 minutes until softened. Place the eggs and soured cream in a bowl with a little seasoning and whisk lightly together. Add the egg mixture to the shallots and cook, stirring with a fork for about 1 minute, bringing the set eggs in from the side of the pan to the centre. When the eggs are just starting to set, remove the pan from the heat – be careful not to overcook the eggs.

3. Serve the scrambled eggs over the hash browns, with the smoked salmon on top. Garnish with crushed black peppercorns and spring onion curls, then serve.

Preparation time: 20 min   **Cooking time:** 20 min
Cals per serving: 397   **Serves:** 6

Hash Browns with Smoked Salmon and Scrambled Eggs

Sausage Hash Browns

butter	50g (2oz)
small onion	1, chopped
potatoes	700g (1½lb), cooked in their skins until almost tender, then diced
chopped fresh thyme	2 tsp
pork sausages	450g (1lb)
red onions	450g (1lb), cut into 5mm (¼in) rings
sunflower oil	for brushing
small tomatoes	450g (1lb), halved

1. Melt the butter in a non-stick frying pan. Fry the onion for 1 minute. Add the potatoes and fry on a moderate heat, turning frequently, for 25 minutes or until crisp and brown. Season and add the thyme.

2. Meanwhile, grill the sausages for about 20 minutes, until browned and cooked to the centre. Brush the onion rings with sunflower oil and grill until cooked and caramelised. Grill the tomatoes at the same time.

3. Serve the sausages on top of the hash browns with the onions and tomatoes on the side.

Preparation time: 15 min   **Cooking time:** 30 min
Cals per serving: 740   **Serves:** 4

Sausages in Red Onion Marmalade

1. Preheat the oven to 200°C/180°C fan oven/Gas Mark 6. Melt half the butter in a roasting tin or a 2 litre (3½ pint) shallow flameproof dish, then fry the sausages until lightly browned. Lift out and set aside. Gently fry the onions in the remaining butter for 10 to 15 minutes or until soft.

2. Stir in the remaining ingredients, season, bring to the boil and bubble for 2 minutes or until reduced by half. Place the sausages on top of the onions so they continue to brown when cooking then place the dish, uncovered, in the oven. Cook for about 45 minutes, stirring occasionally. The onions should be soft, golden and glazed with the pan juices – if the juices are too concentrated, stir in 4 tablespoons of boiling water. Garnish with parsley and serve.

Preparation time: 5 min   **Cooking time:** 1 hr 5 min
Cals per serving: 860   **Serves:** 4

butter	50g (2oz)
good quality sausages	900g (2lb)
large red onions	3, about 700g (1½lb), thinly sliced
chopped fresh or dried thyme	1 tbsp fresh or 1 tsp dried
red wine	225ml (8fl oz)
red wine vinegar	4 tbsp
sugar	1 tbsp
fresh flat-leaf parsley	to garnish

Eggs Benedict

very fresh medium eggs 4, preferably organic
ham slices, or grilled bacon rashers 4
English muffins 4, split and toasted
chopped fresh parsley to garnish

For the hollandaise sauce
white wine vinegar 2 tbsp, plus extra to poach
black peppercorns 9, crushed
large egg yolks 2 (or 3 medium)
unsalted butter 250g (9oz), cubed
lemon juice 2 tsp

1. To make the sauce, put 2 tablespoons of vinegar in a small pan with 2 tablespoons of water and the black peppercorns. Bring to the boil and simmer until the liquid is reduced by half.

2. Whiz the egg yolks in a food processor for 1 minute. Strain the reduced vinegar, adding it to the yolks while the machine is running.

3. In a small pan, melt the butter and cook until it begins to brown around the edges. With the food processor running on full speed, add two-thirds of the melted butter. Add the lemon juice, then the remaining butter. Season and put to one side.

4. Take a wide, shallow pan of boiling water and add 1 tablespoon of vinegar to each 600ml (1 pint) of water. Carefully break an egg into a saucer, make a whirlpool with a large spoon in the boiling water and lower the egg into the water. Reduce the heat and cook gently for 3 minutes or until the white is just set and the yolk soft. Using a draining spoon, carefully lift the egg out of the pan and put in a shallow dish of warm water. Repeat with the remaining eggs.

5. Warm the ham in the microwave for 1 minute on medium, or in a medium oven, 170°C/150°C fan oven/Gas Mark 3, for 10 minutes. Place the ham on the muffin halves, top each with an egg, some hollandaise sauce and the other muffin half. Garnish with parsley and serve.

Preparation time: 10 min   **Cooking time:** 15 min
Cals per serving: 800   **Serves:** 4

BLT-topped Bagels with Hollandaise Sauce

large bagels	3, split
butter	25g (1oz), softened
rashers smoked streaky bacon	12, rind removed
olive oil	2 tsp
tomatoes	3, thickly sliced
ready-made hollandaise sauce	150ml (5fl oz)
mixed lettuce leaves	75g (3oz)
crushed black peppercorns	to garnish

1. Grill the bagels until golden and spread generously with the butter. Cover with a piece of foil and keep warm. Grill the bacon for 2 to 3 minutes on each side or until crisp. Keep warm. Heat the oil in a small frying pan until very hot and fry the tomatoes for about 1 minute on both sides until lightly charred.

2. Place the hollandaise sauce in a small saucepan and heat gently. To assemble, top the warm bagels with a few lettuce leaves, the tomatoes and bacon. Spoon over the warm hollandaise sauce and garnish with the crushed black peppercorns.

Preparation time: 15 min   **Cooking time:** 8 min
Cals per serving: 490   **Serves:** 6

Smoked Trout Bagels

1. Put the cream cheese, mayonnaise and horseradish sauce in a bowl, then beat together until smooth and season well.

2. Spread the mixture over the bottom half of the bagels, arrange the smoked trout on top, then sandwich the bagels together. Serve with the lime wedges on the side.

Preparation time: 10 min   **Cals per serving:** 460   **Serves:** 6

cream cheese	200g pack
mayonnaise	3 tbsp
horseradish sauce	1–2 tbsp
bagels	6, split
cold cure smoked trout	375g pack
lime wedges	to garnish

BLT-topped Bagels with
Hollandaise Sauce

Lazy brunch: Pan-fried Potatoes, Lassi and Sausages in Red Onion Marmalade

Friends for Brunch: Spend time enjoying the food and the company and **as little time as possible** actually preparing. **Keep it fun and informal**, yet totally **indulgent**. The **Bacon and Tuna Hash** is delicious served with the **Lemon and Parmesan Quick Zucchini Bread**, or children love the zingy **Orange Eggy Bread**. The scrumptious **Sausages in Red Onion Marmalade** are **effortless** to prepare, just **slowly baked** in the oven. **Pan-fried Potatoes** are the must-have **comfort food**, excellent **served on the side**, piping **hot from the pan**, to soak up the **juices**. And for something **a little different**, finish with a fresh, **well-chilled Raspberry Lassi**.

Polenta with Mixed Mushrooms

butter	50g (2oz)
assorted mushrooms	1.1kg (2¼lb)
red chilli	1, deseeded and finely chopped
garlic cloves	3, sliced
sun-dried tomatoes	100g (3½oz), roughly chopped
dried or fresh thyme	1 tsp
ready-made polenta	1kg pack
olive oil	3 tbsp
truffle oil	optional
fresh thyme sprigs	to garnish

1. Melt half the butter in a deep-sided frying pan or wok. Add half the mushrooms and cook over a high heat until all the liquid has evaporated; set aside. Repeat with the remaining butter and mushrooms. Fry the chilli and garlic in the pan for 2 minutes, then add to the mushrooms, along with the sun-dried tomatoes and thyme. Mix well and season.

2. Slice the polenta into 16 pieces about 1cm (½in) thick. Heat the oil in a non-stick frying pan and fry the polenta in batches, for 3 to 4 minutes on each side, or until golden.

3. To serve, arrange two slices of polenta per person on a plate, top with the mushroom sauce and drizzle with a little truffle oil, if using. Garnish with thyme sprigs.

Preparation time: 10 min   **Cooking time:** 20 min
Cals per serving: 292   **Serves:** 8

Pan-fried Mushroom
and Feta Omelette

1. Melt the butter in an 18cm (7in) diameter non-stick omelette pan and fry the mushrooms with the garlic until they are a deep golden brown and beginning to go crisp around the edges. Add the sun-dried tomatoes and stir over the heat for 1 to 2 minutes. Meanwhile, preheat the grill.

2. Roughly spread the mushroom mixture over the base of the pan. Beat 2 tablespoons of cold water into the eggs and season with pepper (both feta cheese and sun-dried tomatoes can be salty, so no extra salt should be needed to season the omelette). Pour this over the mushrooms, gently swirling the pan to spread the eggs. Leave to set, undisturbed, on a low heat for 1 to 2 minutes, then sprinkle over the feta. Place the pan under the hot grill for about 1 to 2 minutes or until the eggs are lightly cooked and the feta cheese is just beginning to melt.

3. Sprinkle the omelette with black pepper and scatter with fresh thyme sprigs, to garnish. Cut into wedges and serve immediately.

Preparation time: 5 min   **Cooking time:** 15 min
Cals per serving: 325   **Serves:** 4

butter	50g (2oz)
large mushrooms	225g (8oz), thinly sliced
garlic cloves	3, sliced
sun-dried tomatoes	50g (2oz), chopped
large eggs	4, beaten
feta cheese	100g (3½oz), crumbled
fresh thyme sprigs	to garnish

Hot Egg-fried Rice

oil 2 tbsp
streaky bacon 250g (9oz), shredded
green chilli 1, sliced
green pepper 1, deseeded and diced
spring onions 2, sliced
large eggs 2, beaten
long-grain rice 175g (6oz), cooked
dark soy sauce 3 tbsp

1. Heat the oil in a wok, add the bacon and cook until brown and crisp. Add the chilli, pepper and spring onions and cook for 1 minute. Add the eggs, stirring all the time for 1 minute.

2. Add the cooked rice, soy sauce and seasoning. Heat through and serve.

Preparation time: 5 min   **Cooking time:** 8 min
Cals per serving: 765   **Serves:** 4

Creamy Baked
Egg Starter

1. Preheat the oven to 180°C/160°C fan oven/Gas Mark 4. Butter four ramekins.

2. Place one tomato in each of the four ramekins and season. Carefully break an egg on top of each, then drizzle 1 tablespoon of double cream over each egg. Bake in the oven for 15 to 18 minutes. The eggs will continue to cook once they have been taken out of the oven.

3. Leave to stand for 2 minutes before serving.

Preparation time: 5 min   **Cooking time:** 15–18 min
Cals per serving: 182   **Serves:** 4

butter for greasing
sun-dried tomatoes 4
medium eggs 4
double cream 4 tbsp

Potato and Chorizo
Tortilla

olive oil 6 tbsp
potatoes 450g (1lb), very thinly sliced
onions 225g (8oz), thinly sliced
garlic cloves 2, finely chopped
sliced chorizo 50g (2oz), cut into thin strips
large eggs 6, lightly beaten

1. Heat the oil in a non-stick frying pan, measuring about 18cm (7in) across the base. Add the potatoes, onion and garlic. Stir together until coated in the oil, then cover the pan. Cook gently, stirring from time to time, for 10 to 15 minutes or until the potato is soft. Season with salt.

2. Add the chorizo to the potato mixture. Season the eggs and pour on to the potato mixture. Cook over a moderate heat for 5 minutes or until beginning to brown at the edges and the egg is about three-quarters set. Put the pan under a preheated grill to brown the top. The egg should be a little soft in the middle as it continues to cook and set as it cools.

3. Carefully loosen the tortilla round the edge and underneath with a palette knife or fish slice, cut into wedges and serve.

Preparation time: 10 min   **Cooking time:** 25 min
Cals per serving: 434   **Serves:** 4

Pan-fried
Potatoes

1. Peel and halve the potatoes. Cook in a large pan of boiling, salted water for about 15 to 20 minutes or until tender. Drain, then, when cool enough to handle, cut into walnut-sized chunks.

2. Heat the oil and butter in a large frying pan and cook the warm potatoes in batches, tossing them frequently, for about 10 minutes or until they are evenly golden. Season generously with salt and pepper. Spoon on to sheets of kitchen paper to drain off any excess fat. Serve straight away.

Preparation time: 10 min   **Cooking time:** 30 min
Cals per serving: 356   **Serves:** 10

potatoes 1.6kg (3½lb)
oil 150ml (5fl oz)
butter 75g (3oz)

Potato and
Chorizo Tortilla

French Toast

medium eggs	2
double cream	6 tbsp
caster sugar	2 tbsp
orange	I, rind finely grated
thick day-old white bread	4 slices
or croissants	2, halved
unsalted butter	for frying
fruit or fruit compote	to serve
icing or caster sugar	to dust

1. Whisk together the eggs, cream, caster sugar and orange rind and dip the bread in the mixture. Heat the butter in a frying pan and fry the bread until golden on both sides.

2. Serve with fruit or a fruit compote and dust with icing sugar.

Preparation time: 5 min   **Cooking time:** 5–7 min
Cals per serving: 835   **Serves:** 2

Orange Eggy Bread

1. Lightly whisk the eggs with the milk and orange rind, then dip the raisin bread into the mixture.

2. Heat the butter in a frying pan and fry the bread on both sides until golden. Sprinkle with the caster sugar and serve with orange slices.

Preparation time: 5 min   **Cooking time:** 5 min
Cals per serving: 287   **Serves:** 4

large eggs	2
milk	150ml (5fl oz)
orange	I, rind finely grated
raisin bread	8 slices
butter	for frying
caster sugar	I tbsp
orange slices	to serve

Quick Zucchini,
Lemon and Parmesan Bread

1. Grease and base-line a 900g (2lb) non-stick loaf tin and dust with some plain flour. Preheat the oven to 190°C/170°C fan oven/Gas Mark 5. Place the grated courgettes on kitchen paper and dry well.

2. Place the plain flour, wholemeal flour, sugar, baking powder, salt and lemon rind in a bowl and mix well. Add the courgettes to the dry ingredients with the parmesan and black pepper and mix lightly together with a fork. Make a well in the centre. Whisk together the milk, oil and eggs and pour into the well, stirring into the flour mixture, until smooth.

3. Pour into the prepared tin and level the surface with a knife. Bake for about 50 minutes or until a skewer inserted into the centre of the loaf comes out clean. Leave to cool in the tin for 10 minutes before turning out on to a wire rack. Leave to cool, then sprinkle parmesan on top.

Freezing: Complete the recipe, cool, wrap and freeze.

To use: Remove from the freezer and thaw at cool room temperature overnight before serving.

Preparation time: 25 min, plus 10 min cooling
Cooking time: 50 min   **Cals per serving:** 171   **Makes:** 12 slices

butter	for greasing
plain flour	175g (6oz), sifted plus extra to dust
courgettes	175g (6oz), grated
plain wholemeal flour	75g (3oz)
caster sugar	1 tbsp
baking powder	1 tsp
salt	½ tsp
lemon	1, rind finely grated
parmesan	75g (3oz), freshly grated plus extra for sprinkling
milk	200ml (7fl oz)
olive oil	6 tbsp
medium eggs	2, beaten

Luxurious feast: Hash
Browns with Smoked
Salmon and Scrambled
Eggs and Wholemeal
Banana Muffins

Lazy Lie-in for Two: Make the most of having **time to enjoy** a **late breakfast** at the weekend. **Conjure up** that lovely **Sunday morning feeling** and **indulge yourself** and your partner in a **relaxed** Sunday brunch of **Hash Browns with Smoked Salmon and Scrambled Eggs**, a truly winning combination. Alternatively, try **Eggs Benedict**, served on **warmed muffins** and **topped with homemade hollandaise sauce**. And there is nothing like the aroma of **steaming hot fresh coffee** served in **big mugs** to go with it. Follow on with a **sweet treat** of **Wholemeal Banana Muffins**, and **lashings of toast** spread generously with **butter** and **marmalade**.

Wholemeal Banana Muffins

butter	for greasing, optional
raisins	50g (2oz)
orange	1, rind grated and juice
plain wholemeal flour	125g (4oz)
wheatgerm	25g (1oz)
caster sugar	3 tbsp
baking powder	2 tsp
salt	pinch of
large egg	1, beaten
milk	4 tbsp
sunflower oil	4 tbsp
ripe medium bananas	2, roughly mashed

For the topping

orange marmalade	5 tbsp
banana chips	50g (2oz)
walnuts	50g (2oz), chopped

1. Preheat the oven to 200°C/180°C fan over/Gas Mark 6. Line six muffin tins with paper muffin cases or grease the tins well. Place the raisins in a bowl, pour the orange juice over and leave to soak for 1 hour.

2. Place the orange rind in a bowl with the next five ingredients and mix together. Make a well in the centre.

3. In a separate bowl, mix the egg, milk and sunflower oil, then pour into the well in the flour mixture and stir until just blended. Drain the raisins, reserving 1 tablespoon of the juice, and gently stir into the mixture with the bananas. Do not over-mix.

4. Fill each muffin case two-thirds full. Bake for 20 to 25 minutes or until a skewer inserted into the centre comes out clean. Transfer the muffins to a wire rack to cool slightly.

5. For the topping, gently heat the orange marmalade with the reserved orange juice until melted. Simmer for 1 minute, then add the banana chips and walnuts. Spoon on top of the muffins. Serve while still warm.

Preparation time: 15 min, plus 1 hr soaking
Cooking time: 20–25 min   **Cals per serving:** 370   **Makes:** 6

Golden Honey
Fruits

selection of tropical fruit,
such as pineapple, mango,
papaya and banana 900g (2lb)
runny honey 3 tbsp
Greek yogurt to serve
mixed spice to sprinkle

1. Cut the fruit into wedges. Place on a foil-lined grill pan, drizzle with the honey and cook under a very hot grill until caramelised, about 5 to 8 minutes. Serve with Greek yogurt sprinkled with a little mixed spice. Simmer for 2 to 3 minutes. Garnish and serve.

Preparation time: 5 min   **Cooking time:** 5–8 min
Cals per serving: 191   **Serves:** 4

Orange
Pancakes

1. Sift the flour, salt and caster sugar into a bowl. In a bowl, beat together the eggs and the egg yolk. Make a well in the centre of the flour mixture and add the eggs. Using a whisk or wooden spoon and starting in the centre, gradually mix the eggs with the flour, slowly adding the milk. Beat until you have a batter covered with bubbles. Cover and leave to stand in a cold place for at least 30 minutes.

2. Just before cooking the pancakes, stir in the melted butter (this makes all the difference to the flavour and texture and means you can cook them without greasing the pan each time).

3. Meanwhile, make the orange sauce. Put the butter, orange rind, icing sugar, Grand Marnier, if using, and orange juice into a pan and cook over a low heat until the butter has melted and the sugar has dissolved.

4. Place a non-stick crêpe pan over a high heat and pour in a small ladleful of batter (enough to form a film in the base). When bubbles appear on the surface loosen the edges with a palette knife, flip over and cook briefly on the other side. Fold and slide on to a plate, spoon the warm sauce on top, sprinkle with orange rind and serve. Repeat with the remaining batter.

Preparation time: 15 min, plus 30 min standing
Cooking time: 25 min   **Cals per serving:** 309   **Makes:** 14–16 pancakes

plain white flour 175g (6oz)
salt pinch of
caster sugar 2 tsp
large eggs 2
large egg yolk 1
milk 475ml (16fl oz)
butter 50g (2oz), melted

For the orange sauce
butter 75g (3oz)
small oranges 2, rind grated
icing sugar 75g (3oz)
Grand Marnier 2 tbsp, optional
fresh orange juice 475ml (16fl oz)
finely grated orange rind to sprinkle

Chocolate Pancakes

plain chocolate	150g (5oz)
plain flour	100g (3½oz)
large egg	1
salt	pinch of
skimmed milk	325ml (11fl oz)
butter	25g (1oz)
soft light brown sugar	1 tbsp
medium bananas	4, thickly sliced
brandy	120ml (4fl oz)
vegetable oil	for brushing
icing sugar	to dust
Greek yogurt or quark	to serve
chocolate shavings	to decorate

1. Place 50g (2oz) chocolate in a food processor and whiz until roughly chopped. Add the flour, egg, salt and milk and process until smooth. Cover and chill for 30 minutes.

2. Melt the butter and sugar in a frying pan. Add the bananas and stir-fry over a medium heat for 3 minutes. Add the brandy (take care when doing this as it may ignite in the warm pan) and continue to simmer for about 2 minutes until the bananas soften and the liquid is syrupy. Set aside.

3. Lightly brush an 18cm (7in) non-stick crêpe or small frying pan with oil and heat. Stir the batter and coat the base of the pan thinly, with a ladleful of mixture (equivalent to 4 tablespoons). Cook for 2 minutes or until golden brown, then turn with a palette knife. Cook for a further 1 minute. Transfer to a plate, cover and keep warm. Cook the remaining batter in the same way.

4. Chop the remaining chocolate. Place two spoonfuls of banana filling over one half of each pancake; sprinkle with some of the chocolate. Fold in half, then in half again. Keep warm while filling the remaining pancakes. Dust with icing sugar and serve warm with yogurt and decorate with chocolate shavings.

Freezing: Make and wrap the pancakes as above, then freeze for up to one month.

To use: Thaw at cool room temperature for 3 hours. Complete as above.

Preparation time: 15 min, plus 30 min chilling
Cooking time: 30–40 min
Cals per serving: 115 if making 8; 75 if making 12
Makes: 8–12 pancakes   **Serves:** 4–6

Cinnamon Pancakes
with Rhubarb Compote

1. To make the compote, put the orange juice and caster sugar in a pan with 6 tablespoons of water and heat gently until the sugar has dissolved. Add the rhubarb, bring to the boil, reduce the heat and simmer gently for 5 to 10 minutes or until tender. Lift out the rhubarb and set aside. Add the ginger syrup and bubble for 5 minutes or until syrupy. Add the chopped ginger to the rhubarb and remove from the heat.

2. To make the pancakes, place the flour, sugar, baking powder, bicarbonate of soda, salt and cinnamon in a bowl, mix thoroughly and make a well in the centre. Whisk together the buttermilk and eggs and pour into the well, stirring until smooth. Stir in the melted butter.

3. Heat a little oil in a non-stick frying pan. Ladle the batter into the pan to form 10cm (4in) diameter pancakes. Cook until small bubbles form and the edges begin to turn brown. Turn with a palette knife and cook for a further 1 minute or until cooked through. Lay on kitchen paper and keep warm, covered with foil. Repeat with the remaining batter, adding more oil as required.

4. Sandwich two pancakes together with the warm rhubarb compote. Top with more compote and a spoonful of crème fraîche, dust with cinnamon and serve.

Freezing: Complete step 1, cool, cover and freeze. Complete steps 2 and 3, cool, wrap and freeze.

To use: Thaw the compote and pancakes overnight at cool room temperature and reheat as above.

Preparation time: 30 min   **Cooking time:** 15–20 min
Cals per serving: 403   **Makes:** 12 pancakes   **Serves:** 6

For the compote
fresh orange juice 150ml (5fl oz)
caster sugar 175g (6oz)
fresh rhubarb 700g (1½lb), chopped
stem ginger syrup 2 tbsp
stem ginger 1 tbsp, finely chopped

For the pancakes
plain flour 175g (6oz)
light muscovado sugar 2 tbsp
baking powder 1 tsp
bicarbonate of soda ½ tsp
salt ½ tsp
ground cinnamon 2 tsp
buttermilk 284ml carton
large eggs 2, beaten
butter 50g (2oz), melted
vegetable oil for frying
crème fraîche to accompany
cinnamon to dust

Buttermilk Pancakes

1. Melt 50g (2oz) butter and allow to cool. Mix the flour, bicarbonate of soda, cinnamon, nutmeg and caster sugar together in a bowl.

2. Make a well in the centre and add the melted butter, egg and the buttermilk. Mix, then stir into the flour until well combined and smooth.

3. Preheat the oven to 140°C/120°C fan oven/Gas Mark 1. Brush a non-stick frying pan with oil and drop a tablespoonful of batter into the pan, flipping when golden. Remove and keep warm in the oven between a clean cloth. Repeat with the remaining batter.

4. Preheat the grill to high and cook the bacon until crisp. Drain any excess fat on kitchen paper.

5. Heat half the remaining butter in a frying pan until foaming, then fry half the apples until golden. Take out and keep warm. Repeat with the remaining butter and apples. Return all the apples to the pan, add the syrup, bring to the boil and bubble for 1 minute.

6. Serve the pancakes with apples, bacon and extra maple syrup and garnish with parsley.

Preparation time: 25 min   **Cooking time:** 30 min
Cals per serving: 820   **Makes:** 12 pancakes   **Serves:** 6

butter	125g (4oz)
self-raising flour	175g (6oz), sifted
bicarbonate of soda	1 tsp
ground cinnamon	½ tsp
ground nutmeg	½ tsp
golden caster sugar	50g (2oz)
large egg	1, beaten
buttermilk	284ml carton
vegetable oil	for frying
rindless thin streaky bacon rashers	700g (1½lb)
apples	6, cored and cut into eighths
maple syrup	4 tbsp, plus extra to pour
fresh parsley	to garnish

Lemon and Blueberry Pancakes

plain flour	125g (4oz)
caster sugar	3 tbsp
baking powder	1 tsp
bicarbonate of soda	¼ tsp
lemon	1, rind finely grated
natural yogurt	125ml (4fl oz)
milk	2 tbsp
medium eggs	2
butter	25g (1oz), melted
sunflower oil	to drizzle
butter	for frying
blueberries	100g (3½oz)
crème fraîche	to accompany
lemon rind	to top

For the blueberry syrup

caster sugar	150g (5oz)
blueberries	150g (5oz)
lemon juice	2 tbsp

1. Sift the flour into a bowl, add the caster sugar, baking powder, bicarbonate of soda and lemon rind. Pour in the yogurt, milk and eggs and whisk together. Add the melted butter.

2. Add the sunflower oil and a knob of butter to a frying pan and place over a moderate heat. Add a couple of spoonfuls of the mixture to the pan. Drop a few blueberries onto each pancake. After about 2 minutes, turn and cook for 1 to 2 minutes. Repeat with the remaining mixture.

3. For the blueberry syrup, in a small pan dissolve the caster sugar in 100ml (3½fl oz) water over a low heat. Add the blueberries, bring to the boil and bubble for 1 minute. Add the lemon juice, set aside for 2 minutes, then spoon over the pancakes.

4. Top with crème fraîche and lemon rind.

Preparation time: 15 min   **Cooking time:** 15–20 min
Cals per serving: 213   **Makes:** 8 pancakes   **Serves:** 4

snack attacks

Cherry Chocolate Fudge Brownies

unsalted butter	150g (5oz), plus extra for greasing
plain chocolate with 70% cocoa solids	200g (7oz)
caster sugar	175g (6oz)
vanilla extract	2 tsp
medium eggs	5
plain flour	175g (6oz)
baking powder	½ tsp
glacé cherries, halved	250g (9oz)

For the icing	
plain chocolate with 70% cocoa solids	150g (5oz)
Kirsch	2 tbsp
double cream	4 tbsp
icing sugar and cocoa powder	mixed, to dust
double cream	lightly whipped, to serve

1. Preheat the oven to 180°C/160°C fan oven/Gas Mark 4. Grease and baseline an 18cm (7in) square cake tin, 5cm (2in) deep. Place the butter and chocolate in a heatproof bowl over a pan of simmering water. Allow the chocolate to melt; do not stir. Remove from the heat and stir until smooth. Allow to cool.

2. Whisk the sugar, vanilla extract and eggs until thick, pale and frothy. Stir the chocolate into the egg mixture. Sift the flour and baking powder together and lightly fold into the chocolate mixture with the cherries. Pour the mixture into the tin. Bake for 40 minutes or until just set. Cool slightly in the tin before removing from the tin and icing.

3. To make the icing, place the chocolate and Kirsch in a heatproof bowl over a pan of simmering water. When melted add the cream and 4 tablespoons of water; stir well. Pour over the brownie and leave to set.

4. Cut the brownie into squares, dust with icing sugar and cocoa powder. Serve with double cream.

Freezing: Complete up to the end of step 2, remove from the tin, wrap and freeze.

To use: Thaw at room temperature for 5 hours. Complete the recipe.

Preparation time: 20 min, plus 30 min cooling and 1 hr setting
Cooking time: 50 min   **Cals per serving:** 470   **Serves:** 12

Apple Madeleines

1. Preheat the oven to 200°C/180°C fan oven/Gas Mark 6. Grease the Madeleine tins. Using an electric whisk, beat the eggs and sugar together for about

8 minutes until thick, then stir in the vanilla extract. Quickly, but gently, fold in the flour, baking powder and apple followed by the melted butter, making sure the butter does not settle at the bottom of the bowl.

2. Spoon the mixture into the Madeleine tins. Cook for 8 to 10 minutes or until golden, then remove from the tins and cool on a wire rack. To serve, dust with icing sugar.

Preparation time: 15 min   **Cooking time:** 8–10 min
Cals per serving: 105   **Makes:** 24

unsalted butter	150g (5oz), melted and cooled, plus extra for greasing
large eggs	3
caster sugar	150g (5oz)
vanilla extract	1 tsp
plain flour	150g (5oz), sifted
baking powder	½ tsp
apples such as Cox's	2, peeled, cored and finely chopped
icing sugar	to dust

The Ultimate
Chocolate Brownie

plain chocolate with 70% cocoa solids	400g (14oz)
unsalted butter	200g (7oz), plus extra for greasing
light muscovado sugar	225g (8oz)
vanilla extract	1 tsp
pecan nuts	150g (5oz), chopped
cocoa powder	25g (1oz), sifted, plus extra to dust
self-raising flour	75g (3oz), sifted
large eggs	3, beaten
ice cream	to serve, optional

1. Preheat the oven to 170°C/150°C fan oven/Gas Mark 3. Put the chocolate and butter in a heatproof bowl over a pan of simmering water and stir until melted. Remove from the heat and stir in the sugar, vanilla extract, pecans, cocoa, flour and eggs.

2. Turn the mixture into a greased and baselined (use non-stick baking parchment) 20cm (8in), 5cm (2in) deep, square cake tin and level with the back of a spoon. Bake for about 1 hour 15 minutes or until set to the centre on the surface, but still soft underneath.

3. Leave to cool in the tin for 2 hours. Turn out, dust with cocoa and cut into squares. Serve warm with ice cream or cold.

Preparation time: 15 min, plus 2 hr cooling
Cooking time: 1 hr 20 min   **Cals per serving:** 379   **Makes:** 16

Nutty
Fudge Shortbread

1. Preheat the oven to 180°C/160°C fan oven/Gas Mark 4. Whiz the flour, salt, caster sugar and 125g (4½oz) of the butter in a food processor until it begins to come together. Press the mixture into a 20 x 30cm (8 x 12in) greased Swiss roll tin and smooth over with the back of a spoon. Bake for 20 to 30 minutes or until golden. Leave to cool.

2. Put the remaining butter, muscovado sugar, syrup and condensed milk in a pan and heat gently, but do not boil. Whisk together until combined. Pour over the shortbread, smooth the surface and chill for 3 hours.

3. Melt the chocolate in a heatproof bowl over a pan of simmering water. Mix with the nuts and pour over the fudge mixture. Smooth the top and leave to set. Cut into wedges to serve.

Preparation time: 40 min, plus 3 hr chilling
Cooking time: 40 min   **Cals per serving:** 450   **Makes:** 16 wedges

plain flour	300g (11oz), sifted
salt	pinch of
caster sugar	125g (4oz)
unsalted butter	225g (8oz), softened
light muscovado sugar	125g (4oz)
golden syrup	2 tbsp
condensed milk	170g can
plain chocolate	300g (11oz)
walnut halves	100g (3½oz)
hazelnuts, lightly toasted	100g (3½oz)

Sticky Ginger Ring

unsalted butter	100g (3½oz), diced, plus extra for greasing
soft light brown sugar	95g (3½oz)
black treacle	3 tbsp
milk	100ml (3½fl oz)
brandy	2 tbsp
large egg	1, beaten
plain flour	150g (5oz)
ground ginger	2 tsp
ground cinnamon	2 tsp
bicarbonate of soda	1 tsp
ready-to-eat pitted prunes	75g (3oz), chopped
icing sugar	225g (8oz), sifted
stem ginger	2 pieces, drained from syrup and chopped

1. Preheat the oven to 180°C/160°C fan oven/Gas Mark 4. Using your hands, generously grease a 21cm (8½in), 600ml (1 pint) capacity, round ring mould with butter.

2. Put the butter, sugar and treacle in a small pan and heat gently until melted, stirring all the time. Add the milk and brandy and leave to cool, then beat in the egg.

3. Sift the flour, spices and bicarbonate of soda into a large mixing bowl. Make a well in the centre, pour in the treacle mixture and stir together until all the flour has been combined – it should have a soft dropping consistency. Stir in the prunes.

4. Pour the mixture into the greased ring mould and bake in the oven for 1 hour or until the cake is firm to the touch and a skewer inserted in the centre comes out clean. Leave to cool in the tin for 10 minutes, then loosen the sides of the cake and turn out on to a wire rack.

5. To make the icing, mix the icing sugar with about 2 tablespoons of hot water to create a coating consistency. Drizzle over the cake and down the sides, then decorate with the stem ginger.

Freezing: Wrap the cake in clingfilm and foil before icing. Freeze for up to one month.

To use: Thaw for 3 hours and complete the cake.

Preparation time: 15 min, plus cooling **Cooking time:** 1 hr
Cals per serving: 420 **Serves:** 6

Lemon Angel Cakes

vegetable cooking spray for greasing
plain flour 50g (2oz)
cornflour 1 tbsp
caster sugar 100g (3½oz)
large egg whites 5
salt ¼ tsp
cream of tartar ½ tsp
vanilla extract ½ tsp
rosewater ½ tsp
large cardamom pods 3, seeds finely crushed
lemon 1, rind finely grated
low-fat fromage frais, berries and sun-dried pineapple slices to serve, optional
icing sugar to dust

1. Preheat the oven to 170°C/150°C fan oven/Gas Mark 3. Grease and baseline an 18cm (7in) square cake tin with non-stick baking parchment. Sift the flour, cornflour and 50g (2oz) of caster sugar into a bowl. Set aside.

2. Whisk the egg whites with the salt, cream of tartar, vanilla extract, rosewater and 1 tablespoon of cold water until stiff. Gradually whisk in the remaining sugar and continue to whisk until stiff and glossy. Sift the flour mixture over the egg whites and carefully fold in with the crushed cardamom seeds and grated lemon rind. Spoon into the prepared tin and level the surface.

3. Bake for 35 minutes or until firm to the touch and the cake has shrunk from the sides of the tin. Loosen round the sides with a palette knife and flip the tin upside down on to a cooling rack, leaving the cake in the tin to cool. Lift off the tin and cut the cake into nine squares, then halve each one to make 18 triangles. Serve plain or with fromage frais, berries and pineapple, and dusted with icing sugar.

Freezing: Cook the cake, cut as step 3, then pack and freeze.

To use: Thaw at cool room temperature for 4 hours and serve.

Preparation time: 20 min, plus 30 min cooling
Cooking time: 35 min   **Cals per serving:** 35   **Makes:** 18 triangles

Walnut and Coffee Layer Cake

butter for greasing
walnuts 250g (9oz), plus
extra to decorate
plain flour 100g (3½oz)
large eggs 9
caster sugar 250g (9oz)

For the filling
instant espresso coffee 3 tbsp
boiling water 3 tbsp
unsalted butter 300g (11oz), at room
temperature
golden icing sugar 300g (11oz), sifted

For the icing
icing sugar 175g (6oz), sifted
boiling water 2–3 tbsp

1. Preheat the oven to 170°C/150°C fan oven/Gas Mark 3. Grease and baseline a 23cm (9in) springform cake tin with non-stick baking parchment. Put the walnuts and flour in a food processor and whiz to a fine powder. Put to one side. If you don't have a food processor, grind the nuts through a drum nut grater or cheese grater and mix them with the flour.

2. Separate the eggs, then put the yolks in the bowl of a food processor and five whites in a large mixing bowl. (Freeze the remaining whites for use later.) Add the sugar to the yolks and beat until pale and very thick. Alternatively, whisk together the egg yolks and sugar in a heatproof bowl over a pan of simmering water with an electric hand whisk.

3. Using a metal spoon, fold the walnut and flour mixture into the yolk mixture. Whisk the egg whites to soft peaks. Fold in one-third of the egg white to the yolk mixture, then carefully fold in the rest. Pour the mixture into the lined tin.

4. Bake the cake for 55 to 60 minutes or until a skewer inserted into the centre for 30 seconds comes out clean. Cool in the tin for 15 minutes, then turn out on to a cooling rack.

5. To make the filling, dissolve the coffee in the boiling water and put to one side. Put the butter in a bowl and beat until very soft and creamy. Gradually beat in the icing sugar and 4 teaspoons of the dissolved coffee (reserve the rest) until well combined and fluffy.

6. Cut the cake horizontally into three layers. Put the bottom layer on a serving plate and spread half the coffee filling over it. Gently press the second layer into position and spread with the remaining filling. Lift the top of the cake into position and press down gently.

7. For the icing, put the icing sugar into a bowl, add ½ to 1 teaspoon of the reserved coffee and 2 to 3 tablespoons of boiling water and combine thoroughly. Pour the icing on the cake then, with a round-bladed palette knife, quickly spread in an even layer to the edge, then decorate with walnut pieces. Allow the icing to set (about 2 hours) before serving. The cake will keep for about five days.

Freezing: Freeze the cake at the end of step 6.

To use: Thaw at cool room temperature for 4 hours then complete the cake to serve.

Preparation time: 1 hr, plus 15 min cooling and 2 hr setting
Cooking time: 55–60 min   **Cals per serving:** 741   **Serves:** 12

Homemade treats:
Cherry Chip Cookies
and Walnut and Coffee
Layer Cake make a
coffee morning

Coffee Break: Getting together with **friends** for **a chat and a coffee** is a great chance for you to **show off your baking skills**. Try to serve a good mix of **cakes and biscuits**, such as **Cherry Chip Cookies** and little **Lemon Angel Cakes**, or **Mini Mince Pies** for a festive occasion and some **Apple Madeleines**, even a few **savoury nibbles**, too. The **Walnut and Coffee Layer Cake** is bound to be popular, layered with **sweet, soft coffee cream** and topped with a **frosted coffee icing**. It is rich and **deliciously indulgent**. The **White and Dark Chocolate Cookies**, can be made just before your guests arrive, to **woo them** with that all too enticing **smell of homebaking**.

Orange and Carrot Squares

butter	for greasing
sunflower oil	250ml (9fl oz)
caster sugar	225g (8oz)
large eggs	3
self-raising flour	225g (8oz), sifted
salt	pinch of
carrots	250g (9oz), grated
orange flower water	1 tsp, optional

For the icing

unsalted butter	50g (2oz)
cream cheese	200g pack
icing sugar	40g (1½oz), sifted
oranges	2, rind finely grated
orange juice	2 tbsp

1. Preheat the oven to 180°C/160°C fan oven/Gas Mark 4. Grease and baseline an 18 x 28cm (7 x 11in), 2.5cm (1in) deep, tin. Whisk the oil and sugar together, then whisk in the eggs one at a time. Gently fold the flour and salt, into the mixture, then fold in the carrots and orange flower water.

2. Pour into the tin and bake for 40 minutes or until golden and a skewer inserted in the centre comes out clean. Leave in the tin for 10 minutes, then turn out on to a wire rack to cool.

3. For the icing, beat together the butter and cream cheese until light and fluffy. Beat in the icing sugar, half the orange rind and juice. When the cake is cold, remove the lining paper, cover with a 5mm (¼in) layer of icing and decorate with the remaining orange rind. Cut into 12 squares to serve.

Freezing: Cut the carrot cake into squares, wrap in clingfilm, then in foil and freeze for up to one month.

To use: Thaw at cool room temperature for 2 hours.

Preparation time: 15 min, plus cooling   **Cooking time:** 40 min

Cals per serving: 450   **Makes:** 12 squares

Mini Mince Pies with a Frosted Topping

1. Put the flour in a food processor with the butter and whiz until the mixture resembles fine breadcrumbs. Add the sugar, orange rind and juice and pulse until the mixture just begins to come together. Turn out on to a floured work surface and knead lightly until smooth. Divide the dough into four, wrap and chill for at least 1 hour before using.

2. Preheat the oven to 190°C/170°C fan oven/Gas Mark 5. On a floured work surface, roll the pastry out thinly and stamp into rounds with a 6cm (2½in) cutter. Line 48 small, deep tartlet tins, about 3cm (1¼in) across the base and 2.5cm (1in) deep, with the pastry. Place 1 teaspoon of mince-meat in each and put to one side.

3. To make the topping, very lightly whisk the egg white, then beat in the icing sugar and flour until stiff. Put a little topping on each pie and sprinkle with almonds. Bake in batches of 24 for 15 to 20 minutes or until the pastry is cooked and the topping and almonds golden. Leave in the tins for 10 minutes, then turn out on to a cooling rack.

Preparation time: 1 hr, plus 1 hr chilling and 10 min cooling

Cooking time: 30–40 min   **Cals per serving:** 158   **Makes:** 48

plain flour	450g (1lb), plus extra to dust
chilled butter	375g (13oz), cubed
icing or caster sugar	175g (6oz)
large orange	1, rind finely grated
orange juice	3–4 tbsp
mincemeat	450g (1lb)

For the topping

large egg white	1
icing sugar	200–225g (7–8oz), sifted
plain flour	½ tsp
flaked almonds	75g (3oz)

Orange and Carrot
Squares

Cherry Chip Cookies

unsalted butter	75g (3oz), softened, plus extra for greasing
caster sugar	25g (1oz)
light muscovado sugar	50g (2oz)
vanilla extract	few drops
large egg	1, lightly beaten
self-raising flour	175g (6oz), sifted
orange	1, rind finely grated
white chocolate	125g (4oz), roughly broken
glacé cherries	125g (4oz), chopped
icing sugar	to dust

1. Preheat the oven to 180°C/160°C fan oven/Gas Mark 4. Grease two baking sheets. In a large bowl, beat together the butter, caster sugar, light muscovado sugar and vanilla extract until well combined, using an electric whisk. Gradually beat in the egg until the mixture is light and fluffy.

2. With a metal spoon, lightly fold in the flour, orange rind, chocolate and glacé cherries. Place tablespoonfuls of the mixture on to the baking sheets, spaced well apart and bake for 10 to 12 minutes. The biscuits should be soft under a crisp crust.

3. Cool the cookies on the baking sheet for 1 minute before transferring them to a cooling rack. Dust with icing sugar just before serving.

Preparation time: 20 min, plus 30 min cooling
Cooking time: 10–12 min
Cals per serving: 208 for 12, 178 for 14   **Makes:** 12–14

Tiffin

1. Grease and baseline a 20cm (8in), 4cm (1½in) deep, round cake tin. Put the raisins, dates and brandy in a bowl and leave to soak for 30 minutes.

2. Melt the chocolate, with 125g (4½oz) butter and the syrup in a small pan over a gentle heat.

3. Add the biscuits, orange rind, raisins, dates and any remaining liquid. Mix well, pour into the tin, cool and chill for 1 hour.

4. Melt the chocolate for the topping in a small pan with the remaining butter. Pour this over the biscuit layer in the tin. Chill overnight. Remove from the tin and cut into wedges to serve.

Freezing: Make up to the end of step 4, then wrap and freeze for up to two months.

To use: Thaw at room temperature for 4 hours. Complete the recipe.

Preparation time: 40 min, plus 1 hr cooling and overnight chilling
Cals per serving: 578   **Makes:** 8 wedges

unsalted butter	150g (5oz), plus extra for greasing
raisins	50g (2oz)
dates	75g (3oz), chopped
brandy	4 tbsp
dark chocolate	200g bar
golden syrup	3 tbsp
digestive biscuits	250g (9oz), crushed
large orange	½, rind finely grated

For the topping
dark chocolate, with 70% cocoa solids	150g (5oz)

Macaroons

medium egg whites	2
caster sugar	225g (8oz)
ground almonds	125g (4oz)
almond extract	½ tsp
whole blanched almonds	25

1. Preheat the oven to 180°C/160°C fan oven/Gas Mark 4. Line two baking sheets with baking parchment. Whisk the egg whites until stiff. Gradually fold in the sugar, then stir in the almonds and almond extract to form a paste.

2. Spoon teaspoonfuls of the mixture, spacing them slightly apart, on to the baking trays. Press an almond into the centre of each and bake for 12 to 15 minutes until just golden and firm to touch.

3. Leave to cool. Transfer from the baking trays to wire racks to cool completely. Store in airtight containers until ready to serve.

Freezing: Leave to cool, wrap and freeze for up to two months.

To use: Thaw for 2 hours, then wrap.

Preparation time: 10 min   **Cooking time:** 12 –15 min
Cals per serving: 80   **Makes:** 25

White and Dark Chocolate Cookies

1. Preheat the oven to 180°C/160°C fan oven/Gas Mark 4. Grease three baking sheets. Cream together the butter and sugar. Gradually add the eggs and vanilla extract.

2. Sift in the flour, add the orange rind, then sprinkle in the white and dark chocolate. Mix the dough together with your hands.

3. Knead lightly, then wrap in clingfilm. Chill the cookie mixture for at least 30 minutes.

4. Divide the mixture into 26 pieces and roll each into a ball. Flatten each one slightly to make a disc, then put them on the baking sheets, spaced well apart. Bake for around 10 to 12 minutes or until golden.

5. Leave on the baking sheet for 5 minutes, then transfer to a wire rack to cool completely.

Preparation time: 15 min, plus 30 min chilling
Cooking time: 10–12 min   **Cals per serving:** 140   **Makes:** 26

unsalted butter	125g (4oz), softened, plus extra for greasing
golden caster sugar	125g (4oz)
medium eggs	2, beaten
vanilla essence	2 tsp
self-raising flour	250g (9oz), sifted
orange	1, rind finely grated
white chocolate	100g (3½oz), chopped
dark chocolate	100g (3½oz), chopped

Make time for tea: for the minimum of effort try serving savoury Mini Ham Pastry Croissants, with chocolate Tiffin

Time for Tea: Make teatime as **varied** and as much of a **treat** as you like. **Mix sweet and savoury**, but **keep it fairly light**. Children love the **Oven-baked Root Vegetable Chips**, a healthy alternative to crisps. Serve **toast** with the **Cannellini Bean and Basil Spread**. **Croissants**, usually associated with breakfasts, are a **perfect teatime snack**. These savoury **Mini Ham Pastry Croissants** are made with **puff pastry** and **filled with mustard, ham and eggs**, similar to a **croque monsieur**, and appeal to children and adults, alike. You can **alter the fillings** as you please. More **sophisticated**, are these **rich slices of chocolate Tiffin** made with **brandy-soaked raisins and dates**.

Chocolate and Brandy
Torte

butter	125g (4oz), diced, plus extra for greasing
plain chocolate	225g (8oz), broken into pieces
large eggs	3, separated
light muscovado sugar	125g (4oz)
brandy	4 tbsp
self-raising flour	75g (3oz), sifted
ground almonds	55g (2oz)
icing sugar	sifted, to dust

1. Preheat the oven to 180°C/160°C fan oven/Gas Mark 4. Grease and baseline a 20cm (8in) springform tin. Put the butter and chocolate into a heatproof bowl and place over a pan of simmering water. Stir until melted and smooth. Remove from the heat and put to one side.

2. Whisk the egg yolks and light muscovado sugar until pale and creamy, then whisk in the brandy and melted chocolate on a low speed. Fold the self-raising flour and ground almonds into the chocolate mixture with a large metal spoon. Put the mixture to one side.

3. Whisk the egg whites to soft peaks. Beat a large spoonful of the egg white into the chocolate mixture, then carefully fold in the remainder with a large metal spoon.

4. Pour the mixture into the prepared tin and bake for 45 minutes or until a skewer inserted into the centre comes out clean. Allow the cake to cool in the tin for 10 minutes, then turn out on to a wire rack. Remove the lining paper from the base of the cake when it is completely cold, then dust the top with icing sugar.

Preparation time: 10 min, plus cooling **Cooking time:** 45 min
Cals per serving: 596 for 6, 446 for 8 **Serves:** 6–8

Sweet Mocha
Bread

strong plain white flour 425g (15oz), plus extra to dust
salt 1 tsp
fast-action dried yeast 7g sachet
caster sugar 75g (3oz)
large eggs 3
double cream 150ml (5fl oz)
butter 50g (2oz), melted
oil for greasing

For the filling and topping
caster sugar 75g (3oz)
instant coffee granules 4 tbsp
plain chocolate 200g (7oz), chopped
pecan nuts 50g (2oz), chopped

1. Sift the flour and salt into a bowl. Stir in the yeast and caster sugar. In a separate bowl, lightly beat the eggs, cream and melted butter. Make a well in the centre of the flour mixture, then add the egg mixture. Mix everything together to form a soft dough.

2. Turn the dough out on to a floured work surface and knead for 5 to 10 minutes until smooth and elastic. Transfer the dough to a lightly oiled bowl, cover with clingfilm and leave in a warm place to rise for about 40 minutes or until doubled in size.

3. For the filling, put 50g (2oz) of the caster sugar in a small pan with 5 tablespoons of water and heat gently until the sugar dissolves. Stir in the coffee granules and bring to the boil. Simmer for 1 minute, then remove from the heat and set aside to cool.

4. Grease and line a 20cm (8in) springform cake tin. Turn the dough out on to a floured surface and divide into four pieces. Roll out one piece to a 25cm (10in) round and press into the base of the tin so the edges come slightly up the sides. Scatter over 50g (2oz) of the plain chocolate, then spoon over about one-third of the coffee syrup.

5. Roll out another piece of dough to a 25cm (10in) round and lay this over the first, letting the excess dough come up the sides of the tin and pinching the edges firmly into the first layer of dough. Repeat the layering, finishing with a round of dough. Brush the top lightly with water and scatter with the pecan nuts.

6. Cover the tin with lightly oiled clingfilm and leave to rise in a warm place for about 30 minutes or until the dough nearly reaches the top of the tin. Meanwhile, preheat the oven to 220°C/200°C fan oven/Gas Mark 7.

7. Bake the bread for 15 minutes, then reduce the oven temperature to 170°C/150°C fan oven/Gas Mark 3. Cover the tin with a piece of foil and bake for a further 30 minutes.

8. Put the remaining sugar in a small pan with 4 tablespoons of water and heat gently until the sugar dissolves. Bring to the boil and boil for 1 minute. Remove from the heat and stir in the remaining chocolate. Transfer the bread to a wire rack and drizzle with the chocolate sauce. Leave to cool before slicing and serving.

Preparation time: 25 min, plus 1 hr 10 min rising
Cooking time: 45 min   **Cals per serving:** 475   **Serves:** 10

Border Tart

For the pastry

plain flour	175g (6oz), plus extra to dust
unsalted butter	125g (4oz)
ground almonds	25g (1oz)
caster sugar	25g (1oz)
large egg yolk	1
vanilla ice cream	to serve

For the filling

unsalted butter	100g (3½oz), softened
dark muscovado sugar	100g (3½oz)
large eggs	2, beaten
raisins	200g (7oz)
sultanas	200g (7oz)
small oranges	2, rind finely grated
ground cinnamon	½ tsp
icing sugar	125g (4oz), sifted, plus extra to dust

1. To make the pastry, whiz the flour and butter in a food processor until the mixture resembles fine breadcrumbs, then add the ground almonds, caster sugar and egg yolk with 1 tablespoon of cold water. Pulse until the mixture just comes together (add more water if it needs it). Alternatively, sift the flour into a large bowl, rub in the butter to form fine breadcrumbs and stir in the remaining pastry ingredients.

2. Turn out on to a floured work surface, knead lightly, wrap and chill for at least 30 minutes. Preheat the oven to 190°C/170°C fan oven/Gas Mark 5.

3. Roll out the pastry on a lightly floured work surface to a 25cm (10in) round. Line a 23cm (9in) loose-bottomed, fluted tart tin with the pastry, prick the bottom with a fork and chill for a further 30 minutes.

4. Line the pastry case with greaseproof paper and fill with baking beans. Bake for 15 minutes, remove the paper and beans and cook for a further 10 to 15 minutes or until just cooked in the centre. Cool for 15 minutes.

5. Meanwhile, to make the filling, beat together the butter and sugar, then stir in the eggs, raisins, sultanas, grated rind of one orange and the cinnamon. Tip into the pastry case and bake for 30 minutes until set. (You might need to cover loosely with foil for the last 10 minutes or so to prevent the raisins burning.) Allow to cool a little, then transfer to a wire rack to cool completely.

6. Put the icing sugar in a bowl and mix with about 3 tablespoons of water to make a smooth icing. Drizzle over the tart and allow to set. Serve in slices, sprinkled with the remaining grated orange rind and dusted with icing sugar. Or serve warm with vanilla ice cream.

Preparation time: 30 min, plus 1 hr chilling and 15 min cooling
Cooking time: 1 hr   **Cals per serving:** 594   **Serves:** 8

Extra Moist
Fruity Teabread

Darjeeling tea bag	I
ready-to-eat dried figs	75g (3oz), chopped
sultanas	225g (8oz)
ready-to-eat dried pears	75g (3oz), chopped
orange	I, rind and juice of
butter	125g (4oz), softened
dark muscovado sugar	175g (6oz)
medium eggs	2, beaten
self-raising flour	225g (8oz), sifted
ground mixed spice	I tsp
demerara sugar	to sprinkle

1. Put the tea bag in a jug, add 150ml (5fl oz) boiling water and leave to steep for 3 minutes. Remove the bag and discard.

2. Put the figs, sultanas, pears, rind and juice of the orange in a bowl, then add the tea. Cover and leave to soak for at least 6 hours or overnight.

3. Preheat the oven to 180°C/160°C fan oven/Gas Mark 4, then grease and line a 900g (2lb) loaf tin.

4. Cream the butter and sugar together in a large bowl. Add the eggs and beat well, then add the flour, mixed spice and soaked fruit and mix everything together until thoroughly combined.

5. Put the mixture into the prepared tin and bake in the centre of the oven for 50 minutes. Take out, sprinkle with demerara sugar, cover with foil and return to the oven for 55 minutes or until a skewer inserted in the centre comes out clean. Wrap in clingfilm and store in an airtight container for up to two weeks.

Freezing: Once cold, pack and freeze in a sealed bag. Thaw for 8 hours.

Preparation time: 30 min, plus 6 hrs or overnight soaking
Cooking time: I hr 45 min   **Cals per serving:** 290   **Serves:** 12

Cannellini Bean
and Basil Spread

cannellini beans	400g can, drained and rinsed
garlic cloves	2
olive oil	I tbsp
lemon juice	2 tsp
sea salt	I tsp
fresh basil leaves	handful, torn
dark rye bread	
and mixed salad dressed	
with olive oil vinaigrette	to serve

1. Put the beans, garlic, olive oil, lemon juice, salt and pepper in a food processor. Whiz to make a rough paste, then stir in the basil leaves.

2. Serve with dark rye bread and a large mixed salad dressed with olive oil vinaigrette.

Preparation time: 5 min
Cals per serving: 127   **Serves:** 3

Extra Moist Fruity
Teabread

Mini Ham
Pastry Croissants

flavourless oil for greasing
ready-made puff pastry 225g (8oz)
Dijon mustard 3 tbsp
sliced ham 100g (3½oz)
large egg yolk 1, beaten
sesame seeds and
mustard seeds for sprinkling

1. Preheat the oven to 200°C/180°C fan oven/Gas Mark 6. Oil two baking sheets. Roll out the pastry until it measures 18 x 23cm (7 x 9in). Cut in half lengthways to make two equal strips, spread each with mustard and cut each strip into five diagonally to make 10 triangles.

2. Cut the ham into strips 10cm (4in) long and 5mm (¼in) wide. Place two strips of ham on the long edge of each triangle and roll them up from that edge. Place the croissants on the baking sheets, curling the ends to form crescents. Tuck the point of each triangle underneath to stop the croissants unravelling as they bake.

3. Brush the tops with beaten egg, sprinkle seeds on top then bake for 10 to 15 minutes or until crisp and golden. Serve warm. At this stage you can freeze the croissants, then, when ready to serve, defrost and heat them in a moderate oven for 5 to 6 minutes or until crisp.

Preparation time: 30 min   **Cooking time:** 10–15 min
Cals per serving: 55   **Makes:** 20

Hot Stilton
Bites

1. Preheat the oven to 220°C/200°C fan oven/Gas Mark 7. Place a baking sheet in the oven to heat. Roll out the pastry to a thickness of 1cm (½in) and cut into 5cm (2in) squares. Scatter the stilton and parmesan, cayenne pepper, poppy seeds and mustard seeds over the pastry.

2. Place the bites on the hot baking sheet and bake for 10 minutes or until golden. Leave for a few minutes, then transfer to a serving plate.

Preparation time: 15 min   **Cooking time:** 10 min
Cals per serving: 263   **Serves:** 6

ready-rolled puff pastry 250g (9oz)
stilton cheese 125g (4oz), crumbled
parmesan 25g (1oz), grated
cayenne pepper 1 tsp
poppy seeds 1 tsp
black mustard seeds 1 tsp

Prawns with Avocado and Tomato Salsa

ripe avocado	½
large ripe tomatoes	3, peeled, quartered and chopped
spring onions	2, finely chopped
large red chilli	1, halved, deseeded and finely chopped
lemon	1, juice of
Tabasco sauce	a dash
wheat tortillas	2
vegetable oil	for frying
olive oil	1 tbsp
butter	15g (½oz)
small shallot	1, finely chopped
raw warm water prawns	225g (8oz), thawed if frozen
iceberg lettuce	¼
fresh coriander	1 tsp, chopped, to garnish

1. Chop the avocado flesh and put in a bowl with the tomatoes, spring onions, chilli and half the lemon juice. Mix together, mashing a little with a fork. Season and add a dash of Tabasco.

2. Cut the tortillas into eight triangles, heat the vegetable oil and deep-fry a few at a time until they're crisp and golden, then drain on kitchen paper and put to one side.

3. Heat a frying pan and add the olive oil and butter. Once the butter has melted add the shallot and fry until soft. Add the prawns to the pan and cook over a high heat until they change colour. Add the remaining lemon juice and a dash of Tabasco, then stir well.

4. Shred the lettuce and divide between four bowls, then top with the prawns and avocado and tomato salsa. Surround with tortillas and garnish with the coriander.

Preparation time: 10 min   **Cooking time:** 10 min
Cals per serving: 252   **Serves:** 4

Hot Spiced Nuts

1. Preheat the oven to 190°C/170°C fan oven /Gas Mark 5. Pour the oil into a roasting tin, stir in the salt and spices, then heat in the oven for 2 minutes. Add the nuts to the tin, shaking it to coat the nuts in the seasoned oil. Bake for 7 to 10 minutes, shaking the nuts once until golden.

2. Using a slotted spoon, transfer the nuts to kitchen paper to drain. Sprinkle with salt and serve warm, garnished with chilli slices, or store in an airtight container for up to two days. Reheat in a low oven for 5 minutes before serving.

Preparation time: 5 min   **Cooking time:** 10 min
Cals per serving: 246 for 6, 185 for 8   **Serves:** 6–8

sunflower oil	2 tbsp
Maldon sea salt flakes	1 tsp, plus extra to sprinkle
ground cumin	½ tsp
ground coriander	½ tsp
ground chilli powder	½ tsp
garlic powder and salt	¼ tsp
shelled natural mixed nuts	200g pack
red chilli slices	fried in sunflower oil, to garnish

Red Onion and Parmesan Tarts

For the pastry

plain flour	225g (8oz), sifted
unsalted butter	100g (3½oz), diced and chilled
salt	pinch of
medium egg yolk	1

For the filling

butter	15g (½oz)
olive oil	1 tbsp
medium red onions	4, sliced in fine wedges
lemon juice	1 tbsp
crème fraîche	200ml tub
chopped fresh thyme	1 tbsp, plus thyme sprigs to garnish
parmesan	50g (2oz), freshly grated

1. To make the pastry, put the flour and butter in a food processor and whiz until the mixture resembles breadcrumbs. Put into a bowl, add a pinch of salt, the egg yolk and 7 teaspoons of cold water. Mix well and bring the dough together with your hands. Wrap and chill for 15 minutes.

2. To make the filling, melt the butter and oil together in a pan. Toss the onions in 1 tablespoon of lemon juice, then sauté the onions for 15 minutes. Put to one side.

3. Divide the pastry into six pieces. Roll each piece on a floured board and use to line six 11cm (4¼in) loose-based tartlet tins. Prick the base and sides with a fork. Put on a lipped baking sheet, cover with clingfilm and freeze for 10 minutes.

4. Preheat the oven to 200°C/180°C fan oven/Gas Mark 6. Line tartlet tins with greaseproof paper and baking beans and bake for 10 to 15 minutes. Remove the paper and beans and return to the oven for 5 minutes or until dry in the centre.

5. Increase the oven temperature to 230°C/210°C fan oven/Gas Mark 8. Put half the onions in the pastry cases. Mix the crème fraîche and thyme together, season and spoon half over the onions. Add half the parmesan. Top with the rest of the onions, crème fraîche and parmesan. Bake for 5 to 10 minutes or until golden. Serve garnished with thyme sprigs.

Preparation time: 40 min, plus 25 min chilling and freezing
Cooking time: 30–40 min   **Cals per serving:** 500   **Serves:** 6

Cheddar Wafers

1. Preheat the oven to 200°C/180°C fan oven/Gas Mark 6. Mix together the cheese and thyme. Put 1 teaspoon of cheese mixture in a 5cm (2in) pastry cutter on a non-stick baking sheet. Repeat with more cheese – about five rounds will fit on the sheet at a time. Cook for 2 to 3 minutes or until lacy and pale gold (do not overcook them or they'll taste bitter).

2. Remove sheet from the oven and, using a palette knife, lift the wafers off, then curl them over a rolling pin to shape; set aside to cool. Continue until all the mixture is used. Keep in an airtight container for two days.

Preparation time: 25 min   **Cooking time:** 15–20 min
Cals per serving: 21   **Makes:** 25–30

cheddar	125g (4oz), finely grated
chopped fresh thyme	pinch of

Red Onion and
Parmesan Tarts

Smoked Salmon
Bagel Chips

smoked salmon 200g (7oz), sliced
cream cheese 75g (3oz)
bagel chips 110g pack
cooked beetroot 1, peeled and finely chopped
olive oil 2 tsp
herb oil to drizzle
fresh dill sprigs chopped
dill and lemon rind to garnish

1. Cut the salmon into wide strips. Season the cream cheese with black pepper and spread on to each bagel chip, then top with salmon strips.

2. Mix the beetroot with the olive oil and season with black pepper. Top half the bagel chips with beetroot and dill sprigs. Drizzle herb oil over the rest and top with chopped dill and lemon rind.

3. Once dressed, the bagel chips will keep for 3 hours in a cool place.

Preparation time: 20 min   **Cals per serving:** 67   **Makes:** about 25

Anchovy Rolls

1. Preheat the oven to 200°C/180°C fan oven/Gas Mark 6. Remove the crusts and butter the bread. Spread each slice with mustard, then sprinkle with half the parmesan and place one anchovy fillet on each side of each slice. Roll the bread up tightly and cut in half.

2. Pack the rolls on to a baking sheet, seam-side down, drizzle with oil and sprinkle with the remaining cheese and black pepper. Cook for 15 to 20 minutes until golden. Serve warm.

Preparation time: 15 min   **Cooking time:** 15–20 min
Cals per serving: 79   **Makes:** 28

thin slices white bread 14
butter 125g (4oz), softened
Dijon mustard 2 tbsp
parmesan 4 tbsp, finely grated
anchovies in olive oil 50g can, drained
olive oil for drizzling

Oven-baked
Root Vegetable Chips

large Maris Piper potatoes	700g (1½lb)
large carrots	300g (11oz)
large parsnips	3, about 700g (1½lb) total weight
ground cumin	½ tsp
ground coriander	½ tsp
ground chilli powder	½ tsp
garlic powder	¼ tsp
salt	¼ tsp
ground cloves	pinch of
sea salt	½ tsp
olive oil	4 tbsp

1. Peel the vegetables and cut lengthways into 1cm (½in) x 7.5cm (3in) chips. Mix all the spices and salt together. Put the vegetables in a bowl and toss with the oil and the spice mix, then transfer to two roasting tins.

2. Cook at 220°C/200°C fan oven/Gas Mark 7 for 50 to 55 minutes or until the vegetables are tender and golden. Toss frequently and swap the tins over occasionally, so that the vegetables cook evenly.

3. Drain the vegetables on kitchen paper. Serve warm with Home-made Tomato Ketchup (see below).

Preparation time: 30 min   **Cooking time:** 55 min
Cals per serving: 320   **Serves:** 6

Home-made Tomato
Ketchup

1. Heat the oil in a pan, add the shallots and garlic and cook gently for 5 minutes or until softened. Stir in the tomato purée, fry for 30 seconds, then stir in the tomatoes. Bring to the boil and bubble for 20 miutes or until most of the liquid has evaporated.

2. Cool slightly, then whiz in a blender or food processor until smooth. Return to the clean pan, season, then add the sugar and vinegar. Bring to the boil and simmer for 2 to 3 minutes, then cool.

Preparation time: 10 min   **Cooking time:** 28 min
Cals per serving: 145   **Serves:** 6

oil	2 tbsp
shallots	2, chopped
garlic cloves	3, chopped
tomato purée	2 tbsp
chopped tomatoes	2 x 400g cans
soft dark brown sugar	6 tbsp
white wine vinegar	2 tbsp

midweek meals

Turkey, Ham and Spinach Broth

green or yellow split peas	125g (4oz), soaked overnight in double their volume of cold water
butter	25g (1oz)
onion	225g (8oz), chopped
ground coriander	1 tbsp
pearl barley	40g (1½oz)
ham or turkey stock	2ltr (3½pt)
bay leaf	1
celery stick	1
fresh thyme sprig	1
potatoes	225g (8oz), peeled and cut into chunks
carrots	400g (14oz), peeled and cut into chunks
cooked turkey and ham	150g (5oz) each, cut into chunks
baby spinach leaves	150g (5oz), washed and dried
fresh coriander sprigs and black pepper	to garnish
finely grated parmesan	50g (2oz), optional

1. Drain the split peas and place in a pan with enough cold water to cover. Bring to the boil and simmer for 10 minutes. Drain the peas and discard the liquid. Meanwhile, melt the butter in a separate pan, add the onion and cook for 5 minutes or until soft, but not coloured. Add the ground coriander and cook for 30 seconds.

2. Add the split peas, pearl barley and stock. Tie the bay leaf, celery and thyme sprig together and add to the pan. Bring to the boil and simmer for 40 minutes or until the peas and barley are tender. Add the potatoes and cook for 5 minutes; add the carrots and cook for 5 to 10 minutes more. Season well.

3. Add the turkey, ham and spinach and bring back to the boil. Simmer for 2 to 3 minutes. Ladle into individual bowls and garnish with fresh coriander and pepper and serve with parmesan, if using.

Freezing: Complete the recipe, but omitting the spinach, then cool, pack and freeze.

To use: Thaw overnight at cool room temperature. Reheat, then add the spinach. Simmer for 2–3 minutes. Garnish and serve.

Preparation time: 20 min, plus overnight soaking
Cooking time: 1 hr 15 min   **Cals per serving:** 300   **Serves:** 6

Pumpkin and Butternut Squash Soup

1. Preheat the oven to 220°C/200°C fan oven/Gas Mark 7. Place the pumpkin and squash, the shallots, garlic and the coriander seeds in a large roasting tin and toss with the melted butter. Season the vegetables well and roast for about 30 minutes, until golden and just cooked through.

2. Tip the vegetables into a large pan, then use the hot vegetable stock to rinse all the remaining bits out of the roasting tin. Add this to the vegetables in the pan, then stir in the milk.

3. Put three-quarters of the soup into a food processor or blender and whiz until smooth. Mash the remaining soup mixture, then stir the two together and reheat. Garnish with basil and swirls of soured cream, then serve with small Yorkshire puddings or crusty bread.

Preparation time: 20 min   **Cooking time:** 30 min
Cals per serving: 435   **Serves:** 4

pumpkin	900g (2lb), peeled and roughly diced
butternut squash	750g (1lb 10oz), peeled and roughly diced
shallots	125g (4oz), chopped
large garlic clove	1, chopped
coriander seeds	1 tsp
butter	125g (4oz), melted
hot vegetable stock	600ml (1pt)
milk	600ml (1pt)
fresh basil sprigs and soured cream	to garnish
small Yorkshire puddings or crusty bread	to serve

Pea and Lettuce Soup with Lemon Cream

unsalted butter	100g (3½oz)
unwaxed lemon	1, rind of
bay leaf	1
onion	75g (3oz), finely chopped
frozen peas	800g (1lb 12oz)
lettuce	150g (5oz), washed, dried and shredded
caster sugar	½ tsp
salt	1 tsp
black pepper	
lemon juice	2 tbsp

For the lemon cream

double cream	142ml carton
frozen peas	200g (7oz), cooked for 1 min in boiling water and drained
unwaxed lemon	1, rind finely grated
lemon juice	1 tbsp
unwaxed lemon rind strips	to garnish

1. To make the soup, melt the butter in a large pan. Tie together the lemon rind and bay leaf and add to the butter with the onion. Cook gently for 10 minutes or until the onion is soft and golden. Add the peas, lettuce, sugar, salt and pepper and stir until coated with the butter.

2. Pour in 900ml (1½ pints) of boiling water, return to the boil and simmer for 10 minutes or until the peas are soft. Remove from the heat, take out the lemon rind bundle and discard. Allow the soup to cool a little, whiz in a food processor or blender until smooth. Add the lemon juice.

3. To make the lemon cream, heat the cream in a small pan and allow to bubble for 5 minutes. Add the peas and grated lemon rind, season to taste and cook for 2 minutes. Add the lemon juice and stir through.

4. Reheat the soup, and adjust the seasoning if necessary. Ladle the soup into individual bowls and drizzle the lemon cream over each one. Garnish with the lemon rind strips and serve.

Freezing: Complete the recipe to the end of step 3, then cool, pack and freeze the soup and lemon cream separately.

To use: Thaw at cool room temperature overnight. Reheat the soup and lemon cream separately and complete the recipe.

Preparation time: 15 min   **Cooking time:** 30 min
Cals per serving: 381   **Makes:** 1.7 litres (3pt)

Autumn Vegetable Soup

1. Melt the butter in a large pan, then add the onion, potatoes, bacon, garlic, leek, apple and thyme. Season, stir, then cover and cook over a gentle heat for 15 minutes.

2. Add the cider and bring to the boil. Simmer for 5 minutes, then add the stock and simmer for 15 minutes more until the potato is soft.

3. Pour half the soup into a food processor or blender and whiz until smooth, then add to the remaining soup. Reheat gently, add the cabbage and simmer for a further 3 minutes. Ladle into warm bowls and serve.

Preparation time: 15 min   **Cooking time:** 40 min
Cals per serving: 451   **Serves:** 4

butter	50g (2oz)
medium onion	1, diced
potatoes	450g (1lb), diced
smoked bacon	100g (3½oz) pack, cubed
garlic clove	1, chopped
white of leek	100g (3½oz), chopped
Cox's Orange Pippins	2, cored and chopped
dried thyme	2 tsp
good-quality dry cider	600ml (1pt)
vegetable stock	900ml (1½pt)
Savoy cabbage	125g (4oz), shredded

Garlic Soup with Thyme Croutons

olive oil	4 tbsp
large onions	3, about 700g (1½lb) total weight, chopped
garlic cloves	16, roughly chopped
white wine or cider	150ml (5fl oz)
potatoes	350g (12oz), peeled and roughly chopped
vegetable stock	1.6ltr (2¾pt)
whipping cream	100ml (3½fl oz), plus extra for drizzling

For the thyme croutons

bread slices	3–4, cubed
olive oil	3–4 tbsp
dried thyme	1 tsp
fresh thyme sprigs	

1. In a heavy-based pan, heat the olive oil, add the onions and garlic then cover and cook over a low heat, stirring occasionally, for 15 to 25 minutes, or until translucent and very soft. Keep checking and do not allow to colour. Add the wine and bring to the boil. Bubble until the liquid has reduced by half.

2. Preheat the oven to 200°C/180°C fan oven/Gas Mark 6. Add the potatoes and stock to the onions and garlic, then bring to the boil and simmer, uncovered, for 45 minutes, or until reduced slightly. Meanwhile, make the thyme croutons. Mix the bread cubes in a bowl with the oil and thyme, then place in a preheated baking tray and bake for 10 minutes until golden and crisp. Sprinkle with salt and thyme sprigs.

3. When the soup has cooled a little, pour it into a food processor or blender and whiz until smooth. Add the cream, season well and reheat.

4. Ladle the soup into bowls, drizzle with a little cream, sprinkle the croutons on top and serve.

Freezing: Complete the recipe up to the end of step 3, but do not add the cream and do not reheat. Cool and freeze.

To use: Thaw at cool room temperature overnight. Bring the soup back to the boil, add the cream and simmer for 1 to 2 minutes. Complete the recipe. Make the thyme croutons fresh.

Preparation time: 15 min   **Cooking time:** 1 hr 30 min
Cals per serving: 258   **Serves:** 4

Garlic Soup with
Thyme Croutons

Summer Vegetable Soup with Herb Pistou

sunflower oil	3 tbsp
medium onion	1, finely chopped
waxy potatoes	225g (8oz), finely chopped
carrots	175g (6oz), finely diced
medium turnip	1, finely diced
bay leaves	4
large sage leaves	6
courgettes	2, about 365g (13oz) total weight, finely diced
French beans	175g (6oz), trimmed and halved plus extra to garnish
small fresh peas	125g (4oz), shelled
tomatoes	225g (8oz), peeled, deseeded and diced
small head broccoli	1, broken into florets

For the herb pistou

sea salt	¾ tsp
garlic cloves	6, chopped
chopped fresh basil	1 tbsp
olive oil	150ml (5fl oz)

1. Heat the oil in a large pan, add the onion, potatoes, carrots and turnip and fry over a gentle heat for 10 minutes. Add 1.7 litres (3 pints) of water, season well, bring to the boil and add the bay and sage leaves, then simmer for 25 minutes.

2. Add the courgettes, French beans (remove 12 French beans and cook them separately for garnish), peas and the tomatoes. Return to the boil and simmer for 10 to 15 minutes. Add the broccoli florets 5 minutes before the end of cooking time. Remove the bay and sage leaves and adjust the seasoning, if necessary.

3. To make the herb pistou, using a pestle and mortar or a strong bowl and the end of a rolling pin, pound the sea salt and garlic together until smooth. Add the basil and pound until broken down to a paste, then slowly blend in the olive oil.

4. Pour the soup into bowls, add a spoonful of herb pistou and garnish with the remaining French beans.

Preparation time: 45 min   **Cooking time:** 50 min
Cals per serving: 291   **Serves:** 6

Creamy Corn and Smoked Haddock Chowder

1. Melt the butter in a large pan and gently fry the onion for about 5 minutes until transparent. Add all the sweetcorn, milk and potatoes and season with black pepper. Bring to simmering point and continue to cook over a low heat, stirring occasionally, for about 20 minutes or until the potato is tender.

2. Cut the fish into large pieces, add to the chowder and simmer for another 3 minutes. To serve, ladle the chowder into warm bowls and garnish with the tomato and thyme.

Preparation time: 10 min   **Cooking time:** 35 min
Cals per serving: 560   **Serves:** 4

butter	25g (1oz)
small onion	1, finely chopped
sweetcorn	330g can
creamed sweetcorn	375g can
milk	750ml (1¼pt)
potatoes	450g (1lb), peeled and roughly chopped
smoked haddock	350g (12oz), skinned
diced tomato and fresh thyme	to garnish

Salmon Laksa

olive oil	1 tbsp
bunches spring onions	2, sliced
garlic clove	1, finely chopped
red chilli	1, deseeded and finely chopped
fresh ginger	2.5cm (1in) piece, finely chopped
Thai red curry paste	1–2 tbsp
coconut milk	400ml can
fish or vegetable stock	325ml (11fl oz)
skinned salmon fillet	700g (1½lb), cubed
chopped fresh coriander	2 tbsp
stir-fry rice noodles	150g (5oz)
salt	1 tsp

1. Heat the oil in a large frying pan and fry the spring onions, garlic, chilli, ginger and curry paste for 2 to 3 minutes. Add the coconut milk and stock and bring to the boil.

2. Add the salmon, return to the boil and simmer for 5 to 7 minutes or until the salmon is just cooked. Add the coriander and season to taste.

3. Meanwhile, put the noodles in a bowl with 1 teaspoon of salt, pour over boiling water to cover and leave to stand for 2 minutes. Drain and put in a large bowl, spoon the salmon and soup on top and serve.

Preparation time: 15 min   **Cooking time:** 10–15 min
Cals per serving: 503 for 4, 335 for 6   **Serves:** 4–6

Roasted Tomato Soup with Cod and Pesto

1. Preheat the oven to 220°C/200°C fan oven/Gas Mark 7. Put the tomatoes, two-thirds of the garlic and the onion in a roasting tin, drizzle with 55ml (4 tablespoons) of the olive oil and season well. Cook for 25 minutes, stirring occasionally.

2. Meanwhile, make the pesto: whiz the herbs, remaining garlic, lemon juice and 100ml (3½fl oz) of the remaining olive oil in a food processor to form a thick paste; season to taste.

3. Put the tomatoes in a food processor or blender and whiz briefly to form a thick, chunky purée. Pour into a pan with the stock, stir together and gently heat through.

4. Heat the remaining olive oil in a large non-stick frying pan and fry the seasoned fish for 2 to 3 minutes on each side. To serve, ladle the hot soup into warm bowls, then put a piece of fish in the middle of each. Drizzle with a generous spoonful of pesto and serve.

Preparation time: 20 min   **Cooking time:** 30 min
Cals per serving: 498   **Serves:** 4

ripe tomatoes	800g (1lb 12oz), halved
garlic cloves	3, chopped
small red onion	1, finely chopped
olive oil	200ml (7fl oz)
fresh basil	25g (1oz), chopped
fresh flat-leaf parsley	25g (1oz), chopped
lemon juice	1 tbsp
vegetable stock	450ml (15fl oz)
thick cod steaks	4, about 150g (5oz) each

Coconut Broth and Chicken Noodles

vegetable oil 1 tbsp
Thai red curry paste 2 tbsp
chicken stock 900ml (1½pt)
unsweetened coconut milk 400ml can
**selection of vegetables, such
as carrots, courgettes, beans,** about 350g
broccoli florets, baby corn (12oz) total weight
thread egg noodles 200g (7oz)
**large skinless
chicken breasts** 2, cut into thin strips
fresh coriander leaves to garnish
prawn crackers to serve

1. Heat the oil in a large pan and fry the curry paste for about 10 seconds. Add the chicken stock and coconut milk, bring to boiling point, then lower the heat and simmer for about 5 minutes.

2. Cut the carrots and courgettes into matchsticks and the remaining vegetables into small pieces. Cook the noodles according to packet instructions, then drain and put to one side.

3. Add the chicken to the soup and simmer for 3 minutes or until cooked through. Add the vegetables and mix well. Season to taste.

4. Divide the egg noodles among four large warmed bowls, pour the soup on top, then garnish with coriander and serve with prawn crackers.

Preparation time: 15 min   **Cooking time:** 12 min
Cals per serving: 384   **Serves:** 4

Coconut Broth and
Chicken Noodles

Summer Crunch Salad

French beans	150g (5oz), halved
courgettes	150g (5oz), cut into thin matchsticks
fennel	150g (5oz) cut into thin matchsticks
cherry tomatoes	200g (7oz)
roughly chopped fresh basil	2 tbsp
Parma ham slices	4
soft light brown sugar	1 tbsp
flaked almonds	25g (1oz), lightly toasted
parmesan shavings and fresh basil sprigs	to garnish

For the dressing

lemon juice	2 tbsp
olive oil	100ml (3½fl oz)

1. To make the dressing, whisk all the ingredients together in a small bowl, then cover and set aside.

2. To make the salad, blanch the French beans in boiling salted water for 1 minute, drain, refresh and drain again. Mix all the vegetables together in a large bowl, toss the chopped basil through and season.

3. Place the Parma ham on a baking sheet, sprinkle with the sugar and place under a hot grill for 2 to 3 minutes, or until golden.

4. Mix the dressing and almonds into the salad and serve with the Parma ham, garnished with parmesan shavings and basil sprigs.

Preparation time: 15 min   **Cooking time:** 4 min
Cals per serving: 260   **Serves:** 4

Warm Prawn, Bacon
and Mushroom Salad

1. To make the dressing, whisk all the ingredients together in a small bowl, then cover and set aside.

2. To make the salad, roughly chop the bacon, then dry-fry it in a heavy-based frying pan, stirring, for 5 minutes. Add the walnuts and cook for 2 to 3 minutes or until crisp. Remove from the pan and set aside.

3. Heat the oil in the wiped-out pan, add the shallots and fry, stirring for 5 minutes. Add the garlic and mushrooms and fry for 2 to 3 minutes. Pour in the brandy and cook for 1 to 2 minutes until reduced and syrupy. Add the prawns and stir-fry over a high heat for 2 minutes or until pink. Add the cooked bacon and stir gently to combine.

4. Toss the salad leaves with half the dressing and arrange on plates. Add the remaining dressing to the prawn mixture and spoon on top of the salad. Garnish with the chives.

Preparation time: 30 min   **Cooking time:** 20 min
Cals per serving: 520   **Serves:** 6

unsmoked streaky bacon	175g (6oz)
walnuts	75g (3oz), broken
oil	3 tbsp
shallots	125g (4oz), finely sliced
garlic cloves	2, crushed
brown-cap or chestnut mushrooms	225g (8oz), thickly sliced
brandy	4 tbsp
raw prawns	450g (1lb), peeled and deveined
mixed salad leaves	250g (9oz)
snipped fresh chives	to garnish

For the dressing

Dijon mustard	1 tsp
white wine vinegar	2 tbsp
walnut oil	6 tbsp
olive oil	6 tbsp

Garden Salad with Crisp Crumbs

asparagus tips or French beans	175g (6oz), trimmed and thickly sliced on the diagonal
sugarsnap peas	175g (6oz), halved on the diagonal
cucumber	1, peeled, halved, deseeded and sliced on the diagonal
bunches watercress	3, washed, dried and broken into sprigs
fennel bulb	1, quartered and thinly sliced
cherry tomatoes	225g (8oz), halved
red onions	175g (6oz), quartered and finely sliced
finely grated lemon rind	to garnish

For the crisp crumbs

olive oil	2 tbsp
garlic cloves	2, crushed
chorizo sausage	125g (4oz), chopped
breadcrumbs	75g (3oz)
lemon	1, rind grated
chopped fresh flat-leaf parsley	2 tbsp

For the dressing

lemon	1, juice of
Dijon mustard	1 tsp
caster sugar	1 tsp
olive oil	120ml (4fl oz)

1. To make the crisp crumbs, heat the oil in a frying pan, add the garlic, chorizo sausage and breadcrumbs and cook for 3 to 4 minutes, or until golden. Add the grated lemon rind and parsley and cook for a further 1 minute. Remove and drain on kitchen paper.

2. To make the dressing, mix all the ingredients together and set aside.

3. To make the salad, blanch the asparagus and sugarsnap peas in boiling salted water for 1 minute. Drain and immediately refresh in cold water, then drain again.

4. Place the asparagus, sugarsnap peas, cucumber, watercress, fennel, tomatoes and onions in a large bowl. Just before serving, toss in the dressing, top with the crumbs and garnish with lemon rind.

Preparation time: 45 min   **Cooking time:** 5 min, plus 15 min cooling
Cals per serving: 367   **Serves:** 6

Roasted Vegetable Salad with Mustard Mayonnaise

mixed vegetables, such as
fennel, courgettes, leeks,
aubergines, baby turnips, about 900g (2lb)
new potatoes and onions total weight
garlic cloves 2, unpeeled
fresh marjoram or
rosemary sprigs 4–5
olive oil 6 tbsp
flaked sea salt 1 tsp
mixed crushed peppercorns to taste
balsamic vinegar 2 tbsp
mixed charcuterie such as
bresaola, pastrami,
Parma ham, chorizo about 200g (7oz)
and salami total weight, to serve
fresh marjoram sprigs
and green olives to garnish
warm crusty bread to serve

For the mustard mayonnaise
mayonnaise 150ml (5fl oz)
Dijon mustard 2 tbsp

1. Preheat the oven to 220°C/200°C fan oven/Gas Mark 7. For the vegetables, quarter the fennel, chop the courgettes, leeks and aubergines, trim the turnips and cut the onions into petals, leaving the root intact. Place all the vegetables, garlic, rosemary or marjoram, oil, salt and peppercorns in a roasting tin and gently toss together to combine well.

2. Roast the vegetables for 30 to 35 minutes or until the vegetables are golden, tossing frequently. Sprinkle over the balsamic vinegar, then return to the oven for a further 5 minutes.

3. To make the mustard mayonnaise, mix together the mayonnaise and mustard, then season and set aside.

4. Arrange the meats on a platter. Surround with the roasted vegetable salad garnished with marjoram sprigs and green olives. Serve with the mustard mayonnaise and crusty bread.

Preparation time: 10 min **Cooking time:** 40 min
Cals per serving: 555 **Serves:** 4–6

Roasted Vegetable Salad
with Mustard Mayonnaise

The ideal meal for unexpected guests: Meatballs with Olive and Pesto Pasta and a crisp green salad

Unexpected Guests: When friends **drop in out of the blue** and you want to **knock up something quick** and filling to eat, **a good standby** is a **simple risotto** with **Garlic and Parmesan and** a **Caesar Salad** or **Tomato and Mozzarella Pasta Salad**. Alternatively, there is nothing **more satisfying** than a plate of **steaming hot pasta**. This dish of **Meatballs with Olive and Pesto Pasta**, is so easy **to prepare**. Here, the pasta is the **wide-ribboned pappardelle noodles**, but you could **choose any** other **ribbon pasta** instead. Serve in a **big serving dish** with a **green salad** on the side, with a **rich French dressing**, and hey presto **a good meal** in **no time at all**.

Melon, Mint and Crispy Ham Salad

red wine vinegar 3–4 tbsp
caster sugar ½ tsp
chopped fresh mint 3 tbsp
salt pinch of
olive oil 120ml (4fl oz)
Serrano or Parma ham 2 × 70g packs
ripe charentais melons 1½
spring onions 3, finely sliced and soaked in iced water
tropical mixed peppercorns 1 tsp, crushed
Manchego or parmesan cheese shavings 50g (2oz)
fresh mint sprigs to garnish

1. To make the salad dressing, whisk together the vinegar, sugar, chopped mint, salt and oil. Set aside.

2. Preheat the grill. Grill half the Serrano ham for 1 to 2 minutes, or until crisp, then set aside. Grill the remaining slices, then set aside to cool. Break into large pieces.

3. Quarter the whole melon, then cut the melon half into two (you should end up with six pieces). Cut each piece into three wedges and remove the skin. Place three wedges on each plate and top with the ham.

4. To serve, whisk the dressing again and drizzle over the melon. Top with the spring onion curls, then sprinkle with crushed peppercorns and Manchego cheese shavings and garnish with mint sprigs.

Preparation time: 20 min   **Cooking time:** 4 min
Cals per serving: 364   **Serves:** 6

Halloumi and Avocado Salad

1. To make the dressing, whisk the lemon juice together with the olive oil and mint, then season with pepper.

2. Coat the halloumi with the flour. Heat the oil in a large frying pan and fry the cheese for 1 minute on each side or until it forms a golden crust.

3. Meanwhile, in a large bowl, add half the dressing to the salad leaves and avocado and toss together. Arrange the hot cheese on top and drizzle over the remaining dressing. Garnish with parsley and serve.

Preparation time: 10 min   **Cooking time:** 2 min
Cals per serving: 558   **Serves:** 4

lemon juice 3 tbsp
olive oil 100ml (3½fl oz)
chopped fresh mint 3 tbsp
halloumi cheese 250g pack, sliced into 8
seasoned flour 1 tbsp
oil 2 tbsp
mixed leaf salad 200g bag
avocados 2, peeled and sliced
fresh flat-leaf parsley to garnish

Caesar
Salad

For the croutons
olive oil 3 tbsp
paprika 1 tsp
cayenne pepper pinch of
1 day-old rustic white bread 125g (4oz), cubed

For the dressing
olive oil 200ml (7fl oz)
garlic cloves 8, crushed
anchovy fillets in oil 8, drained and chopped
balsamic vinegar 1 tbsp
Dijon mustard 2 tbsp
lemon 1, juice of
medium egg 1

To finish
cos lettuce leaves 450g (1lb), dried
parmesan 50g (2oz), finely grated

To garnish
crushed black peppercorns
fresh chives

1. Preheat the oven to 220°C/200°C fan oven/Gas Mark 7. To make the croutons, place the olive oil, paprika and cayenne pepper in a bowl and mix together well. Add the bread and toss until well coated in the oil. Place the cubes on a baking sheet and bake for 6 to 8 minutes until crisp and golden. Set aside until required.

2. To make the dressing, place the olive oil in a small pan with the garlic and anchovies and heat gently for 5 to 6 minutes until the anchovies have been broken down. Transfer to a bowl; cool. Add the vinegar, mustard and lemon juice and whisk together until thickened.

3. Cook the egg in boiling water for 2 minutes. Cool under cold, running water, then remove the shell and break open the egg. Drop the yolk directly into the cool dressing and whisk until smooth – do not worry if some of the white goes in too.

4. Place the lettuce leaves in a bowl, scatter over the croutons and parmesan; toss together with the dressing. Garnish with the crushed black peppercorns and chives, then serve immediately.

Preparation time: 10 min   **Cooking time:** 16 min
Cals per serving: 508   **Serves:** 6

Apple, Fennel, Ham and Pecan Salad

large crisp apples	2, about 450g (1lb), total weight, quartered, cored and sliced
fennel	450g (1lb), halved; core removed and thinly sliced lengthways
shelled pecan nuts	75g (3oz)
cooked ham	300g (11oz), cut into wide strips
chicory head	1, divided into leaves
fresh flat-leaf parsley	to garnish

For the dressing

runny honey	1 tsp
German or Dijon mustard	2 tsp
cider vinegar	3 tbsp
vegetable oil	135ml (4½fl oz)
poppy seeds	2 tsp

1. To make the dressing, whisk together the honey, mustard, vinegar and seasoning in a small bowl. Whisk in the vegetable oil then the poppy seeds. Set aside.

2. Place all the ingredients for the salad in a large bowl, toss well with the dressing and correct the seasoning, if necessary. Garnish with parsley and serve.

Preparation time: 30 min   **Cals per serving:** 345   **Serves:** 6

Apple, Fennel, Ham
and Pecan Salad

Warm Spicy Chorizo Sausage
and Chickpea Salad

olive oil	5 tbsp
chorizo or spicy sausage	200g (7oz), thinly sliced
red onion	225g (8oz), chopped
large red pepper	1, deseeded and roughly chopped
garlic cloves	3, finely chopped
cumin seeds	1 tsp
chickpeas	2 × 440g cans, drained and rinsed
chopped fresh coriander	2 tbsp
lemon	1, juice of

1. Heat 1 tablespoon of the olive oil in a non-stick frying pan and cook the chorizo sausage over a medium heat for 1 to 2 minutes or until lightly browned. Remove with a slotted spoon and set aside. Fry the onion in the chorizo oil for 10 minutes or until browned.

2. Add the pepper, garlic, cumin seeds and chickpeas to the onion and cook for a further 5 minutes, stirring frequently to prevent sticking. Remove from the heat and add the chorizo.

3. Add the coriander, lemon juice and remaining olive oil. Season well and serve immediately.

Preparation time: 20 min   **Cooking time:** 17 min
Cals per serving: 566   **Serves:** 4

Quick Jerk
Chicken Salad

1. Season the chicken breasts and rub them with jerk seasoning. Heat the grill to maximum. Place the chicken breasts under the grill and cook for 5 minutes on each side or until cooked to the centre. Set aside.

2. Meanwhile, cook the potatoes in boiling salted water for 10 minutes or until tender. Drain, cool a little and cut into chunks. Mix the mayonnaise and mustard together, then add to the potatoes, stir and set aside.

3. Heat the oil in a large frying pan, add the onion and fry for 5 minutes. Add the mushrooms and cook for a further 2 minutes, then season.

4. Place the potato and mushroom mixtures in a bowl and add the spinach. Toss with the chives, add the lemon juice and season. Cut the chicken into thick slices on the diagonal and serve with the salad.

Preparation time: 10 min   **Cooking time:** 27 min
Cals per serving: 600   **Serves:** 4

chicken breast fillets,	4, skin on
jerk seasoning	4 tsp
Jersey Royals	450g (1lb)
mayonnaise	100ml (3½fl oz)
wholegrain mustard	2 tbsp
vegetable oil	2 tbsp
onion	200g (7oz), sliced
brown cap mushrooms	125g (4oz)
young spinach leaves	225g (8oz)
chopped fresh chives	3 tbsp
lemon juice	to taste

Oriental Beef
Salad

dark soy sauce	4 tbsp
hot horseradish sauce	1 tsp
fresh root ginger	2.5cm (1in) piece, chopped
lime	½, juice of
sirloin steaks	2, about 175g (6oz) each
noodles	200g (7oz)
oil	3 tbsp
spring onions	4, sliced
pak choi or spinach	200g (7oz), thickly sliced
toasted sesame seeds	1 tbsp, to garnish

1. To make the dressing, combine the soy sauce, horseradish sauce, ginger and lime juice in a bowl. Spoon half the dressing over the steaks and set the remainder aside.

2. Cook the noodles according to packet instructions. Drain, run under cold water and set aside.

3. Heat 1 tablespoon of the oil in a non-stick frying pan. Fry the steaks for 2 minutes on each side for medium rare, or 3 to 4 minutes if you prefer them well done. Remove and set aside. Wipe out the pan, add the remaining oil and fry the spring onions for 1 minute. Add the pak choi and noodles and cook for 1 minute or until the pak choi is just wilting and the noodles are warmed through. Season to taste.

4. Slice the steaks into 1cm (½in) strips; add to the noodles and pak choi. Pour the remaining dressing over, garnish with sesame seeds and serve.

Preparation time: 15 min   **Cooking time:** 6–10 min
Cals per serving: 304   **Serves:** 4

Tomato and Mozzarella Pasta Salad

lemon juice 2 tsp
basil-flavoured olive oil 100ml (3½fl oz)
garlic cloves 2, crushed
penne pasta 350g (12oz)
mozzarella 250g (9oz), cut into chunks
vine-ripened tomatoes 700g (1½lb), skinned, deseeded and cut into chunks
large red chilli ½, deseeded and finely sliced
large green chilli ½, deseeded and finely sliced
crushed black pepper and basil leaves to garnish

1. Place the salt and pepper in a small bowl, whisk in the lemon juice, followed by the flavoured oil and garlic, then set aside.

2. Bring a large pan of salted water to the boil, add the pasta and cook according to packet instructions. Drain, place in a bowl and toss with 2 tablespoons of the dressing (this will prevent the pasta from sticking); set aside to cool. Place the mozzarella in a large bowl with the remaining dressing and set aside.

3. When ready to serve, add the pasta to the mozzarella with the tomatoes and chillies. Toss together and season well. Garnish with crushed black pepper and basil leaves, then serve.

Preparation time: 20 min   **Cooking time:** 10–12 min
Cals per serving: 712   **Serves:** 4

Warm Oyster Mushroom and Spinach Salad

1. Bake the focaccia cubes at 200°C/180°C fan oven/Gas Mark 6 for 6 to 8 minutes, or until lightly toasted.

2. In a small bowl, whisk together the vinegar, mustard, salt and pepper until well combined, then whisk in the sunflower oil and half the walnut oil. Put to one side.

3. Cook the bacon in a non-stick frying pan for 2 to 3 minutes, add the remaining walnut oil and heat for 1 minute, then add the mushrooms. Stir-fry the mixture over a brisk heat for 2 to 3 minutes or until wilted and the bacon is brown and crisp. Take the pan off the heat, stir in the walnut pieces and season.

4. Put the spinach in a large bowl, add the bacon and mushrooms and toss together with the dressing. Pile into a serving dish and sprinkle with focaccia croutons. Serve immediately.

Preparation time: 20 min   **Cooking time:** 8 min
Cals per serving: 840   **Serves:** 4

focaccia bread 4 slices, cubed
balsamic vinegar 2 tbsp
Dijon mustard 1 tsp
sunflower oil 3 tbsp
walnut oil 6 tbsp
streaky bacon rashers 225g (8oz), de-rinded and cut into short, thin strips
oyster mushrooms 350g (12oz)
walnut pieces 25g (1oz)
baby spinach 450g (1lb), washed and dried

Warm Oyster
Mushroom and
Spinach Salad

Garlic Mushrooms on Ciabatta

garlic cloves	3, crushed
chopped fresh chives	2 tbsp
lemon	1, rind finely grated, juice of ½
unsalted butter	125g (4oz), melted
field mushrooms	6, thinly sliced
ciabatta loaf	1, sliced and grilled
chopped fresh parsley and salad leaves	to garnish

1. Preheat the oven to 180°C/160°C fan oven/Gas Mark 4. In a jug, combine the garlic, chives, lemon rind and juice, butter, salt and pepper.

2. Place the mushrooms in an ovenproof dish, pour the butter mixture over, cover with foil and cook for 40 to 45 minutes or until the mushrooms are tender.

3. Serve the mushrooms piled high on grilled ciabatta with chopped parsley and salad leaves, to garnish.

Preparation time: 10 min   **Cooking time:** 40–45 min
Cals per serving: 292   **Serves:** 6

Grilled Sweet Potatoes with Feta and Olives

1. Cut the sweet potato lengthways into eight wedges. Put them in a pan of boiling water, bring back to the boil, simmer for 3 minutes, then drain and rinse in cool water. Drain, dry well and brush lightly with olive oil. Season, then barbecue or grill for 10 to 15 minutes or until well browned on all sides and cooked through.

2. Meanwhile, mash the cheese, herbs, chopped black olives, garlic and olive oil together. Serve the sweet potato with the feta cheese mixture, garnished with parsley.

Preparation time: 15 min   **Cooking time:** 13–18 min
Cals per serving: 348   **Serves:** 4

large sweet potato	1, about 500g (1lb 2oz) total weight
olive oil	4 tbsp, plus extra for brushing
feta cheese	200g (7oz)
herbes de Provence	2 tsp
pitted black olives	50g (2oz), chopped
garlic clove	1, crushed
fresh flat-leaf parsley	to garnish

Chicken, Mango and Mayo
Open Sandwich

mayonnaise 2–3 tbsp
thick slice organic white bread 1, toasted
cold leftover chicken fillet or smoked chicken 150g (5oz), sliced
ripe mango ¼, peeled and sliced
chopped fresh parsley or chopped fresh coriander to serve

1. Spread some of the mayonnaise thickly on the toasted bread and lay the chicken and mango slices on top in layers.

2. Top with a little more mayonnaise, season well with salt and pepper and sprinkle with the chopped parsley, to serve.

Preparation time: 10 min **Cals per serving:** 570 **Serves:** 1

Focaccia Rolls
with Goat's Cheese and Almond Pesto

1. To make the almond pesto, place all the ingredients except the almonds, lemon juice and seasoning in a food processor and whiz until smooth. Add the almonds and process again. Add the lemon juice and season to taste.

2. Preheat the oven to 220°C/200°C fan oven/Gas Mark 7. To make the focaccia rolls, use a rolling pin to roll each slice of focaccia to about 3mm (⅛in) thick. Spread each slice with a little of the goat's cheese, followed by some tapenade and half a slice of ham. Roll up tightly and secure with cocktail sticks. Place on a baking sheet and cook for 10 to 15 minutes or until golden. Pile on to a serving plate and garnish with basil leaves. Serve with the almond pesto for dipping.

Preparation time: 30 min **Cooking time:** 10–15 min
Cals per serving: 253 **Makes:** 12

olive focaccia loaf 1, cut into 12 thin slices
rindless, soft goat's cheese 125g (4oz)
black olive tapenade 3 tbsp
slices wafer-thin ham 6
fresh basil leaves to garnish

For the almond pesto
fresh basil 3 × 15g packs
small shallot 1, chopped
balsamic vinegar 1 tbsp
Dijon mustard 2 tsp
garlic clove 1, chopped
olive oil 150ml (5fl oz)
blanched almonds 50g (2oz), toasted
lemon juice to taste

Napolitana Pizza

1. Tip the flour into a large bowl, stir in the yeast and salt then make a well in the centre. Pour 150ml (5fl oz) warm water into the well and use your fingertips to mix everything together and form a dough.

2. Turn out on to a lightly floured surface and knead for 5 minutes, or until smooth. The dough should be quite soft. Lightly oil a large bowl, put the dough into the bowl, turn it over to coat in the oil and then cover with clingfilm and a clean tea-towel. Put in a warm, draught-free place for 45 minutes or until doubled in size.

3. Preheat the oven to 240°C/220°C fan oven/Gas Mark 9 and put a large baking sheet in the oven to heat. Meanwhile, mix the tomatoes with the garlic and season with black pepper.

4. Lightly oil a large heavy-based baking sheet. On a lightly floured surface, roll the dough into a rectangle, about 33 x 35.5cm (13 x 14in) and transfer to the baking sheet. Spread the tomato mixture over the dough, sprinkle with oregano and top with the mozzarella, anchovies and olives. Drizzle the oil over the pizza.

5. Put the baking sheet on the hot baking sheet, and cook the pizza in the oven for 20 to 25 minutes or until the mozzarella is golden and bubbling and the dough is lightly browned underneath. Leave for 5 minutes before serving.

Preparation time: 15 min, plus 45 min rising and 5 min standing
Cooking time: 20–25 min   **Cals per serving:** 460   **Serves:** 4

strong white bread flour	225g (8oz), sifted, plus extra to dust
easy-blend yeast	7g sachet
salt	½ tsp
olive oil	4 tbsp, plus extra for greasing
chopped plum tomatoes	400g can, drained
garlic cloves	2, crushed
fresh oregano sprigs	2–3
mozzarella	125g (4oz), diced
anchovy fillets	50g can, drained and cut in half lengthways
pitted black olives	50g (2oz)

Napolitana
Pizza

Onion, Feta Cheese and Pinenut Tarts

puff pastry	450g (1lb)
plain flour	to dust
olive oil	4 tbsp, plus extra for brushing
onions	700g (1½lb), sliced
pinenuts	25g (1oz)
raisins	25g (1oz), optional
feta cheese	50g (2oz), crumbled
pitted black olives	25g (1oz)
sun-dried tomatoes	25g (1oz), chopped
capers	25g (1oz), rinsed and drained
fresh oregano sprigs	to garnish

1. Roll out the puff pastry on a lightly floured work surface, then cut out four circles, each 15cm (6in) diameter. Chill for 30 minutes.

2. Preheat the oven to 220°C/200°C fan oven/Gas Mark 7 and place two baking sheets in the oven to heat. Meanwhile, heat the oil in a large, heavy-based frying pan. Add the onions and fry gently for 10 to 15 minutes, stirring from time to time, until they are golden and caramelised all over. Set aside to cool, then stir in the pinenuts, raisins, if using, feta cheese, olives, sun-dried tomatoes and the capers.

3. Prick the pastry circles with a fork and brush with a little oil. Divide the onion mixture among the pastry circles, leaving a 1cm (½in) margin round the edges, then season well.

4. Place the tarts on the hot baking sheets and return to the oven. Cook for 15 minutes or until the pastry is crisp, golden and risen around the edges. To serve, garnish with oregano sprigs.

Freezing: Complete the recipe to the end of step 4, without garnishing, then cool, wrap and freeze.

To use: From frozen, reheat at 220°C/200°C fan oven/Gas Mark 7 for 10 minutes.

Preparation time: 15 min, plus 30 min chilling
Cooking time: 35 min   **Cals per serving:** 710   **Serves:** 4

Cheat's Courgette and Goat's Cheese Pizza

pizza bases 2 x 20cm (8in)
Dijon mustard 4 tsp
large red onion 1, thinly sliced
courgettes 225g (8oz), very thinly sliced
spicy sausages 2
soft goat's cheese 200g (7oz)
fresh thyme leaves only
olive oil to drizzle

1. Preheat the oven to 200°C/180°C fan oven/Gas Mark 6 and preheat two baking sheets. Place the pizza bases on the baking sheets and spread them with the mustard. Sprinkle over the onion and courgettes, then season with salt and pepper.

2. Remove the sausages from their casing, crumble the mixture equally between the two pizza bases with the goat's cheese. Sprinkle the thyme over and drizzle with olive oil.

3. Cook in the oven for 45 minutes until the crust and the sausages are browned and the vegetables are cooked. Swap the pizzas around in the oven halfway through cooking, so that they cook evenly. Serve straight from the oven.

Preparation time: 15 min   **Cooking time:** 45 min

Cals per serving: 665   **Serves:** 4

Quick Pizza
Puffs

ready-rolled puff pastry 500g pack
ready-made tomato sauce 4 tbsp
roughly chopped pitted
black olives 4 tbsp
capers or caper berries 2 tbsp, rinsed
and drained
mozzarella cheese 125g (4oz), sliced
anchovy fillets 8
chopped mixed dried herbs 2 tsp
fresh thyme sprigs

1. Preheat the oven to 200°C/180°C fan oven/Gas Mark 6 and preheat a baking sheet. Unroll the pastry and, using a small saucer as a guide, cut out four 15cm (6in) circles.

2. Spread the pastry circles with the tomato sauce, then sprinkle with the olives and capers. Top each pizza with a slice of mozzarella cheese and two anchovy fillets. Season with pepper and sprinkle with the herbs and the thyme sprigs.

3. Carefully put the pizzas on the preheated baking sheets and cook for 20 to 25 minutes or until the pastry is golden and crisp. Serve hot.

Preparation time: 10 min   **Cooking time:** 20–25 min
Cals per serving: 599   **Serves:** 4

Quick Pizza Puffs

Lasagne

olive oil	2 tbsp
onions	225g (8oz), chopped
harissa paste	1 tbsp
minced beef	450g (1lb)
large garlic clove	1, crushed
tomato purée	1 tsp
chopped tomatoes	2 × 400g cans
bay leaves	2
large eggs	4
butter	50g (2oz), plus extra for greasing
plain flour	50g (2oz)
milk	900ml (1½pt)
parmesan	75g (3oz), grated
freshly grated nutmeg	to taste
pre-cooked lasagne sheets	6, about 125g (4oz) total weight

1. Preheat the oven to 190°C/170°C fan oven/Gas Mark 5. Heat the oil in a frying pan, add the onion and harissa paste and cook gently for 5 minutes until soft. Stir in the mince, garlic and tomato purée. Fry for 10 to 15 minutes, stirring from time to time, until the mince is well browned. Add the tomatoes and bring to the boil. Add the bay leaves, season, cover and simmer for 45 minutes or until the sauce is syrupy. If necessary, remove the lid, bring the mixture to the boil, then bubble for the last 5 minutes.

2. Meanwhile, boil the eggs for 6 minutes. Cool them quickly under cold, running water, then carefully peel off the shell. Roughly chop the eggs, cover and then set aside.

3. Melt the butter in a pan, stir in the flour to make a paste, then blend in the milk. Bring to the boil, stirring, then simmer for 5 minutes. Beat in 50g (2oz) parmesan, the salt and pepper and a pinch of nutmeg.

4. Butter a 3 litre (5¼ pint) ovenproof dish. Prepare the lasagne according to the packet instructions. Spoon one-third of the meat sauce into the dish with one-third of the white sauce, then lay two pieces of the lasagne on top. Spoon another third of the meat sauce and a third of the white sauce on top. Scatter over half the chopped egg. Repeat with two more sheets of lasagne, the remaining meat sauce and the remaining egg. Top with the remaining lasagne, then spoon over the remaining white sauce. Sprinkle with the remaining parmesan.

5. Place the dish on a baking sheet, then cook for 30 to 35 minutes, or until golden.

Freezing: Complete the recipe to the end of step 4, then cool, wrap and freeze.

To use: Defrost overnight at cool room temperature. Add an extra 5–10 min to the cooking time.

Preparation time: 25 min   **Cooking time:** 1 hr 55 min
Cals per serving: 637 for 6, 478 for 8   **Serves:** 6–8

Summer Vegetable and Pasta Bake

pasta shapes	125g (4oz)
baby carrots	75g (3oz), washed and trimmed
asparagus	75g (3oz), trimmed and cut into 7.5cm (3in) pieces
broccoli	175g (6oz), cut into small florets
artichoke hearts in water	200g can, drained and roughly chopped
ready-made cheese sauce	350ml tub
olive oil	1 tbsp
gruyère	25g (1oz), grated
sunflower seeds	10g (½oz), toasted
fresh breadcrumbs	50g (2oz)

1. Preheat the oven to 200°C/180°C fan oven/Gas Mark 6. Cook the pasta shapes, according to packet instructions. Drain and place in an ovenproof dish.

2. Place the carrots in a pan of boiling water and cook for 3 minutes. Add the asparagus and broccoli and cook for a few minutes until just tender. Drain well.

3. Stir the cooked vegetables, artichoke hearts and cheese sauce into the pasta and season. Mix the oil, gruyère and sunflower seeds into the breadcrumbs, then sprinkle over the vegetables.

4. Bake for 20 minutes. Serve immediately.

Preparation time: 10 min   **Cooking time:** 30 min
Cals per serving: 350   **Serves:** 4

Pasta with Smoked Haddock and Spinach

1. Cook the pasta in a large pan of boiling salted water according to packet instructions. Season the haddock with pepper, then slice diagonally into 4cm (1½in) pieces.

2. Meanwhile, melt the butter in a frying pan, add half the haddock and cook over a medium heat for 4 to 5 minutes. Set aside and cook the remaining haddock in the same way.

3. Drain the pasta. Place the spinach in the pan and cook over a low heat for 1 to 2 minutes or until just wilted. Return the pasta to the pan, then stir in the soured cream, chives, lemon juice, salt and nutmeg and stir well. Gently stir the haddock into the pasta and serve immediately with lemon wedges.

Preparation time: 10 min   **Cooking time:** about 15 min
Cals per serving: 370   **Serves:** 4

pasta shapes	225g (8oz)
smoked haddock	450g (1lb), skinned
butter	10g (½oz)
baby spinach	450g (1lb)
soured cream	142ml carton
snipped fresh chives	2 tbsp
lemon juice	1 tbsp
nutmeg	pinch of
lemon wedges	to serve

Penne, Cheese and Ham Bake

butter	50g (2oz), plus a little extra for the spinach
plain flour	25g (1oz)
English mustard powder	1 tbsp
milk	450ml (15fl oz)
cheddar	125g (4oz), grated
double cream	142ml carton
cooked sliced ham	125g (4oz), chopped
nutmeg	pinch of
penne pasta	350g (12oz)
baby spinach	150g (5oz)
parmesan	25g (1oz)

1. Preheat the oven to 200°C/180°C fan oven/Gas Mark 6. Melt the butter in a pan, stir in the flour and cook for a couple of minutes on a medium heat.

2. Add the mustard powder and milk and stir until smooth. Whisk the sauce as it comes to the boil, then simmer gently for 10 minutes. Remove from the heat, then beat in the cheddar gradually, until it melts, add the cream and ham, then season with nutmeg and salt and pepper.

3. Cook the pasta in a large pan of boiling salted water according to packet instructions; drain thoroughly. Meanwhile, melt a knob of butter in a large pan, add the spinach and cook for 3 minutes until wilted.

4. Mix together the sauce, pasta and spinach and pour into a shallow ovenproof dish. Grate the parmesan over the top and bake for 20 to 30 minutes or until golden.

Preparation time: 15 min   **Cooking time:** 45–55 min
Cals per serving: 874 for 4, 582 for 6   **Serves:** 4–6

Penne, Cheese and
Ham Bake

Happy families: Provençal Fish
Stew with crusty bread and a
good old nursery pudding, Apricot
and Cardamom Crumble

Family Supper: 'Keep it simple' is the **clue** to a **successful and enjoyable** family meal. A **one-pot supper** is the ideal choice – try **Shepherd's Pie** or a **Bonfire Pumpkin and Cheese Bake** served with **Creamy Baked Potatoes**. This **Provençal Fish Stew** is **really easy to make** and **popular** with all the family: **meltingly delicious cod** slowly cooked in a **rich tomatoey sauce** with **potatoes**, topped with **crispy croutons** and **drizzled with fresh herb oil**. Serve with **fresh bread** to **mop up the juices**. For pud, choose **comfort food**, such as **Apricot and Cardamom Crumble**, served with a jug of **hot custard,** or the **Roast Apples with Butterscotch Sauce**.

Spaghettini Carbonara with Salami Crisps

large eggs	2
large egg yolks	2
single cream	6 tbsp
garlic cloves	2, crushed
parmesan	50g (2oz), grated
sunflower oil	2 tbsp
Italian salami	125g (4oz), cut into thin strips
red onions	3, cut into wedges
thin pasta such as spaghettini	350g (12oz)
parmesan curls	to garnish

1. Place the eggs, egg yolks, cream, garlic and parmesan in a bowl and beat together until smooth. Season well and set aside.

2. Heat the oil in a large frying pan. Add the salami strips and cook for 5 minutes, stirring, until they are golden and crisp. Drain thoroughly on kitchen paper. Cook the onions in the same pan for 5 minutes or until crisp, then drain on kitchen paper.

3. Cook the pasta in a large pan of boiling salted water according to packet instructions, then drain and toss in the egg mixture. Return to the pan and cook, stirring, over a low heat for 2 to 3 minutes or until the sauce thickens slightly. Season with plenty of black pepper.

4. Serve the pasta in bowls, topped with the salami strips and onion. Garnish with parmesan curls.

Preparation time: 15 min   **Cooking time:** 15 min
Cals per serving: 825   **Serves:** 4

Orechiette with Peppers, Capers and Anchovies

red peppers	3, halved and deseeded
yellow peppers	2, halved and deseeded
orechiette pasta	350g (12oz)
olive oil	2 tbsp
garlic cloves	2, crushed
dried crushed red chillies	½ tsp
anchovy fillets in oil	50g can, drained and chopped
chopped plum tomatoes	400g can
capers	2 tbsp, drained and rinsed
lemon juice	to taste
anchovy fillets	to garnish

1. Preheat the grill to high. Place the peppers on a baking sheet, skin-side up, and grill for 6 to 8 minutes or until the skins turn black all over. Put the peppers in a bowl, cover and set aside for 15 minutes (the steam will help to loosen the skin). Peel the peppers and slice into thin strips.

2. Cook the pasta in a large pan of boiling salted water according to packet instructions. Meanwhile, heat the oil, add the garlic and chillies and fry for 30 seconds. Add the anchovies, tomatoes and the peppers and cook for a further 1 to 2 minutes. Drain the pasta and add to the sauce with the capers, toss together, then check the seasoning and add lemon juice to taste. Garnish with the anchovy fillets and serve immediately.

Preparation time: 20 min, plus 15 min standing
Cooking time: 30 min   **Cals per serving:** 520   **Serves:** 4

Parmesan Polenta with Minted Summer Vegetables

vegetable stock	900ml (1½pt)
polenta	125g (4oz)
double cream	3 tbsp
parmesan	125g (4oz), grated
chopped fresh mint	2 tbsp

For the minted vegetables

butter	50g (2oz)
shallots	50g (2oz), finely chopped
garlic cloves	2, thinly sliced
shelled fresh broad beans or shelled fresh peas	125g (4oz)
asparagus tips or French beans	125g (4oz), cut diagonally
baby carrots	125g (4oz)
caster sugar	1 tbsp
chopped fresh mint	2 tbsp
grainy mustard	2 tsp
white wine vinegar	1 tbsp
fresh mint sprigs	to garnish

1. To make the Parmesan polenta, bring 600ml (1pint) of the stock to the boil in a large pan, then reduce to a simmer. Add the polenta in a slow, steady stream, stirring all the time for about 5 minutes until thick. Stir in the remaining stock and cream, then cook for a further 10 minutes, stirring all the time, until the polenta resembles mashed potato. Add the parmesan and mint, then season. Remove from the heat and keep warm.

2. To make the minted vegetables, melt the butter in a large pan and add the shallots and garlic. Cook for 5 minutes then add the vegetables, sugar and 4 tablespoons of water. Bring to the boil, cover and cook for about 5 minutes or until the vegetables are tender and the liquid becomes syrupy.

3. Toss the hot vegetables with the chopped mint, mustard and vinegar and season well. Serve immediately with the polenta and garnish with mint sprigs.

Preparation time: 10 min   **Cooking time:** 15 min
Cals per serving: 645   **Serves:** 4

Risotto with Saffron, Lemon and Basil

unsalted butter	50g (2oz)
olive oil	I drop
medium onion	I, very finely chopped
fresh chicken stock	about Iltr (1¾pt)
arborio rice	225g (8oz)
dry white wine	150ml (5fl oz)
saffron threads	2 large pinches
lemon	½, rind finely grated
lemon juice	to taste
fresh basil leaves	a decent handful, roughly chopped
parmesan	50g (2oz), freshly grated

1. Melt half the butter with the olive oil in a large pan, then add the onion and cook it gently for a few minutes. Meanwhile, pour the stock into another large pan and bring to a simmer over a low heat. When the onion is soft and translucent, add the rice and stir well to ensure each grain is coated in butter. Pour in the wine and continue to stir over a lowish heat until it has almost evaporated.

2. Begin to add the hot stock, a ladleful at a time, stirring as you do so. The rice will absorb the liquid as it cooks, so keep stirring to keep it moving, and add more stock as you need to. After about 15 minutes add the saffron threads and continue cooking and stirring.

3. When the rice is almost done (start tasting after about 18 minutes, but don't panic if it takes more than 20 minutes), add the lemon rind and juice and the basil leaves. Stir well and when you are happy with the consistency – not too dry nor too sloppy – turn off the heat. Check for seasoning (it may need a little extra salt), then add the remaining butter and the parmesan. Stir again and serve straight away.

Preparation time: 15 min   **Cooking time:** 25 min
Cals per serving: 802   **Serves:** 2 generously

Garlic and Parmesan Risotto

1. Heat the stock and keep it hot over a low heat. Meanwhile, melt half the butter in a large heavy-based pan and stir in the onion. Cook for 8 to 10 minutes until very soft, but not too coloured, then stir in the garlic and rice. Stir thoroughly over the heat to fry the rice lightly in the butter for 2 to 3 minutes.

2. Pour in a ladleful of the hot stock and let it simmer gently, stirring all the time, until the rice has absorbed most of it. Keep adding the stock in this way until the rice is tender, but still has a little bite to it; this will take 20 to 25 minutes and the end result should look creamy and soft.

3. Remove from the heat, then stir in the remaining butter, along with the parmesan, seasoning and parsley, and serve.

Preparation time: 5 min   **Cooking time:** 35 min
Cals per serving: 385   **Serves:** 4

light vegetable stock	750–900ml (1¼–1½pt)
butter	50g (2oz)
onion	I, finely chopped
garlic cloves	3, crushed
arborio rice	225g (8oz)
parmesan	50g (2oz), grated
chopped fresh parsley	4–5 tbsp

Risotto with Saffron,
Lemon and Basil

Chicken and Leek Pilaff

vegetable oil 3 tbsp
skinless chicken thighs 350g (12oz), cut into
1 cm (½in) strips
streaky bacon 225g (8oz), cut
into strips
medium leeks 450g (1lb), washed
and thinly sliced
small mushrooms 175g (6oz),
cut into quarters
ground cumin 1 tsp
cayenne ½ tsp
tomato paste 2 tbsp
easy-cook long grain rice 225g (8oz)
chopped plum tomatoes 400g can
chicken stock 600–750ml (1–1¼pt)
chopped fresh chives 2 tbsp, plus extra
to garnish

1. Heat the oil in a large deep frying pan or flameproof casserole. Add the chicken, season with black pepper and cook for 1 to 2 minutes. Add the bacon, and cook over a high heat for 5 minutes. Add the leeks and mushrooms and continue to cook over a high heat for 5 minutes.

2. Stir in the spices and tomato paste and cook for 3 to 4 minutes, stirring frequently. Add the rice and cook, stirring, for 1 minute or until it turns opaque. Stir in the tomatoes, stock and seasoning. Bring to the boil, cover and simmer gently for 30 to 35 minutes, or until the rice is tender. (The amount of stock required depends on the absorbency of the rice you're using.) Add the chopped chives and more seasoning, if necessary. Garnish with chives and serve.

Preparation time: 15 min   **Cooking time:** 55 min
Cals per serving: 685   **Serves:** 4

Stir-fried Salmon and Broccoli

sesame oil 2 tsp
red pepper 1, deseeded and finely sliced
jalapeno chilli ½, finely sliced
garlic clove 1, crushed
broccoli florets 125g (4oz)
spring onions 2, sliced
salmon fillets 2, about 125g (4oz) each, cut into strips
Thai fish sauce 1 tsp
soy sauce 2 tsp

1. In a large frying pan or wok, heat the oil and add the red pepper, chilli, garlic, broccoli and spring onions. Stir-fry the vegetables over a high heat for 3 to 4 minutes. Add the salmon fillets, Thai fish sauce and soy sauce.

2. Cook for 2 minutes more, stirring gently, then serve with wholewheat noodles.

Preparation time: 10 min   **Cooking time:** 6 min
Cals per serving: 201   **Serves:** 2

Quick Fish Cakes

1. Put the haddock in a wide pan, cover with cold salted water and add the peppercorns. Bring to the boil and simmer for 5 to 7 minutes until the haddock is opaque and flakes easily. Lift the fish from the pan and put it in a bowl.

2. Add the prawns, lemon juice, capers, parsley, mayonnaise and mashed potato to the fish and season well. Mix everything together.

3. On a lightly floured work surface, shape the haddock mixture into 12 cakes, using a 7.5cm (3in) plain cutter to help. Pop the cakes in the freezer for 20 minutes.

4. To make the relish, put all the ingredients in a bowl and mix together. Chill until needed.

5. Preheat the oven to 180°C/160°C fan oven/Gas Mark 4. Pour 2.5cm (1in) of sunflower oil into a large non-stick frying pan and heat until a cube of bread browns in 50 seconds. Fry the fish cakes in batches, turning once, until golden. Keep warm. Garnish with watercress and serve with the cucumber relish.

Preparation time: 20 min, plus 20 min chilling
Cooking time: 15 min   **Cals per serving:** 360   **Serves:** 6

haddock fillet 1kg (2¼lb), skinned
mixed peppercorns 1 tsp
large cooked prawns 175g (6oz)
small lemon 1, juice of
roughly chopped capers 1 tbsp, rinsed and drained
chopped fresh parsley 4 tbsp
mayonnaise 2 tbsp
prepared mashed potato 400g (14oz)
plain flour to dust
sunflower oil for frying
watercress to garnish

For the cucumber relish
cucumber ½, diced
caster sugar 1 tsp
extra-virgin olive oil 2 tbsp
white wine vinegar 1 tbsp

Teriyaki Salmon with Spinach and Noodles

salmon fillet	550g (1lb 4oz)
teriyaki sauce	3 tbsp
light soy sauce	3 tbsp
vegetable oil	2 tbsp
sesame oil	1 tbsp
chopped fresh chives	1 tbsp
chopped fresh root ginger	2 tbsp
garlic cloves	2, crushed
baby spinach leaves	350g bag
yakisoba noodles	3 × 160g packs
furikake seasoning	

1. Cut the salmon fillet into 1cm (½in) slices. Gently mix with the teriyaki sauce, then cover, chill and leave to marinate for 1 hour.

2. Mix together the soy sauce, 1 tablespoon of the vegetable oil, sesame oil, chives, ginger and garlic. Set aside.

3. Heat the rest of the vegetable oil in a wok. Lift the salmon from the marinade and add to the pan. Cook over a high heat until lightly coloured. Push to the side of the pan.

4. Add the spinach, cover and cook for 2 minutes over a high heat until wilted. Push to the side of the pan and add the noodles, along with 6 tablespoons of water and the seasoning sachets from the noodle packets. Cook, stirring until the noodles have loosened and warmed through. Add the soy sauce mixture and stir to combine, mixing in the spinach at the same time, but leaving the salmon at the side of the pan.

5. Divide the noodles among four deep bowls, then lay the salmon on top. Sprinkle with furikake seasoning and serve.

Preparation time: 10 min, plus 1 hr marinating
Cooking time: 8 min **Cals per serving:** 450 **Serves:** 4

Peppered Mackerel

1. Lightly crush 2 teaspoons of the peppercorns in a pestle and mortar. Sprinkle one side of each mackerel with half the crushed peppercorns.

2. Heat the oil in a frying pan. Add the fish, peppered-side down and cook for 5 to 7 minutes over a medium-high heat. Sprinkle the mackerel with the remaining crushed peppercorns, turn the fish over and continue to fry for 5 to 7 minutes. Remove from the pan and keep warm.

3. Wipe out the pan, add the crème fraîche, bring to the boil and stir in the remaining peppercorns.

4. Spoon the pepper sauce over the mackerel, garnish with the lemon wedges and serve.

Preparation time: 10 min **Cooking time:** 15 min
Cals per serving: 660 **Serves:** 4

whole mixed peppercorns	4 tsp
mackerel	4, about 250g (9oz) each, gutted
sunflower oil	1 tbsp
full-fat crème fraîche	200ml (7fl oz)
lemon wedges	to garnish

Teriyaki Salmon with
Spinach and Noodles

Puff-topped Seafood

mixed raw seafood	225g (8oz)
salmon fillet	125g (4oz), cubed
cooked, shelled mussels	125g (4oz)
double cream	2 tbsp
plain flour	to dust
ready-rolled puff pastry	375g (13oz)
large beaten egg	1, to glaze

For the herb and garlic butter

butter	40g (1½oz), softened
garlic cloves	2, crushed
chopped fresh parsley or chives	1 tbsp

1. Preheat the oven to 220°C/200°C fan oven/Gas Mark 7. Mix the seafood, salmon and mussels with the cream and season. On a lightly floured work surface, roll out the ready-rolled pastry a little more thinly. Using the top of a 450ml (15fl oz) ovenproof bowl as a guide, cut out four circles at least 5mm (¼in) bigger all round.

2. Divide the seafood between four 450ml (15fl oz) ovenproof bowls. To make the herb and garlic butter, beat together the butter and garlic and herbs. Top the seafood with the herb and garlic butter. Brush the rim of each bowl and 5mm (¼in) down the outside with beaten egg. Place a pastry circle on top of each bowl and press it down the sides. Make a steam hole in the centre and glaze the pastry with beaten egg.

3. Bake for 12 to 15 minutes until the pastry is well risen and golden. Serve immediately.

Preparation time: 20 min   **Cooking time:** 12–15 min
Cals per serving: 570   **Serves:** 4

Salmon and Cod Pie with Watercress Mash

1. Preheat the oven to 190°C/170°C fan oven/Gas Mark 5. Place the fish in a roasting tin. Add the bay leaf, peppercorns and onion, milk and wine and season. Cover and cook for 25 minutes or until the fish is cooked. Lift the fish with a slotted spoon and set aside. Increase the oven temperature to 200°C/180°C fan oven/Gas Mark 6. Strain the milk and reserve. Flake the fish into large pieces and place in a 2.3 litre (4 pint) ovenproof dish and season.

2. Melt the butter in a pan, add the flour and stir until smooth. Cook for 1 minute, then stir in the cream and reserved milk; season. Bring to the boil, stirring continuously, then simmer for 1 to 2 minutes, or until thick. Add the spring onions to the sauce and pour over the fish.

3. To make the watercress mash, mix everything together; season well. Spoon over the fish and cook for 40 minutes, or until piping hot.

Preparation time: 30 min   **Cooking time:** 1 hr 10 min
Cals per serving: 787   **Serves:** 6

cod and salmon fillets	about 700g (1½lb) each, skinned
bay leaf	1
peppercorns	6
onion	1, peeled and halved
milk	450ml (15fl oz)
white wine	100ml (3½fl oz)
butter	75g (3oz)
plain flour	3 tbsp
double cream	3 tbsp
spring onions	1 bunch, thinly sliced

For the watercress mash

cheddar	50g (2oz), grated
yellow mustard seeds	2 tsp, crushed
watercress	100g (3½oz), chopped
mashed potato	1.1kg (2½lb)

Seafood and Lime Kebabs

peeled raw king prawns	225g (8oz), deveined
monkfish fillet	550g (1lb 4oz), cubed
lime	½, juice of
garlic clove	1, crushed
chilli oil	2 tbsp
teriyaki sauce	2 tbsp
egg noodles	175g (6oz), soaked in boiling water for 10 min
oil	for deep frying
limes	2, quartered
lemon	1, cut into 8 wedges
green chilli	1, deseeded and finely chopped
spring onion curls and fresh flat-leafed parsley	to garnish

1. Place the king prawns and monkfish in a bowl. Combine the lime juice, garlic, chilli oil and teriyaki sauce and pour over the top. Stir well to coat and leave in a cool place for up to 1 hour.

2. Drain the noodles well. Heat the oil in a wok or heavy-based frying pan and fry the noodles, in batches until golden. Drain on kitchen paper.

3. Remove the seafood from the marinade and thread on to eight skewers interspersed with lime and lemon wedges. Heat a griddle or grill.

4. Grill the kebabs for 3 minutes each side, turning once during cooking and brushing with the marinade. Garnish with green chilli, spring onions and parsley and serve with the deep-fried noodles.

Preparation time: 25 min, plus 1 hr marinating
Cooking time: 6 min   **Cals per serving:** 200   **Serves:** 4

Provençale Fish Stew

1. Preheat the oven to 180°C/160°C fan oven/Gas Mark 4. Whiz the herbs together in a food processor for about 10 seconds. With the motor still running, add the olive oil gradually until smooth. Put in a bowl, season, cover and chill. Spread the bread out, in a single layer, on a baking sheet and season. Cook for 15 minutes until crisp and golden, turning the bread halfway through. Leave to cool.

2. For the stew, put the potatoes in a large pan of salted water, bring to the boil and simmer for about 10 minutes until cooked. Drain and cool.

3. Put the wine and Pernod, if using, in a large pan and bring to the boil, then simmer for 10 minutes to allow the alcohol to boil away. Add the passata, fish stock, thyme and 300ml (10fl oz) of water, season and bring to the boil, then simmer for 10 minutes.

4. Add the potatoes, reduce the heat a little and let them warm through for 5 minutes. Just before serving, add the cod and cook for a further 5 minutes or until white and firm. Stir very carefully so you don't break up the fish pieces. Season well. Spoon the stew into bowls, top with the garlic croutons and drizzle liberally with herb oil to serve.

Preparation time: 20 min   **Cooking time:** 55 min
Cals per serving: 574   **Serves:** 6–8

chopped mixed fresh herbs	5 tbsp
olive oil	100ml (3½fl oz)
ready-made garlic bread	1 loaf, cut into rough chunks
For the fish stew	
large potatoes	700g (1½lb), peeled and cut into small chunks
dry white wine	300ml (10fl oz)
Pernod	2 tbsp, optional
passata	900ml (1½pt)
ready-made fresh fish stock	2 × 284ml tubs
chopped fresh thyme	3 tbsp
cod fillet	700g (1½lb), skinned and cut into 2.5cm (1in) cubes

Seafood
Gumbo

butter	125g (4oz)
plain flour	50g (2oz)
Cajun spice	1–2 tbsp
onion	1, chopped
green pepper	1, cored, deseeded and chopped
spring onions	5, sliced
chopped fresh parsley	1 tbsp
garlic clove	1, crushed
beef tomato	1, chopped
garlic sausage	125g (4oz), finely sliced
American easy-cook rice	75g (3oz)
vegetable stock	1.1ltr (2pt)
okra	450g (1lb), sliced
bay leaf	1
fresh thyme sprig	1
salt	2 tsp
cayenne pepper	½ tsp
lemon	½, juice of
whole cloves	4
frozen mixed seafood, such as mussels, squid and prawns	550g (1lb 4oz), defrosted and drained

1. Heat the butter in a 2.6 litre (4½ pint) heavy-based pan. Add the flour and Cajun spice and cook for 1 to 2 minutes until golden brown. Add the onion, green pepper, spring onions, parsley and garlic. Cook for 5 minutes.

2. Add the tomato, garlic sausage and rice and stir well to coat. Add the stock, okra, bay leaf, thyme, salt, cayenne pepper, lemon juice and cloves and season with black pepper. Bring to the boil and simmer, covered, for 12 minutes or until the rice is tender.

3. Add the seafood and cook for 2 minutes to heat through. Serve in deep bowls.

Preparation time: 10 min   **Cooking time:** 25 min
Cals per serving: 570   **Serves:** 4

Creamy Baked Potatoes with Mustard Seeds

baking potatoes	6, about 1.4kg (3lb) total weight
sunflower oil	2 tbsp
coarse sea salt	1 tbsp
large garlic cloves	4–5, unpeeled
butter	50g (2oz)
crème fraîche	6 tbsp
mustard seeds	2 tbsp, toasted and lightly crushed
fresh oregano sprigs	to garnish

1. Preheat the oven to 200°C/180°C fan oven/Gas Mark 6. Prick the potato skins, rub with oil and sprinkle with salt. Cook for 40 minutes. Place the garlic in a baking tin and cook for 20 minutes.

2. Slice the tops off the potatoes, scoop the flesh into a warm bowl, squeeze the garlic out of the skin and add to the potato with the butter, crème fraîche and mustard seeds. Mash and season. Return the mixture to the hollowed out skins.

3. Return the potatoes to the oven and cook for 15 minutes or until golden brown. Garnish with the oregano sprigs and serve.

Freezing: Complete to the end of step 2, cool quickly, wrap and freeze.

To use: Thaw at cool room temperature overnight. Cook at 200°C/180°C fan oven/Gas Mark 6 for 20–25 min or until hot to the centre.

Preparation time: 15–20 min   **Cooking time:** 1 hr 15 min
Cals per serving: 330   **Serves:** 6

Cheesy Baked Potatoes

1. Preheat the oven to 200°C/180°C fan oven/Gas Mark 6. Prick the potatoes, rub with olive oil and sprinkle with a little salt.

2. Place the potatoes on a baking sheet and cook for 1 to 1½ hours, or until a skewer glides easily through the centre of the largest potato.

3. Cut the potatoes in half lengthways. Using a spoon, scoop out the flesh and place it in a bowl, reserving the skins.

4. Add the butter and milk and mash well. Stir in the gammon, spring onions, half the cheddar and the herbs. Season with pepper.

5. Spoon the mixture back into the potato skins and sprinkle the remaining cheddar over the top.

6. Return the potatoes to the oven for a further 20 to 25 minutes until golden brown.

Preparation time: 20 min   **Cooking time:** 1 hr 55 min
Cals per serving: 606   **Serves:** 4

large baking potatoes	4, scrubbed
a little olive oil	for rubbing
butter	50g (2oz)
milk	5 tbsp
cooked gammon	125g (4oz), cubed, fat removed
spring onions	4, sliced diagonally
mature cheddar	125g (4oz), grated
chopped fresh mixed herbs	1 tbsp

Meatballs with Olive and Pesto Salad

premium-quality coarse pork sausages	450g (1lb)
olive oil	2 tbsp
red onion	350g (12oz), sliced
dried pappardelle noodles	225g (8oz)
black olives	125g (4oz)
chopped fresh parsley, or chives (or a mix of both)	2 tbsp
pesto sauce	2 tbsp
snipped and whole fresh chives	to garnish

1. Slit the sausages from top to bottom with a sharp knife, then peel off the skin. Break each sausage in half and roll each piece into a ball, then flatten the balls slightly with the palm of your hand.

2. Heat the oil in a non-stick frying pan and fry the meatballs for about 10 minutes until cooked through. Lift out and set aside on a plate. Add the onion to the pan and fry for about 10 minutes until soft and golden. Add the onion to the meatballs.

3. Cook the pasta in a large pan of boiling salted water according to packet instructions. Drain and return to the pan. Stir the olives, herbs and pesto into the pasta, heat for 1 minute, then place on a large serving plate. Arrange the meatballs and onions on top and pour over any juices that have collected on the plate. Season with black pepper. Serve at once, garnished with chives.

Preparation time: 15 min   **Cooking time:** 30 min
Cals per serving: 715   **Serves:** 4

Savoury Bread and Butter Pudding

1. Preheat the oven to 180°C/160°C fan oven/Gas Mark 4. Spread the bread generously with butter and sparingly with mustard. Put half the slices in the base of a 2 litre (3½ pint) ovenproof dish. Top with the ham and half the cheese, then with the remaining bread, butter side up.

2. Whisk together the milk, eggs, nutmeg and plenty of salt and black pepper. Stir in the herbs, then slowly pour over the bread. Scatter the remaining cheese on top and leave to soak for 15 minutes.

3. Put the dish in a roasting tin that is filled halfway up the sides with hand-hot water, then bake for 1 to 1¼ hours, or until puffed up, golden brown and just set in the centre.

Preparation time: 15 min, plus 15 min soaking
Cooking time: 1 hr 15 min   **Cals per serving:** 430   **Serves:** 6

white bread (such as sourdough)	150–175g (5–6oz), thickly sliced, crusts on
butter	60g (2½oz), softened
Dijon mustard	
ham (no water added)	200g pack, chopped
mature cheddar	125g (4oz), grated
milk	568ml carton
large eggs	5, beaten
grated nutmeg	pinch of
chopped fresh herbs, such as parsley, marjoram or thyme	2 tbsp

Lentil Chilli

oil-water spray	for frying
red onions	2, chopped
ground coriander	1 tsp
ground cumin	1 tsp
ground paprika	½ tsp
garlic cloves	2, crushed
sun-dried tomatoes	2, chopped
crushed dried chilli flakes	½ tsp
red wine	120ml (4fl oz)
vegetable stock	300ml (10fl oz)
brown or green lentils	2 x 410g cans, drained and rinsed
chopped tomatoes	2 x 400g cans
sugar	to taste
plain low-fat yogurt and chopped fresh coriander or fresh flat-leaf parsley	to garnish
cooked rice	to serve

1. Spray a pan with the oil-water spray and cook the onions for 5 minutes. Add the coriander, cumin and paprika. Combine the garlic, sun-dried tomatoes, chilli, wine and stock and add to the pan. Cover and simmer for 5 to 7 minutes. Uncover and simmer until the onions are very tender and the liquid is almost gone.

2. Stir in the lentils and tomatoes and season. Simmer, uncovered, for 15 minutes until thick. Stir in the sugar, then remove from the heat.

3. Ladle out a quarter of the mixture and whiz in a food processor or blender. Combine the puréed and unpuréed portions. Garnish with the yogurt and herbs and serve with rice.

Preparation time: 10 min   **Cooking time:** 30 min
Cals per serving: 170   **Serves:** 6

Bonfire Pumpkin and Cheese Bake

1. Preheat the oven to 220°C/200°C fan oven/Gas Mark 7. Boil the potatoes, pumpkin and onion together in salted water in a shallow flameproof casserole for 3 to 4 minutes. Drain off all the liquid and roughly mix in the ham and cheese.

2. Beat a little cold water into the crème fraîche to give a thick pouring consistency. Season with pepper, then pour over the vegetables. Place the casserole on the hob and bring to the boil.

3. Transfer to the oven and cook uncovered for 40 minutes, or until bubbling and golden. Two or three times during the cooking time, stir the crust that forms on top into the dish to add to the flavour. To check the dish is cooked, press the tip of a knife into the centre of a potato, which should be tender. Serve with French bread and a green salad if you like.

Preparation time: 15 min   **Cooking time:** 45 min
Cals per serving: 656   **Serves:** 4

new potatoes	450g (1lb), halved
pumpkin	450g (1lb), peeled and thinly sliced
large onion	1, about 175g (6oz) total weight, thinly sliced
smoked ham	125g (4oz), thinly sliced
buttery cheese, such as taleggio, gruyère or fontina	225g (8oz), thinly sliced
crème fraîche	300ml (10fl oz)
French stick loaf	1
and green salad	to serve, optional

Lentil Chilli

Spiced One-pot
Chicken

Thai red curry paste 3 tbsp
orange juice 150ml (5fl oz)
garlic cloves 2, crushed
chicken pieces 6, about 2.3kg (5lb)
total weight, bone in
squash or pumpkin 700g (1½lb), cut into
5cm (2in) cubes
red onions 5, peeled and quartered
capers 2 tbsp, drained
and chopped

1. Preheat the oven to 220°C/200°C fan oven/Gas Mark 7. In a small bowl, mix together the Thai curry paste, orange juice and garlic. Put the chicken pieces in the marinade, cover and set aside for 15 minutes.

2. Put the vegetables in a large roasting tin, then remove the chicken from the marinade and place on top of the vegetables. Pour over the marinade and season. Mix everything together so it is covered with the marinade and scatter the capers over.

3. Cook for 1 hour 10 minutes, turning occasionally or until the chicken is cooked to the centre and the skin is golden.

Preparation time: 10 min, plus 15 min marinating
Cooking time: 1 hr 10 min   **Cals per serving:** 648   **Serves:** 6

Greek Lemon
Chicken Pie

lemon	1, preferably unwaxed
whole chicken	1.6kg (3½lb)
carrot	1, thickly sliced
celery stick	1, thickly sliced
onion	½
black peppercorns	8
butter	150g (5oz)
leeks	450g (1lb), sliced
plain flour	50g (2oz)
milk	150ml (5fl oz)
stale wholemeal or ciabatta bread	125g (4oz)
garlic cloves	2, crushed
walnuts	25g (1oz), toasted and roughly chopped
fresh oregano sprigs	to garnish

1. Remove the lemon rind using a swivel peeler, squeeze the juice and reserve. Tuck the lemon rind inside the chicken, then put it in a large pan with the carrot, celery, onion and peppercorns. Add enough cold water to cover the chicken thighs and cover the pan with a lid. Bring to the boil, then simmer for 45 minutes, or until the juices run clear when the thigh is pierced. Lift the chicken from the pan and put to one side to cool. Bring the stock to the boil and bubble until about 600ml (1 pint) is left, then strain and reserve the liquid.

2. Preheat the oven to 200°C/180°C fan oven/Gas Mark 6. In a frying pan, melt 50g (2oz) of the butter and fry the leeks for 4 to 5 minutes or until lightly coloured. Stir in the flour and cook, stirring, for 2 to 3 minutes, then add the reserved chicken stock and milk. Bring to the boil, stirring all the time. Simmer for 2 to 3 minutes, or until the sauce thickens. Season, add the remaining lemon juice and allow to cool.

3. Remove the skin from the chicken and cut the flesh into bite-sized pieces. Stir the chicken into the sauce, then spoon this into a 2.6 to 3 litre (4½–5¼ pint) ovenproof dish.

4. Melt the remaining butter. Crumble the bread and mix with the butter, adding the garlic and walnuts. Sprinkle over the chicken. Cook for 20 minutes, then cover with foil and cook for 10 to 20 minutes or until golden. Garnish with oregano sprigs.

Freezing: Complete the recipe but don't cook the pie. Wrap and freeze.

To use: Thaw overnight at cool room temperature. Add an extra 5–10 minutes to the cooking time and cover the top with foil if the pie begins to turn too brown.

Preparation time: 30 min, plus 1 hr cooling
Cooking time: 1 hr 40 min   **Cals per serving:** 710   **Serves:** 6–8

Food for all seasons: Pea and Lettuce Soup with crusty rolls and Apple, Fennel, Ham and Pecan Salad; An apple and a good Cheddar to finish

Quick Lunches: Whether it's just for **yourself or a few friends**, choose nutritious dishes that are **quick and easy to prepare**. **Soup** is ideal for any weather; you could choose either a **warming Pumpkin and Butternut Squash Soup** or this light and refreshing **Pea and Lettuce Soup**, both of which make a **great starter** or **meal in one**. Serve with lots of **fresh bread**. A crunchy and **revitalising salad** is a **welcome addition**. This **fresh**, slightly sweet, **Apple, Fennel, Ham and Pecan Salad** is no exception. Or serve a **Garden Salad** with **Onion, Feta Cheese and Pinenut Tarts**. Finish with a **crisp apple** and a good **cheddar** for a **well-rounded meal.**

Spicy Bean and Chorizo Casserole

chorizo sausages	6, about 50g (2oz) each
onion	1, chopped
garlic cloves	2, crushed
red pepper	1, deseeded and cut into strips
smoked paprika	1 tsp
red wine vinegar	1 tsp
chopped tomatoes	400g can
sun-dried tomatoes	4, drained and chopped
tomato purée	1 tbsp
treacle	1 tbsp
dark muscovado sugar	1 tbsp
bay leaf	1
pinto beans	435g can, drained
breadcrumbs	4 tbsp
chopped fresh parsley	2 tbsp

1. Heat a 2.6 litre (4½ pint) flameproof casserole dish for 2 to 3 minutes, add the chorizo sausages and cook lightly until browned. Add the onion, garlic and pepper, then fry until softened and golden. Add the smoked paprika and red wine vinegar, then stir well and cook for 30 seconds.

2. Add the tomatoes, sun-dried tomatoes, tomato purée, treacle, sugar and bay leaf. Season with salt and pepper. Bring to the boil, cover and simmer gently for 20 minutes.

3. Stir in the beans, then cover and cook for a further 10 minutes. Preheat the grill. Uncover the casserole, sprinkle the breadcrumbs and parsley over the casserole and grill for 2 to 3 minutes until the breadcrumbs are crisp and golden.

Preparation time: 10 min   **Cooking time:** 40 min
Cals per serving: 400   **Serves:** 4

Spicy Bean and
Chorizo Casserole

Leek and Ham
Galette

leeks 700g (1½lb), trimmed and cut into 2cm (¾in) thick slices

butter 50g (2oz)

plain flour 50g (2oz)

milk 100ml (3½fl oz)

chopped fresh marjoram 2 tbsp

beaufort or gruyère cheese 100g (3½oz), cubed, plus 4 tbsp, grated

good quality cooked sliced ham 2 x 150g packs, thickly shredded

plain flour to dust

chilled puff pastry 1 x 425g pack, containing two sheets

egg 1, beaten with a pinch of salt

1. Preheat the oven to 220°C/200°C fan oven/Gas Mark 7. Cook the leeks in a large pan of boiling salted water for 2 to 3 minutes or until just beginning to soften. Drain, reserving the cooking liquid. Plunge the leeks into cold water, drain and dry very well on kitchen paper or spin in a salad spinner.

2. Melt the butter in a large pan, take off the heat and mix in the flour to form a smooth paste. Mix in 450ml (15fl oz) leek water and the milk, stirring until smooth. Bring to the boil, simmer for 1 to 2 minutes, cover and cool for 20 minutes or until cold. Add the marjoram, leeks, the cheese and ham and season with salt and pepper.

3. On a lightly floured surface, roll out one sheet of puff pastry to a rectangle measuring 30.5 x 33cm (12 x 13in). Cut into two rectangles, one measuring 15 x 30.5cm (6 x 12in) and the other one measuring 18 x 30cm (7 x 12in). Repeat with the other sheet of pastry.

4. Take the smaller rectangles and put them on two greased baking sheets. Spoon on the ham mixture, leaving a 2cm (¾in) pastry border all the way round. Brush the edges of the pastry with the beaten egg. Cover the filling with the larger rectangles of pastry and press the edges together firmly. Cut several slashes in the top of the pastry to prevent the filling seeping out while the galette is cooking. Crimp the edges of the pastry to seal, then cover and freeze for 20 minutes until firm.

5. Remove from the freezer, brush all over again with the beaten egg, make a good-sized steam hole in the centre of each parcel and sprinkle with the grated cheese.

6. Bake the galettes for 20 to 30 minutes or until brown and crisp.

Freezing: At the end of step 4, cover in clingfilm and freeze on the baking tray. When firm, remove from baking tray. Wrap in baking parchment, then in clingfilm.

To serve: Defrost for 3 hours at room temperature on baking parchment. Put a flat baking tray in the oven to preheat to 220°C/200°C fan oven/Gas Mark 7 and complete step 5 of recipe. Put galette on the hot tray (this will keep the pastry base crisp) and bake for 40 minutes.

Preparation time: 40 min, plus 20 min cooling and 20 min freezing
Cooking time: 40 min   **Cals per serving:** 200   **Makes:** 2   **Serves:** 8

Shepherd's Pie with Mint Sauce

vegetable oil	2 tbsp
onions	2, chopped
carrots	2, chopped
garlic cloves	2, chopped
celery stick	1, chopped
minced lamb	900g (2lb)
large flat mushrooms	400g (14oz), chopped
plain flour	2 tbsp
red wine	150ml (5fl oz)
chopped tomatoes	400g can
mint sauce	1 tbsp

For the mash

floury potatoes	1.4kg (3lb), peeled and cut into large chunks
butter	150g (5oz)
warm milk	150ml (5fl oz)
chopped fresh chives	4 tbsp
cheddar	75g (3oz), grated

1. Heat the oil in a pan. Add the onions, carrots, garlic and celery. Fry for 10 minutes or until soft. Add the lamb and separate using a fork. Cook over a high heat for 10 minutes or until the mince is browned and there is a little liquid left. Add the mushrooms and cook for 1 to 2 minutes.

2. Add the flour and cook for 1 minute, then add the wine and tomatoes. Season, bring to the boil, cover and simmer for 50 minutes, or until tender. Uncover and cook for a further 5 to 10 minutes, if necessary, to bubble away any excess liquid. Add the mint sauce.

3. Meanwhile, prepare the mash. Put the potatoes in a pan of cold, salted water. Bring to the boil, cover and simmer for 20 to 30 minutes or until soft. Drain, return to the pan and heat for 1 minute to dry them off. Mash well, then beat in the butter, milk and chives. Season well.

4. Put the mince in individual ovenproof dishes and top with the mash. Roughen the surface with a fork and sprinkle with the cheese. Grill for 3 minutes, or until the tops are golden. Alternatively, brown in the oven at 190°C/170°C fan oven/Gas Mark 5 for 20 to 25 minutes. If cooking from cool room temperature, allow an extra 10 minutes in the oven.

Preparation time: 45 min   **Cooking time:** 1 hr 40 min
Cals per serving: 761   **Serves:** 6

Spiced Lamb in Pitta

1. Pulse the pepper in a food processor with the onion, garlic, cumin and olive oil to form a coarse paste. Add the chopped mint. Mix together this paste and the lamb; season and shape into 16 patties. Chill for 30 minutes. Barbecue or grill for 4 to 5 minutes on each side.

2. Chop the tomatoes, stir in the parsley and season with salt and pepper. Warm the pitta bread, wrap into a cone and secure with a cocktail stick. Fill each pitta with four patties, a drizzle of yogurt and a mint sprig and serve with the tomatoes on the side.

Freezing: Complete to the end of step 1, but do not barbecue or grill. Place the patties on a tray to freeze, then pack.

To use: Thaw at cool room temperature for 4 hours. Complete the recipe.

Preparation time: 20 min, plus 30 min chilling
Cooking time: 10 min   **Cals per serving:** 573   **Serves:** 4

small green pepper	1, deseeded and chopped
small onion	½, chopped
garlic cloves	3, chopped
ground cumin	2 tsp
olive oil	3 tbsp
chopped fresh mint	1 tbsp
lean minced lamb	550g (1lb 4oz)
very ripe tomatoes	450g (1lb), chopped
chopped fresh flat-leaf parsley	2 tbsp
large pitta breads	4
Greek yogurt and mint sprigs	to serve

Coriander-crusted Lamb

olive oil 3 tbsp, plus
extra for greasing

large aubergine 1, cut into
2.5cm (1in) cubes

cumin seeds 1 tsp

garlic clove 1, crushed

boneless lamb steaks 2, about 300g (11oz),
total weight

ground coriander 1 tsp

small red onion 1, sliced into rings

lemon wedges and

fresh coriander to garnish

hummus and toasted

flat bread cut into strips, to serve

1. Heat the oil in a frying pan and fry the aubergine for 8 minutes, or until beginning to soften. Add the cumin seeds and garlic, increase the heat and fry the mixture for 5 minutes, or until the aubergine is cooked and golden. Remove from the heat and set aside.

2. Meanwhile, cut each lamb steak into two. Coat with the ground coriander and season with the salt and pepper.

3. Using kitchen paper, wipe a griddle pan or barbecue with olive oil and heat. Fry the lamb on a moderate to high heat for 4 to 5 minutes on each side. Put on serving plates and place the onion rings on the lamb with the aubergines. Garnish with lemon wedges and coriander. Season with black pepper and serve with hummus and toasted flat bread.

Preparation time: 10 min **Cooking time:** 23 min
Cals per serving: 666 **Serves:** 2

Lamb with Spicy Couscous

1. Trim the lamb fillets, rub in 1 tablespoon of the oil and season well. In a heavy non-stick pan, fry the lamb for 15 minutes, turning regularly. Remove from the pan and leave to rest for 5 minutes.

2. Meanwhile, toss the aubergine in the cumin and cinnamon to coat, and fry in 2 tablespoons of the oil for 10 minutes, or until softened. Prepare the couscous according to packet instructions.

3. Add the aubergine, chilli, 2 tablespoons of the mint, the raisins and the remaining oil to the couscous. Season well, to taste. Slice the lamb and place on the couscous. Drizzle with yogurt, sprinkle with the remaining chopped mint and mint sprigs and serve.

Preparation time: 20 min **Cooking time:** 25 min
Cals per serving: 745 **Serves:** 4

fillets of lamb 2, about 400g
(14oz) each

olive oil 5 tbsp

aubergine 1, cut into
1cm (½in) dice

ground cumin 1 tsp

ground cinnamon ½ tsp

couscous 225g (8oz)

large red chilli 1, deseeded
and finely chopped

chopped fresh mint 3 tbsp

raisins 75g (3oz), soaked in hot
water and drained

yogurt and fresh mint sprigs to garnish

Coriander-crusted Lamb

packed to go

Greek Spinach and Feta Pie

olive oil 2 tbsp, plus
extra for brushing
small onions 2, chopped
ready-prepared spinach 500g pack
large eggs 2, plus extra beaten egg
to glaze
feta cheese 200g (7oz), crumbled
dill seeds 2 tsp
fresh filo pastry 270g pack

1. Preheat the oven to 200°C/180°C fan oven/Gas Mark 6. Heat the oil in a pan and cook the onions for 5 to 10 minutes, or until transparent. Add the spinach and cook for 3 minutes, or until wilted. Set aside to cool.

2. In a separate bowl, combine the two eggs with the feta cheese and half the dill seeds, then season with black pepper. Add the spinach and onion to the feta cheese mixture and stir until well combined.

3. Cut the pastry into 30.5 x 15cm (12 x 6in) sheets. Layer four sheets on a large baking sheet, brushing each piece with olive oil.

4. Spoon the spinach and feta mixture over the pastry and spread evenly with a palette knife. Cover with six more layers of pastry, brushing each sheet with olive oil.

5. Glaze the pie with the beaten egg and sprinkle the remaining dill seeds on top. Cook for 30 to 40 minutes, or until golden.

Preparation time: 15 min   **Cooking time:** 50 min
Cals per serving: 309   **Serves:** 6

Asparagus, Mushroom and Tomato Pizza

thin pizza base	25cm (10in)
olive oil	2 tbsp
firm tomatoes	225g (8oz), thickly sliced
asparagus tips	150g (5oz), blanched
large flat mushrooms	100g (3½oz), roughly chopped
chopped fresh tarragon	1 tbsp
mozzarella	150g pack, drained and sliced

1. Preheat the oven to 200°C/180°C fan oven/Gas Mark 6. Put the pizza base on a baking sheet and brush with 1 tablespoon of the olive oil. Scatter over the tomatoes, asparagus, mushrooms and tarragon, then season with salt and black pepper.

2. Arrange the mozzarella on top, season with more black pepper and drizzle with the remaining oil. Bake for 18 to 20 minutes or until the cheese is lightly browned.

Preparation time: 15 min **Cooking time:** 18–20 min
Cals per serving: 469 **Serves:** 4

Roquefort, Prosciutto and Spinach Pizza

1. Preheat the oven to 200°C/180°C fan oven/Gas Mark 6. Make up the pizza dough according to packet instructions and knead on a floured surface for 5 minutes. Roll out into a 30–35cm (12–14in) diameter circle. Place on a greased and floured baking sheet and press up the edges to make a rim. Put in a warm place and set aside while making the tomato sauce.

2. To make the tomato sauce, place the tomatoes, shallot, garlic, olive oil and wine in a roasting tin and cook for 30 minutes, then put the mixture in a food processor and whiz until smooth. Transfer to a bowl, stir in the tomato paste and sugar and season with salt and black pepper.

3. Increase the oven temperature to 220°C/200°C fan oven/Gas Mark 7. Spread the sauce over the pizza base, cook for 8 to 10 minutes on a preheated baking sheet. Top with the Roquefort, raisins and prosciutto and cook for 5 to 8 minutes until the prosciutto is crisp. Scatter over the spinach and pinenuts, drizzle with olive oil and cook for 5 minutes more.

Freezing: Complete the recipe, cool, pack and freeze.

To use: Cook from frozen at 200°C/180°C fan oven/Gas Mark 6 for 30 minutes or until hot.

Preparation time: 25 min **Cooking time:** 50 min
Cals per serving: 340 **Serves:** 6

pizza base mix	145g packet
flour	to dust
oil	for greasing
For the tomato sauce	
plum tomatoes	225g (8oz), halved
shallot	1, chopped
large garlic clove	1, halved
olive oil	1 tbsp
dry white wine	150ml (5fl oz)
tomato paste	2 tbsp
caster sugar	pinch of
For the topping	
ripe Roquefort	100g (3½oz), cubed
raisins	1 tbsp
prosciutto slices	6
spinach leaves	25g (1oz), trimmed, washed and dried
pinenuts	1 tbsp, toasted
olive oil	1–2 tbsp

Courgette
Puff Pie

courgettes	450g (1lb), sliced
olive oil	3 tbsp
ready-rolled puff pastry	375g pack
medium eggs	2
crème fraîche	2 tbsp
gruyère	75g (3oz), grated
garlic cloves	2, crushed
chopped fresh parsley	4 tbsp
breadcrumbs	50g (2oz)

1. Preheat the oven to 200°C/180°C fan oven/Gas Mark 6. Put the courgettes on a large baking sheet and drizzle with the oil. Put in the oven and roast for 8 minutes.

2. Transfer the courgettes to a sheet of greaseproof paper and put the unwashed baking sheet to one side.

3. Roll out the pastry on a floured board until it measures 30cm (12in) square. Lift the pastry carefully on to the baking sheet.

4. Crack one egg into a bowl and spoon in the crème fraîche, whisk lightly, then add 50g (2oz) of the cheese, along with the garlic and parsley. Season with salt and black pepper and mix together until well combined.

5. Arrange the courgettes down the middle of the pastry and pour the egg and crème fraîche mixture over. Scatter the breadcrumbs and remaining cheese on top. Gather the pastry sides up and over the filling to create a thick pastry rim. Chill for 10 minutes.

6. Beat the remaining egg and brush over the pastry. Bake for 30 minutes or until the pastry is crisp and golden brown.

Preparation time: 25 min, plus 10 min chilling
Cooking time: 40 min   **Cals per serving:** 650   **Serves:** 4

Salmon and Asparagus Pie

plain flour	275g (10oz) plus extra to dust
butter	200g (7oz), chilled and cubed
large eggs	2, beaten separately

For the filling

large eggs	2, beaten
large yolks	2, beaten
crème fraîche	200ml tub
chopped fresh dill	3 tbsp
butter	25g (1oz)
large button mushrooms	200g (7oz), thickly sliced
thick asparagus tips	150g (5oz), approx 11cm (4½in) long
fresh salmon fillet	450g (1lb), cut into wide strips 11cm (4½in) long

1. Whiz the flour, butter and a pinch of salt in a food processor until the ingredients resemble very fine breadcrumbs. Add one beaten egg and 2 tablespoons of cold water and pulse until the mixture just begins to come together. Turn out on to a floured work surface and knead very lightly. Cut a chunk from the pastry – about one-third of the total. Wrap both pieces and chill for at least 30 minutes.

2. Preheat the oven to 200°C/180°C fan oven/Gas Mark 6. Roll out the larger piece of pastry on the floured work surface to form a 28cm (11in) diameter circle, then use it to line a 20cm (8in), 5cm (2in) deep, loose-bottomed tin. Tidy the edges and prick the pastry base with a fork.

3. Line the pastry with greaseproof paper and baking beans, banking the beans up against the sides. Place the pastry tin on a baking sheet and bake for 25 minutes. Remove the paper and beans, brush the inside of the pastry with a little of the other beaten egg. Return to the oven for 5 to 10 minutes, or until the pastry is almost cooked, then cool. To make the filling, mix the eggs and yolks with the crème fraîche and dill, then season. Heat the butter in a frying pan, and fry the mushrooms over a high heat for 1 to 2 minutes. Season with salt and black pepper and set aside to cool.

4. Put the asparagus in a pan of boiling water, return to the boil, then drain. Plunge into iced water for a few minutes, then drain. Arrange half the salmon in a cartwheel pattern in the bottom of the pastry. Scatter the mushrooms over, arrange the asparagus in the same pattern on top, then finish with the remaining salmon. Pour over the crème fraîche mixture to within 1cm (½in) of the top of the pastry case. Brush the inside rim of the pastry with some of the remaining beaten egg. Roll out the remaining pastry, cut into a 25cm (10in) circle and position on top of the filling.

5. Seal the raw pastry gently to the inside rim of the cooked pastry. Brush with the remaining beaten egg, make a steam hole in the middle of the pie and decorate with a knife. Put the baking tray in the oven, set at 200°C/180°C fan oven/Gas Mark 6, to preheat. Bake the pie on the tray for 40 minutes until golden and the filling is cooked – cover with foil if it becomes too brown. To check the pie is cooked, insert a skewer in the centre for 30 seconds – it should feel hot. Place the pie on a cooling rack, in the tin, for 1 hour to serve warm or 3 hours, then remove from tin and slice up for a picnic.

Preparation time: 40 min, plus 30 min chilling and 1 hr cooling
Cooking time: 1 hr 10 min
Cals per serving: 812 for 6, 609 for 8   **Serves:** 6–8

Smoked Mackerel with Potato and Horseradish Salad

small new potatoes	450g (1lb)
horseradish sauce	2 tbsp
half-fat crème fraîche	
or cream	2 tbsp
lemon juice	1 tbsp
olive oil	4 tbsp
crisp apples	2
smoked mackerel fillets	2
watercress	100g pack

1. Cook the potatoes in boiling, salted water for 15 to 20 minutes or until tender. Drain and set aside.

2. In a bowl, mix the horseradish sauce, crème fraîche, lemon juice, olive oil and seasoning. Roughly chop the apples and warm potatoes, place in a large bowl and toss with the horseradish dressing.

3. Skin and flake the mackerel fillets, add to a separate bowl with the watercress, toss together lightly and serve on plates with the potato and horseradish salad on the side.

Preparation time: 15 min **Cooking time:** 20 min
Cals per serving: 500 **Serves:** 4

Parma Ham, Marinated Onion and Rocket Salad

1. Halve the onions and put in a large bowl with the rocket, Parma ham, parmesan shavings and the dressing. Toss together and serve at once.

2. To make the dressing, place the reserved onion marinade, olive oil, salt and pepper in a bowl and whisk together until combined.

Preparation time: 10 min **Cals per serving:** 280 **Serves:** 4

small marinated onions	150g (5oz) drained, reserving 1 tbsp of the marinade
rocket	200g (7oz)
Parma ham slices	8, about 100g (3½oz) total weight
parmesan shavings	75g (3oz)
olive oil	4 tbsp

Family fun: Banana and
Hazelnut Teabread, Chicken
Tikka Pockets and lashings
of Homemade Lemonade

Family Day Out: Always take **plenty of food** on a family day out **(fresh air** has a tendency to **stimulate the appetite)**. Choose food that is **easy to pick up.** Pack lots of bread, **French sticks are ideal** and can be **split open and packed** with any number of fillings from **Cheese and Chargrilled Pepper** to **Tuna Mayo**. Try **wraps** instead of sandwiches: **tortillas** filled with imaginative **salads and cheeses**. Also **easy to munch** are the **Chicken Tikka Pockets**, little pitta breads filled with **spicy chicken**. And for tea, **fruit tartlets**, and **Banana and Hazelnut Teabread** will fill any gaps. Take **lots to drink, too** – the **Homemade Lemonade** is the **perfect thirst-quencher** on a hot day.

Panzanella Salad

day-old country loaf 100g (3½oz), cubed
ripe tomatoes 450g (1lb),
roughly chopped
capers 2 tbsp
chopped fresh thyme 1 tsp
small red onion 1, thinly sliced
garlic cloves 2, crushed
small red chillies 2, deseeded and
finely chopped
extra-virgin olive oil 4 tbsp
pitted black olives 125g (4oz)
sun-dried tomatoes 50g (2oz),
roughly chopped
fresh basil leaves 8, torn
parmesan 25g (1oz)
fresh thyme sprigs
and crushed black pepper to garnish

1. Put the bread in a large bowl with the tomatoes, capers, thyme, onion, garlic, chillies, olive oil, black olives and sun-dried tomatoes. Season well, then toss together and leave in a cool place for 30 minutes.

2. Toss the salad thoroughly again and scatter the torn basil leaves and parmesan shavings over. Garnish with thyme sprigs and crushed black pepper, then serve.

Preparation time: 20 min, plus 30 min chilling
Cals per serving: 330 **Serves:** 4

Italian Chicken Salad

1. Whisk together the lemon juice, olive, walnut and sunflower oils and season. Set aside. Lightly toast the walnuts under the grill then chop very roughly.

2. Mix the grapes together with the gorgonzola, thyme and salad leaves. Using a sharp knife, slice each chicken breast thickly on the diagonal. Toss the salad with the prepared dressing and serve in bowls, topped with the sliced chicken, the remaining thyme sprigs and a good sprinkling of ground black pepper.

Preparation time: 15 min, plus 5 min standing
Cooking time: 25 min **Cals per serving:** 902 **Serves:** 4

lemon juice 3 tbsp
olive oil 1 tbsp
walnut oil 3 tbsp
sunflower oil 3 tbsp
walnuts 50g (2oz)
mixed seedless black and
green grapes 200g (7oz), halved
gorgonzola 125g (4oz), crumbled
chopped fresh thyme 1 tsp
mixed salad leaves 250g bag
roasted chicken breasts 4, skin on

Panzanella Salad

Salad Niçoise

garlic clove	1, crushed
lemon	½, rind finely grated
fresh tuna steaks or	450g (1lb) fresh
good quality canned tuna	2 × 200g cans, drained
olive oil	2 tbsp, plus extra for frying
fresh thyme sprig	1
small red peppers	2, halved and deseeded
vine-ripened tomatoes	350g (12oz), peeled
large eggs	2
fresh basil sprigs	2
cucumber	½, deseeded and cut into chunks
whole small olives	50g (2oz), pitted
salad onions	6, roughly chopped
anchovies	50g can, drained
shelled broad beans	450g (1lb), cooked and outer skin removed
rocket or salad leaves	50g (2oz)

For the dressing

lemon juice	2 tbsp
Dijon mustard	1 tsp
extra-virgin olive oil	6 tbsp

1. If using fresh tuna, rub the garlic and lemon rind over the steaks, season with black pepper, put in a bowl and spoon over the olive oil. Cover and leave in a cool place for 3 to 4 hours. Transfer to a small pan, add the thyme and barely cover with oil. Slowly increase the heat until the tuna is sizzling, then turn the tuna over and remove the pan from heat. Leave for 5 minutes; remove the fish with a slotted spoon, place on a plate and leave until cool.

2. Place the peppers under a preheated grill, skin-side up, and grill until the skins are blackened. Put in a bowl, cover with clingfilm and leave until cool. Thickly slice or quarter the tomatoes, put in a single layer on a plate and salt lightly. Leave for 30 minutes, then drain and pat dry with kitchen paper. Meanwhile, peel the peppers, cut into thick strips and set aside.

3. Bring a small pan of water to the boil, add the eggs (make sure they're covered with water) and simmer for 8 minutes. Cool under cold running water, shell and cut into quarters. To make the dressing, put the lemon juice and mustard in a small bowl, season with salt and pepper, then mix thoroughly. Add the oil and whisk until the dressing thickens.

4. Break the canned or the cooked fresh tuna into large flakes. Pound the basil leaves with 1 teaspoon of salt in a wide wooden salad bowl, then add the peppers, tomatoes, eggs, cucumber, olives, salad onions, anchovies and broad beans. Add just enough dressing to moisten the finished salad and toss gently. Check the seasoning and serve on a bed of rocket leaves.

Preparation time: 40 min, plus marinating and cooling
Cooking time: 30 min
Cals per serving: 530 for 4, 353 for 6   **Serves:** 4–6

Sushi

Japanese rice for sushi 150g (5oz), washed and drained

rice vinegar 2 tbsp

mirin (rice wine) 4 tbsp

golden caster sugar 1 tbsp

nori sheets 4

soy sauce

pickled ginger to serve

For the filling

wasabi paste 1 tsp, plus extra to serve

very fresh raw (or smoked) salmon 150g (5oz), thinly sliced

cucumber ½, peeled, deseeded and cut into long strips

large spring onions 2, cut into long strips

1. Pour 350ml (12fl oz) of cold water into a pan and add the rice. Bring to the boil and cover, then gently simmer for 10 to 12 minutes or until the rice is cooked and all the water has evaporated. Remove from the heat and stir in the rice vinegar, mirin and caster sugar. Let the rice cool, then fluff up using chopsticks or a fork.

2. Lay a sheet of nori, shiny side down, in the centre of a sushi mat (if you don't have one use a clean tea-towel). Wet your hands, then pick up a quarter of the rice and spread it across two-thirds of the nori (you can use a teaspoon if you prefer), then flatten the rice down evenly.

3. Make an indentation along the top end of the rice and spread with a little wasabi, then lay a quarter of the salmon, cucumber and spring onion across the width.

4. Place your fingers over the filling to hold it in place, then, using your thumbs, pick up the mat at the end closest to you. Roll it away from you, pressing in the filling gently but firmly as you do so.

5. Continue rolling until the filling is encased in nori, using the mat to help make a cylinder. Unroll the mat. Repeat with the remaining nori, rice and filling to make four rolls in total.

6. Using a sharp wet knife, trim the end of each roll, cut into three equal pieces, then cut each in half at an angle. Serve with soy sauce, mixed with a little wasabi, and pickled ginger.

Preparation time: 30 min   **Cooking time:** 15 min
Cals per serving: 55   **Makes:** 24 pieces

Roasted Vegetable
and Tuna

1. Preheat the oven to 240°C/220°C fan oven/Gas Mark 9. Put the aubergine and pepper into a roasting tin, drizzle with 2 tablespoons of the olive oil and roast on the top shelf of the oven for 20 minutes.

2. Add the courgettes, tomatoes and garlic, then return to the oven. Cook for a further 30 to 40 minutes, gently stirring the vegetables from time to time until they're soft and lightly charred.

3. Gently toss the tuna and thyme through the vegetables. Serve warm or at room temperature on slices of foccacia, and garnish with thyme.

Preparation time: 20 min   **Cooking time:** 55 min
Cals per serving: 420   **Serves:** 2

aubergine	½, about 150g (5oz) total weight, chopped
red pepper	1, deseeded and roughly chopped
olive oil	3 tbsp
courgettes	150g (5oz), sliced
plum tomatoes	150g (5oz), roughly chopped
garlic cloves	8
tuna or salmon	100g can, drained and flaked
chopped fresh thyme	½ tsp
foccacia bread	4 slices
fresh thyme sprigs	to garnish

Picnic
Sandwich

1. Slice the foccacia in half horizontally and spread one half with the pesto. Layer with the tomatoes and cheese, ham and rocket, then top with the other half of the loaf to create a sandwich.

2. Garnish with rosemary and rock salt, then serve, cut into wedges.

Preparation time: 10 min   **Cals per serving:** 195 **Serves:** 2

focaccia	1 loaf
basil or sun-dried tomato pesto	1 tbsp
ripe tomatoes	75g (3oz), sliced
fontina, emmenthal or other mild cheese	40g (1½oz), thinly sliced
sliced ham	40g (1½oz)
salad leaves, such as rocket	25g (1oz)
fresh rosemary sprigs and rock salt	to garnish

Turkey
and Bacon

streaky bacon rashers 2
plain flour 2 tsp
turkey breast strips 125g (4oz)
olive oil 2 tsp
redcurrant jelly
or cranberry sauce 2 tsp

1. Cut the bacon into short strips. Heat a frying pan over a medium heat and fry the bacon for 1 to 2 minutes until beginning to brown. Remove from the heat.

2. Season the flour with pepper and dust the turkey with the seasoned flour. Add the oil to the pan with the bacon in and stir-fry the turkey for 2 to 3 minutes until cooked through and the bacon is crisp. Use warm or cool and chill until needed. Top with a little redcurrant jelly to serve.

Preparation time: 5 min   **Cooking time:** 5–6 min
Cals per serving: 250   **Serves:** 2

Tuna Mayo

1. Flake the tuna into a bowl. Add the vegetables and toss to combine. Mix together the mayonnaise, yogurt and ketchup, then add this to the tuna mixture and stir until well combined. Serve in bread of your choice.

Preparation time: 10 min   **Cals per serving:** 170 **Serves:** 4

tuna in sunflower oil 198g can, drained
sweetcorn niblets 2 tbsp, thawed if frozen
cucumber piece 5cm (2in), diced
red pepper ½ deseeded and diced
mayonnaise 3 tbsp
natural yogurt 3 tbsp
tomato ketchup 1 tsp

Chicken and
Peanut Butter

smooth or crunchy
peanut butter 3 tbsp
cold roast chicken 125g (4oz), sliced
mild chilli sauce 1 tsp, optional
coconut milk 2 tbsp, optional

1. Spread the bread with a generous layer of peanut butter and top with roast chicken, or, for a saté-like flavour, combine the peanut butter, chilli and coconut milk until smooth and spread over the roast chicken before filling the sandwiches.

Preparation time: 5 min   **Cals per serving:** 325   **Serves:** 2

Cheese and
Char-grilled Pepper

red pepper 1, deseeded
sun dried tomato dressing or French dressing 1 tsp
mozzarella 150g pack, drained and sliced

1. Cut the pepper into quarters and flatten with the palm of your hand. Place under a preheated grill, skin-side up, and grill for 3 to 5 minutes until the skin blackens and burns. Place the peppers in a bowl, cover with clingfilm and leave until cool.

2. Peel the peppers, then cut the peppers into thick strips and toss in the salad dressing. Fill the sandwiches with slices of mozzarella and top with the grilled peppers.

Preparation time: 10 min, plus cooling
Cooking time: 5 min   **Cals per serving:** 200   **Serves:** 2

> **Note:** Sandwich Fillings
> Why not vary the type of bread used: try soft or crusty rolls, pitta breads or even tortilla wraps. Calories given are for the filling only.

Mediterranean
Country Loaf

1. Slice off the top of the loaf and remove the crumb from the middle and lid of the loaf. Drizzle the insides with half the oil and season.

2. Layer the inside of the loaf with salad leaves, half the ham, cheese and pimientos. Repeat the layering until you reach the top of the loaf. Drizzle with the remaining oil. Season and replace the top of the loaf.

3. Wrap tightly in clingfilm, place a heavy board on top to act as a weight and chill for 1 hour. Remove the clingfilm and cut into wedges to serve.

Preparation time: 10 min, plus 1 hr chilling
Cals per serving: 746   **Serves:** 4

round crusty country loaf 1, unsliced
olive oil 6 tbsp
salt and black pepper
mixed salad leaves 100g bag
cooked sliced ham 300g (11oz)
mild cheddar or Jarlsberg 175g (6oz), sliced
pimiento peppers 425g can, drained and shredded

Alfresco feast: chilled Champagne with Salmon and Asparagus Pie, Parma Ham, Marinated Onion and Rocket Salad and strawberries and cream for dessert

Posh Picnic: You can really **indulge your fantasies** on an **alfresco** picnic. Be as daring as you like, just ensure the **food is transportable**. Pack the real crockery and cutlery and plenty of **Champagne, well packed in ice.** Perfect for a picnic are **Sushi,** which look as good as they taste. A **homemade pie** is also ideal picnic fare, such as this **Salmon and Asparagus Pie, delicately flavoured** with dill. You have the pick of summer produce to make great salads, too. The **Parma Ham, Marinated Onion and Rocket Salad** is a meal in itself, or, for a starter, try the **Smoked Mackerel with Potato and Horseradish Salad.** And what is more summery than **strawberries and cream**, to finish?

Chicken Tikka Pockets with Coconut Dressing

crème fraîche 120ml (4fl oz)
coconut milk 5 tbsp
pitta breads 4
mixed salad leaves 200g bag
chicken tikka fillets 2 × 210g packs, sliced
spring onions 2, finely sliced
mango chutney 2 tbsp
flaked almonds 15g (½oz)
raisins 25g (1oz)

1. Mix together the crème fraîche and coconut milk in a small bowl and season well. Set aside.

2. Split each pitta bread open to form a pocket, then fill each pocket with a generous handful of mixed salad leaves. Put the slices of chicken tikka fillets on top of the salad, sprinkle the spring onions over, add the mango chutney, drizzle with the crème fraîche mixture, then top with a sprinkling of flaked almonds and raisins. Serve.

Preparation time: 10 min   **Cals per serving:** 560   **Serves:** 4

Chicken Fajitas

1. Put the chicken breasts into a shallow dish, sprinkle with the seasoning and toss together. Heat the oil in a large non-stick frying pan, add the chicken and cook for 5 minutes or until golden brown and tender.

2. Add the pepper and cook for 2 minutes. Pour in all the sauce, bring to the boil and simmer for 5 minutes or until thoroughly heated. Add a splash of boiling water if the sauce becomes too thick.

3. Stir in the spring onions and cook for 2 minutes more.

4. Place the chicken on a plate and leave to cool. Fill the tortillas with the chicken, salsa, guacamole and soured cream. Roll up the tortilla, and pack for a picnic, or pack the filling ingredients separately and let everyone fill their own.

Preparation time: 10 min   **Cooking time:** 10 min
Cals per serving: 660   **Serves:** 4

skinless, boneless 4, about 700g
chicken breasts (1½lb) total weight, cut into chunky strips
Mexican seasoning 2 tsp
sunflower oil 1 tbsp
red pepper 1, deseeded and sliced
ready-made Mexican sauce 360g jar
bunch spring onions 1, trimmed and halved
flour tortillas 320g pack of 8
tomato salsa 150g pot
guacamole dip 125g (4oz)
soured cream 142ml tub

Pastrami
Tortilla Wraps

guacamole dip 200g tub
canned pimientos 2 tbsp, chopped
wheat tortillas 4
pastrami or salt beef 2 × 100g packs
small red onion 1, very thinly sliced
**endive, fresh mint sprigs
and lime wedges** to garnish

1. Mix the guacamole and pimientos together and season.

2. Divide the mixture between the tortillas and arrange the pastrami on top. Sprinkle with the onion and roll each tortilla up like a sausage. Wrap individually in clingfilm and chill.

3. To serve, remove the clingfilm and cut the tortillas in half. Serve with the endive, mint sprigs and lime wedges.

Preparation time: 20 min, plus 30 min chilling
Cals per serving: 345   **Serves:** 4

Courgette and
Parmesan Frittata

1. Melt 25g (1oz) of the butter in an 18cm (7in) non-stick frying pan and fry the onion until soft. Add the courgettes and fry gently for 5 minutes or until they begin to soften.

2. Preheat the grill. Add the remaining butter to the pan. Season the eggs and pour these into the pan, cook for 2 to 3 minutes or until golden underneath and cooked round the edges.

3. Scatter the cheese over the frittata and put under the preheated grill for 1 to 2 minutes, or until just set. Garnish with parmesan, cut the frittata into quarters, and serve warm or cold with crusty bread.

Preparation time: 10 min   **Cooking time:** 12 min
Cals per serving: 260   **Serves:** 4

butter 40g (1½oz)
small onion 1, finely chopped
courgettes 225g (8oz), finely sliced
medium eggs 6, beaten
parmesan 25g (1oz), freshly grated, plus shavings to garnish
crusty bread to serve

Raspberry Muffins
with Streusel Topping

plain flour	250g (9oz), sifted
light brown soft sugar	175g (6oz)
baking powder	3½ tsp
salt	½ tsp
ground cinnamon	1 tsp
medium eggs	2, beaten
milk	175 ml (6 fl oz)
sunflower oil	100 ml (3 ½ fl oz)
fresh raspberries	125 g (4oz)

For the streusel topping

demerara sugar	40g (1½ oz)
plain flour	40g (1½ oz)
orange	1 rind, grated
butter	25g (1oz), melted

1. Preheat the oven to 200°C/180°C fan oven/Gas Mark 6. Line 12 muffin tins with 150ml (5fl oz) paper muffin cases.

2. To make the topping, place the sugar, flour and orange rind in a bowl. Pour in butter and stir with a fork until crumbly.

3. Place the flour, sugar, baking powder, salt and cinnamon in a bowl, mix well and make a well in the centre. Whisk the eggs, milk and oil together and pour into the well. Whisk until smooth.

4. Add the raspberries to the mixture and carefully and quickly fold through, using a large metal spoon. Fill each muffin cup with the mixture and sprinkle with a little topping. Bake for 20 to 25 min or until golden and firm to the touch. Remove the muffins from the tray and transfer to a wire rack. Leave to cool for 10 min. Serve warm.

Freezing: Complete the recipe, allow to cool thoroughly, then wrap and freeze.

To use: Thaw at cool room temperature overnight. Cover with foil and warm through at 180°C/160 °C fan oven/Gas Mark 4 for 10 to 15 min.

Preparation time: 30 min   **Cooking time:** 20–25 min
Cals per serving: 300   **Makes:** 12

Plum and Cardamom Fool

dessert plums 1kg (2¼lb), stoned and sliced
caster sugar 125g (4oz)
cardamom pods 4, split, seeds removed and crushed
lemon juice 2 tbsp
ready-made fresh custard 150g tub
Greek yogurt 2 × 200g tubs
amaretti biscuits to serve

1. Put the plums, caster sugar, cardamom seeds and lemon juice in a pan. Cover and bring to the boil. Simmer for 20 to 25 minutes, or until the plums are soft, but still holding their shape. Pour into a cold bowl and leave for 30 minutes.

2. Strain the plums, reserving the juices. Set aside eight slices to decorate. Purée the plums in a food processor and pour into a bowl. Boil the reserved juices for 3 to 4 minutes until reduced to 3 tablespoons, then stir into the plum purée along with the custard and one tub of the yogurt. Stir until smooth.

3. Spoon the mixture into four glass tumblers and chill for up to 2 hours. Decorate with swirls of the remaining yogurt and the reserved plum slices and serve with amaretti biscuits.

Preparation time: 15 min, plus 2 hr 30 min chilling and standing
Cooking time: 25 min   **Cals per serving:** 370   **Serves:** 4

Exotic Fruit Salad

1. To make the syrup, put the sugar in a pan with 600ml (1 pint) of water and the mint, five spice, bay leaves, lemongrass and ginger. Heat gently until the sugar has dissolved. Bring to the boil and simmer for 5 minutes. Remove from the heat and set aside to infuse for at least 1 hour, preferably longer.

2. Put all the fruit in a bowl, strain the cooled syrup on top, then cover and chill for at least 2 hours. If you want to, decorate with lemongrass sticks, to serve.

Preparation time: 30 min, plus 1 hr infusion and 2 hr chilling
Cooking time: 7 min   **Cals per serving:** 214   **Serves:** 6

For the syrup
caster sugar 125g (4oz)
fresh mint sprigs 6
ground Chinese five spice ½ tsp
small fresh bay leaves 2
lemongrass sticks 4, split in half and bruised, plus extra to decorate
grated fresh root ginger ½ tsp

For the salad
ripe pineapple 1, about 900g (2lb) total weight, flesh cored and cut into chunks
ripe papaya 2, deseeded, peeled and sliced
galia melon 1, peeled, deseeded, and cut into chunks

Buttermilk Scones

self-raising flour	300g (11oz), sifted, plus extra to dust
baking powder	1 tsp
butter	50g (2oz), chilled and diced, plus extra for greasing
golden caster sugar	25g (1oz)
buttermilk	284ml carton
milk	to glaze
blueberry jam	to serve

For the vanilla mascarpone

mascarpone	250g tub
vanilla pod	1

1. Preheat the oven to 220°C/200°C fan oven/Gas Mark 7. Put the flour, baking powder and a pinch of salt in a large bowl and mix together. Add the butter and rub in until the mixture resembles fine breadcrumbs. Or put all the ingredients in a food processor, whiz for 30 seconds, then tip into a mixing bowl.

2. Add the sugar and buttermilk and use a knife to mix everything together quickly. Knead lightly on a floured board and shape into a round.

3. Roll out the dough to about 2.5cm (1in) thick. Put 25g (1oz) flour in a small bowl and dip in a 6cm (2½in) plain cutter. Stamp out a round and repeat stamping out rounds until all the dough is used up.

4. Put the rounds on two greased baking sheets, brush the tops with milk and bake for 12 to 15 minutes, or until golden and risen.

5. To make the vanilla mascarpone, put the mascarpone in a bowl and beat with a wooden spoon to soften. Cut the vanilla pod in half, split open and use the end of a teaspoon to scrape out the seeds. Add the seeds to the bowl and beat well to mix everything together.

6. Cool the scones on a wire rack and serve with vanilla mascarpone and blueberry jam. Best eaten on the day of making.

Freezing: When cool, freeze for up to three months.

To use: Thaw for 2 hours.

Preparation time: 15 min   **Cooking time:** 12–15 min
Cals per serving: 200   **Makes:** 8

Banana and Hazelnut Teabread

1. Preheat the oven to 180°C/160°C fan oven/Gas Mark 4. Mix the butter and sugar together in a bowl. Add all but 1 tablespoon of the hazelnuts and all the remaining ingredients and mix.

2. Turn into a lined and greased 900g (2lb) loaf tin and sprinkle with the remaining nuts.

3. Bake for 1 hour 40 minutes, or until cooked. Test it by piercing the centre with a skewer – it should come out clean.

4. Leave the teabread in the tin for one minute then turn out on to a wire rack to cool. Serve sliced and spread with butter.

Preparation time: 10 min, plus cooling   **Cooking time:** 1 hr 40 min
Cals per serving: 364 for 8, 291 for 10   **Serves:** 8–10

butter	125g (4oz), plus extra to serve
soft brown sugar	125g (4oz)
hazelnuts	50g (2oz), chopped
self-raising flour	225g (8oz)
baking powder	1 tsp
cinnamon	1 tsp
large eggs	2
sultanas	75g (3oz)
ripe bananas	2, mashed
semi-skimmed milk	2 tsp

Buttermilk
Scones

Working lunch: Focaccia
Rolls, Raspberry Muffins
and plenty of fresh raw
fruit and vegetables

Desk-side Snacks: Everyone needs a few little **energy-boosting snacks** throughout the day to keep them going. Keep them as **healthy and nutritious** and as varied as possible. Choose **interesting breads** to make **sandwiches**, such as **focaccia, ciabatta and crusty country loaves**, and fill them with **salads, ham, cheese and peppers** that are filled with the **flavours of the Mediterranean**. **Raw vegetables** and pieces of **fresh fruit** are **great** to pick-on – **easy to prepare and easy to eat**. You could make a **dip** for the **vegetables** or **fruit**. **Pasta Salad** is ideal for lunch. And for tea, a **Raspberry Muffin**, enjoyed with a **hot cup of tea**, will see you through to **hometime**.

Cheesy Knots

plain flour	125g (4oz)
paprika	pinch of
butter	50g (2oz), cubed
gruyère	50g (2oz), grated
a little milk	for brushing
sesame and poppy seeds	optional

1. Preheat the oven to 200°C/180°C fan oven/Gas Mark 6. Place the flour in a food processor with the paprika and butter. Whiz for a few seconds until the mixture resembles breadcrumbs. Add the cheese and whiz again to mix.

2. With the motor running add enough cold water to mix to a soft dough (about 2 to 3 tablespoons).

3. Divide the dough into 16 pieces and roll each one into a sausage shape about 13cm (5in) long. Carefully twist each one into the shape of a knot and place on a baking sheet. Repeat with the remaining dough. Brush each one with a little milk and sprinkle with seeds, if using. Bake for 10 to 15 minutes or until crisp and pale golden. Allow to cool on the tray for a few minutes before transferring to a wire rack to cool completely.

Preparation time: 10 min   **Cooking time:** 15 min
Cals per serving: 60   **Makes:** 16

Pork Bites
with Fruity Coleslaw

1. Preheat the oven to 190°C/170°C fan oven/Gas Mark 5. Place the sausagemeat, cornflakes, cheddar and sage in a mixing bowl and mix well.

2. Shape the mixture into 20 small balls. Season the flour with black pepper and roll the balls in the seasoned flour. Place on a baking sheet and bake for 20 minutes until golden and cooked through. Allow to cool, then chill until needed.

3. To make the coleslaw, place the cabbage, carrot and fruit in a bowl, and toss to combine. Mix together the yogurt and mayonnaise and add to the bowl. Toss to coat the vegetables and fruit in the mixture. Pack the meat balls and coleslaw in small separate tubs. Remember to pack a spoon or fork for the coleslaw.

Preparation time: 20 min   **Cooking time:** 20 min
Cals per serving: 510   **Serves:** 4

sausagemeat	350g (12oz)
cornflakes	50g (2oz), crushed
cheddar	50g (2oz), grated
dried sage	1 tsp
plain flour	2 tbsp

For the coleslaw

white cabbage	150g (5oz), shredded
carrot	1, peeled and cut into thin matchsticks
small apple	1, cored and sliced
mandarin orange	1, peeled
or clementine	and segmented
natural yogurt	3 tbsp
mayonnaise	3 tbsp

Sausage and Bean Parcels

potatoes	225g (8oz), peeled and diced
cooked chipolata sausages	3
baked beans	150g can
fresh filo pastry sheets	4
oil	for brushing

1. Preheat the oven to 200°C/180°C fan oven/Gas Mark 6. Cook the potatoes in boiling water for 5 to 6 minutes, or until tender. Drain and refresh in cold water, drain again.

2. Cut the sausages into thin slices and place in a bowl. Add the potatoes and beans and mix together well.

3. Layer two sheets of filo pastry on top of each other, brushing each with a little oil. Brush the top with oil and cut into 13cm (5in) squares.

4. Place a spoonful of the filling on to each square and gather up the edges pinching them together to form a bundle. Place on a baking sheet. Repeat with the remaining filo and filling. Bake for 10 to 12 minutes until the pastry is golden.

Variation: For a vegetarian alternative, add 75g (3oz) cubed cheddar in place of the sausage or use vegetarian sausages.

Preparation time: 15 min   **Cooking time:** 17 min
Cals per parcel: 90   **Makes:** 12

Pasta Salad

1. Cook the pasta in a large pan of boiling salted water according to packet instructions. Cool under cold running water and drain well. Blanch the beans and baby corn in boiling water for 3 minutes, then drain and cool under cold water, drain again.

2. Place the pasta in a bowl with the prepared vegetables and the cheese and/or ham if using. Mix together the mayonnaise, yogurt and fruity sauce and pour over the pasta. Toss well before packing into small tubs. Don't forget to pack a fork.

Variation: For a vegetarian pasta salad omit the ham. Add a few extra vegetables such as diced carrot, diced cucumber, peas and some canned, drained beans.

Preparation time: 10 min   **Cooking time:** 15 min
Cals per serving: 330   **Serves:** 4

pasta bows	150g (5oz)
green beans	50g (2oz), trimmed and halved
baby corn	8, cut into chunks
cherry tomatoes	6, halved
button mushrooms	4, halved
cheddar	75g (3oz), cubed, optional
ham slices	2, cut into strips, optional
mayonnaise	3 tbsp
natural yogurt	2 tbsp
brown fruity sauce	1 tsp

Sticky
Chicken

chicken drumsticks 8, about 75g (3oz) each
tomato ketchup 2 tbsp
fruity brown sauce 2 tbsp
clear honey 2 tsp
sunflower oil 2 tsp

For the rice salad
brown rice 125g (4oz)
green beans 75g (3oz), trimmed and
cut into short lengths
cucumber ½, diced
olive oil 3 tbsp
white wine vinegar 1 tbsp
Dijon mustard ½ tsp

1. Preheat the grill to medium. Skin the chicken, if you prefer, and cut two or three slashes in the chicken flesh with a sharp knife. Combine the ketchup, brown sauce, honey and oil in a small bowl.

2. Cook the chicken under the preheated grill for 10 minutes, turning once or twice. Then brush all over with the ketchup mixture. Continue to cook under a medium heat for 10 to 15 minutes or until the chicken is cooked through. To check if the chicken is cooked pierce the thickest part with a skewer – if cooked, the juices should run clear.

3. Leave to cool then cover and chill until required.

4. Meanwhile, make the rice salad. Add the rice to a pan of boiling water, return to the boil. Stir once, then reduce the heat and simmer for 20 minutes. Add the beans to the water and cook for a further 2 minutes. Drain and cool under running water, drain well. Toss in the cucumber.

5. Mix together the olive oil, vinegar and mustard. Pour the dressing over the rice and toss well. Wrap the chicken in foil and place the rice salad in a small tub. Remember to pack a fork for the salad.

Preparation time: 15 min   **Cooking time:** 30 min
Cals per serving: 375   **Serves:** 4

Sticky Chicken

Easy Fruit Tartlets

flour	to dust
shortcrust pastry	350g (12oz)
cooking apple	1, about 350g (12oz) total weight, peeled, cored and diced
or peach slices	410g can peaches, drained and roughly chopped
apricot jam	4 tbsp

1. Preheat the oven to 180°C/160°C fan oven/Gas Mark 4. On a lightly floured work surface, roll the pastry out to a 30cm (12in) square and cut into 16 equal-sized squares. Dampen the corners of the pastry with water. Fold up the sides of each square and pinch the corners to form shallow square tartlet cases. Prick the bases with a fork. Place close together, so that the sides are touching each other on a baking sheet. (This will help the sides to stand up during cooking.) Alternatively, place the pastry into shallow bun tins.

2. Divide the apple between the tartlet cases and top with a little apricot jam. Bake in the centre of the oven for 20 to 25 minutes, or until the pastry is crisp and golden.

3. Allow to cool on the baking sheet for 5 minutes before transferring to a wire rack to cool completely.

Preparation time: 15 min   **Cooking time:** 20–25 min
Cals per serving: 78   **Makes:** 16

Dainty Cup Cakes

1. Preheat the oven to 190°C/170°C fan oven/Gas Mark 5. Line a muffin tin with 12 muffin cases. Put the butter and sugar in a bowl and cream together until pale, light and fluffy.

2. Add the eggs, one at a time, and beat together, folding in a little flour if the mixture looks as if it is going to curdle.

3. Fold in the flour, lemon rind and juice and mix everything together.

4. Spoon the mixture into the cases and bake for 15 to 20 minutes until pale golden, risen and springy to the touch. Cool on a wire rack.

5. To make the frosted flowers, if using, whisk the egg white in a clean bowl for 30 seconds until frothy. Brush the white over the flower petals and put them on a wire rack resting on top of a piece of greaseproof paper. Dust heavily with caster sugar then leave the flowers to dry.

6. To make the icing, put the icing sugar in a bowl with the food colouring of your choice. Mix in the lemon juice to create a smooth dropping consistency. Spoon the icing on to the cakes. Decorate with frosted flowers and serve when the icing is completely set.

Preparation time: 15 min   **Cooking time:** 15–20 min
Cals per serving: 320   **Makes:** 12

butter	175g (6oz), softened
golden caster sugar	175g (6oz)
medium eggs	3
self-raising flour	175g (6oz), sifted
lemon	1, juice of and rind finely grated

For the frosted flowers, optional

egg white	1
edible flowers, such as violas	6
caster sugar	to dust

For the icing

icing sugar	225g (8oz), sifted
food colouring	1 drop
lemon juice	2–3 tbsp

main events

Chicken and Salsa Verde Crostini

walnut bread loaf	1, cut into 15 × 1cm (½in) slices
olive oil	2 tbsp
sea salt flakes	1 tbsp
cooked chicken breast	175g (6oz), cut into 15 slices
sun-dried tomatoes in oil	125g (4oz), drained and sliced into 15 pieces
walnuts	50g (2oz), lightly toasted and finely chopped, to garnish
fresh flat-leaf parsley	to garnish

For the salsa verde
roughly chopped fresh coriander	3 tbsp
fresh mint	3 tbsp, roughly chopped
fresh basil leaves	3 tbsp, roughly torn
garlic clove	1, roughly chopped
Dijon mustard	2 tbsp
anchovy fillets	3
capers	1 tbsp
olive oil	4 tbsp
lemon	½, juice of

1. To make the salsa verde, whiz all the ingredients in a food processor or blender until smooth. Cover and chill.

2. To make the crostini, place the slices of bread on a baking sheet, brush on both sides with olive oil and sprinkle with sea salt. Place under a hot grill for 1 minute on each side or until lightly toasted.

3. To serve, place a slice of chicken on each crostini base, top with a spoonful of salsa verde and a slice of sun-dried tomato, then garnish with a sprinkling of walnuts and parsley.

Preparation time: 20 min, plus chilling
Cooking time: 2 min   **Cals per crostini:** 99   **Makes:** 15

Tomato and Basil Crostini

1. In a large bowl, stir one crushed garlic clove and 2 tablespoons of the olive oil into the tomatoes. Season well and allow to stand for 10 minutes.

2. Lightly toast the ciabatta slices on both sides, halve the remaining garlic cloves, then rub both sides of the toast with the cut side of the garlic and drizzle with a little olive oil. Add the basil to the tomato mixture and spoon it on top of the ciabatta, then serve.

Preparation time: 15 min, plus 10 min standing
Cooking time: 3 min   **Cals per crostini:** 190   **Serves:** 4

garlic cloves	3
extra-virgin olive oil	2 tbsp, plus extra for drizzling
ripe tomatoes	550g (1lb 4oz), roughly chopped
ciabatta bread slices	4–8
shredded fresh basil	2 tbsp

Goat's Cheese and Red Onion Crostini

red onion 1, about 300g (11oz) total weight, finely sliced

olive oil 2 tbsp, plus extra for drizzling

ciabatta bread slices 8

garlic cloves 2, halved

soft goat's cheese 75g (3oz)

chopped fresh thyme to garnish

1. Put the onion on a baking sheet, drizzle with 2 tablespoons of olive oil and grill for 5 minutes or until soft and just beginning to char.

2. Lightly toast the ciabatta slices, then rub both sides of the toast with the cut side of the garlic halves and drizzle with a little olive oil.

3. Spread the goat's cheese on each crostini; top with onion and black pepper. Drizzle with oil and garnish with thyme to serve.

Preparation time: 20 min   **Cooking time:** 5 min
Cals per crostini: 166   **Makes:** 8

Cannellini and Chorizo Crostini

1. Fry the chorizo in a non-stick frying pan until crisp. Remove and drain any excess fat on kitchen paper.

2. Lightly toast the ciabatta slices, then rub each piece on both sides with the cut side of the garlic cloves and drizzle with a little olive oil.

3. Toss the beans with the parsley and remaining olive oil and season well.

4. Spread each crostini with a little mayonnaise. Top with the chorizo and the beans to serve.

Preparation time: 20 min   **Cooking time:** 5 min
Cals per crostini: 195   **Makes:** 8

chorizo sausages 70g pack, thinly sliced

ciabatta bread slices 8

garlic cloves 2, halved

olive oil 2 tbsp, plus extra for drizzling

cannellini beans 100g can, drained

chopped fresh flat-leaf parsley 2 tbsp

thick mayonnaise to serve

Lime and Gin
Marinated Salmon

gin 2 tbsp
lime 1, rind finely grated
sea salt flakes 1 tbsp
pink peppercorns 1 tbsp, lightly crushed
raw salmon fillet 150g (5oz), skin and bones removed
Japanese rice for sushi 150g (5oz), washed and drained
rice vinegar 2 tbsp
golden caster sugar 1 tbsp
pickled ginger slices 15
wasabi paste 1 tbsp
snipped fresh chives to garnish

1. Mix together the gin, lime rind, sea salt and pepper in a bowl. Add the salmon, cover and chill overnight.

2. Pour 350ml (12fl oz) water into a large pan and add the rice. Bring to the boil, then cover and simmer for 10 to 12 minutes. Remove from the heat and stir in the rice vinegar and the caster sugar. Leave until cool, then cover.

3. Using a sharp carving knife, cut the salmon into 30 very thin slices (there's no need to remove the seasonings).

4. Wet your hands and mould the rice into 15 walnut-sized balls. Flatten each one with the palm of your hand to form discs. Top each disc with two slices of marinated salmon, a slice of pickled ginger and a little wasabi paste. Garnish with chives to serve.

Preparation time: 30 min, plus overnight marinating and 45 min cooling   **Cooking time:** 12 min   **Cals per serving:** 55   **Makes:** 15

Gravadlax with Cucumber Salad

1. Arrange the cucumber on a large plate. Mix together the white wine vinegar, caster sugar and chopped dill, then season to taste. Pour the dressing over the cucumber and leave to marinate for 15 minutes.

2. Mix the dill and mustard sauce into the crème fraîche and season.

3. Lightly toast the mini blinis. Arrange the marinated cucumber on four individual serving plates with the slices of gravadlax, the crème fraîche sauce and the blinis. Garnish with dill sprigs to serve.

Preparation time: 15 min, plus 15 min marinating
Cals per serving: 605   **Serves:** 4

small cucumber 1, washed, drained, deseeded and thinly sliced
white wine vinegar 3 tbsp
caster sugar 1 tbsp
chopped fresh dill 3 tbsp
gravadlax with dill and mustard sauce 2 x 125g packs
crème fraîche 4 tbsp
mini blinis 12
fresh dill sprigs to garnish

Gravadlax with
Cucumber Salad

Spicy Crab Cakes with Chilli Mayo

sunflower oil 1 tbsp
spring onions 3, finely sliced
garlic cloves 2, crushed
red chilli 1, deseeded
and chopped
crabmeat 350g (12oz)
tomato ketchup 2 tsp
mayonnaise 4 tbsp
Worcestershire sauce 1 tsp
fresh white breadcrumbs 50g (2oz)
**sliced red chilli and
spring onion curls** to garnish

For the coating
seasoned flour 50g (2oz)
large egg 1, beaten
fresh white breadcrumbs 125g (4oz)
vegetable oil for frying

For the chilli mayo
sweet chilli sauce 2 tbsp
chopped fresh coriander 1 tbsp
lime 1, juice of and rind
finely grated
mayonnaise 5 tbsp

1. Heat the oil in a pan, fry the spring onions for 3 minutes, stirring all the time. Remove from the heat, stir in the garlic and chilli, transfer to a large bowl and leave to cool. Add the crabmeat, ketchup, mayonnaise, Worcestershire sauce and breadcrumbs. Stir until well combined and season.

2. Using your hands, shape the mixture into 12 cakes, place on a baking sheet, cover and chill for at least 1 hour.

3. To coat, dip the cakes into the seasoned flour, then the beaten egg and breadcrumbs. Return to the baking sheet and chill for 30 minutes.

4. Meanwhile, make the chilli mayo. In a bowl, combine all the ingredients. Season, cover and chill. This can be made a day in advance.

5. Heat 2.5cm (1in) of oil in a pan. Fry the cakes in batches for 2 to 3 minutes on each side or until golden. Remove and drain on kitchen paper. Garnish with the sliced chilli and spring onion curls and serve with the Chilli Mayo.

Preparation time: 30 min, plus 1 hr chilling
Cooking time: 15 min   **Cals per serving:** 765   **Serves:** 6

Potted Seafood

1. Lightly oil and baseline six 150ml (5fl oz) ramekins. In a bowl, combine the lemongrass, ginger, chilli, garlic, sugar, pepper, lime juice and fish sauce and season with black pepper, then whisk in the olive oil.

2. Toss the seafood with the dressing and check the seasoning. Spoon the seafood into the ramekins and press down. Drizzle with any remaining dressing, cover, lightly weigh down and chill for at least 1 hour.

3. Run a knife around the insides of the ramekins and turn the seafood out on to a bed of coriander and chervil sprigs. Garnish with lime wedges to serve.

Preparation time: 30 min, plus 1 hr chilling
Cals per serving: 212   **Serves:** 6

olive oil 6 tbsp, plus
extra for greasing
lemongrass stick 1, finely chopped
chopped fresh root ginger 1 tsp
red chilli 1, deseeded and
finely chopped
garlic cloves 2, crushed
caster sugar 2 tsp
lime 1, juice of
fish sauce 1 tbsp
mixed cooked seafood 700g (1½lb)
**fresh coriander, chervil
sprigs and lime wedges** to garnish

Smoked Salmon and Scallop Parcels

queen scallops, with corals attached	6 large or 12 small, about 225g (8oz) total weight
large ripe avocado	1
garlic clove	1, crushed
spring onions	4, finely chopped
green chilli	1, deseeded and finely chopped
grapeseed oil	1 tbsp
lime	1, rind finely grated and juice of
large slices smoked salmon	6, about 300g (11oz) total weight
a squeeze of lime	to taste
salad leaves, such as rocket	to garnish

For the coriander dressing

fresh coriander sprigs	25g (1oz)
small garlic clove	1, crushed
grapeseed oil	4 tbsp
lime juice	1 tbsp
caster sugar	pinch of

1. To make the coriander dressing, place all the dressing ingredients in a food processor or blender and whiz until smooth. Set aside.

2. For the parcels, remove any tough membrane from the scallops and season. Place in a steamer and cook for about 5 minutes or until the flesh is just white. Alternatively, put the scallops on a heatproof plate, cover with another plate and steam over a pan of simmering water for about 3 minutes on each side Drain and set on kitchen paper to cool.

3. Meanwhile, place the avocado, garlic, spring onions, chilli, oil, lime rind and juice in a bowl. Crush the avocado with a fork, then mix together. Season well.

4. Lay the smoked salmon slices on a work surface, place a large scallop or two small ones on each slice and spoon the avocado mixture on top. Roll the salmon around the filling.

5. To serve, place the salmon parcels on serving plates and squeeze a little lime juice over each. Drizzle with the coriander dressing and garnish with salad leaves and a sprinkling of black pepper.

Preparation time: 40 min   **Cooking time:** 6 min
Cals per serving: 235   **Serves:** 6

Warmed Chicken Liver Salad

1. To make the dressing, whisk together the vinegar, mustard, 4 table-spoons of the oil, and seasoning in a small bowl, then put to one side.

2. In a non-stick frying pan, fry the bacon until beginning to brown, stirring. Add the remaining oil and the chicken livers and stir-fry for 2 to 3 minutes until just pink in the centre. Season.

3. In a large bowl, toss the endive, rocket and spring onions with the dressing. Quickly combine the warm livers and bacon and serve at once.

Preparation time: 15 min   **Cooking time:** 8 min
Cals per serving: 506   **Serves:** 4

balsamic vinegar	1–2 tbsp
Dijon mustard	1 tsp
olive oil	5 tbsp
streaky bacon lardons	200g (7oz)
chicken livers	2 x 225g tubs, drained, trimmed and diced
curly endive	½
rocket	100g (3½oz)
bunch spring onions	1, sliced

Butternut Squash with Beetroot and Goat's Cheese

butternut squash	1, peeled, deseeded and cut into wedges
olive oil	4 tbsp
raw beetroot	2, peeled and cut into thin wedges
rocket	50g (2oz)
balsamic vinegar	2 tbsp
firm goat's cheese	150g (5oz), sliced

1. Preheat the oven to 220°C/200°C fan oven/Gas Mark 7. Put the squash in a roasting tin, drizzle with 2 tablespoons of the oil and season with salt and black pepper. Put the beetroot in another tin, toss in 1 tablespoon of the oil and season. Cook the vegetables for 25 to 35 minutes, or until slightly charred, swapping shelves halfway through the cooking.

2. Put the rocket in a bowl, add the remaining oil and balsamic vinegar and toss together well.

3. Grill the goat's cheese on a baking sheet for 1 minute or until the edges just begin to melt.

4. Arrange the vegetables on top of the rocket and top with the melted cheese to serve.

Preparation time: 20 min **Cooking time:** 35 min
Cals per serving: 327 **Serves:** 4

Goat's Cheese Parcels

1. Preheat the oven to 220°C/200°C fan oven/Gas Mark 7. Plunge the spinach into a pan of boiling water, bring back to the boil and boil for 1 minute, then drain and run under very cold water. Once cold, squeeze out all the excess liquid and finely chop. Put to one side.

2. Heat the oil in a pan, add the onion and garlic and cook for 5 minutes, until translucent, then cool. Combine the spinach, onion mixture and goat's cheese in a bowl and season generously.

3. Cut the filo pastry into 23 x 13cm (9 x 5in) squares. Brush one square with melted butter, cover with a second square and brush with more melted butter. Put to one side and cover with a damp cloth to prevent drying out. Repeat with the remaining squares, making 12 sets in all.

4. Put a dessertspoonful of the filling in the centre of each square and join up the corners to form a square parcel. Brush the pastry with more butter, sprinkle with sesame seeds and chill for 20 minutes. Bake for 5 minutes until the pastry is crisp and brown and garnish with rocket

fresh spinach leaves	125g (4oz)
sunflower oil	2 tbsp
onion	1, finely chopped
large garlic clove	1, chopped
soft goat's cheese	250g (9oz)
filo pastry	275g (10oz)
butter	50g (2oz), melted
sesame seeds	for sprinkling
rocket	to garnish

Preparation time: 45 min, plus 20 min cooling and 20 min chilling
Cooking time: 10 min **Cals per serving:** 226 **Serves:** 6

Butternut Squash with
Beetroot and Goat's Cheese

Bloody Mary
Terrine

baby plum or cherry tomatoes	700g (1½lb), halved
garlic cloves	2, chopped
golden caster sugar	2 tbsp
salt	2 tsp
olive oil	2 tbsp, plus extra for greasing
red peppers	1kg (2¼lb), quartered, cored and deseeded
fresh basil leaves	25g (1oz), shredded

For the Bloody Mary mix

large lemon	1, juice of
powdered gelatine	25g (1oz)
tomato juice	300ml (½pt)
vodka	6 tbsp
tomato ketchup	3 tbsp
Worcestershire sauce	2 tbsp
Tabasco sauce	½ tsp

1. Place the tomatoes in a roasting tin. Sprinkle the garlic, caster sugar, salt and black pepper over and drizzle with olive oil. Cook under a hot grill for about 10 minutes, or until the tomatoes have softened and some of the skins look charred. Put to one side to cool.

2. Grill the peppers, skin-side up for 7 to 10 minutes, or until the skins are charred. Turn them over and grill for a further 5 minutes. Place the peppers in a plastic bag and seal for 15 minutes. When they are cool enough to handle, peel off the skins.

3. To make the Bloody Mary mix, put the lemon juice into a measuring jug and add enough cold water to make up to 100ml (3½fl oz). Pour this into a heatproof bowl, sprinkle the gelatine over and leave for 5 minutes. Set the bowl over a pan of simmering water until the liquid runs clear. Put aside to cool.

4. In a large bowl, mix together the tomato juice, vodka, tomato ketchup, Worcestershire sauce, Tabasco and seasoning. Stir the cooled, dissolved gelatine into the Bloody Mary mix, then pour into a jug and put the mixture to one side.

5. Lightly oil a 1.1 litre (2 pint) terrine mould and line with clingfilm. Put one-quarter of the roasted peppers into the terrine and pour in enough Bloody Mary mix to cover. Add a layer of basil, followed by a third of the tomatoes and cover with the Bloody Mary mix. Continue the layering, finishing with peppers on top.

6. Tap the terrine mould bottom on a work surface to distribute the liquid evenly, fold up the clingfilm edges to cover the surface and chill for 4 hours, or until set. To serve, peel back the clingfilm from the top and invert the terrine on to a chopping board, peel off the remaining clingfilm and cut into slices.

Preparation time: 40 min, plus 4 hr chilling
Cooking time: 35 min   **Cals per serving:** 160   **Serves:** 8

Grilled Chicory, Stilton and Caramelised Walnut Salad

white onions	2, quartered and broken into petals
chicory head	1, quartered
red chillies	2, halved and deseeded
radicchio	1, quartered
caster sugar	1 tsp
strong blue vegetarian cheese, such as stilton	125g (4oz), crumbled
fresh flat-leaf parsley	to garnish

For the thyme and lemon dressing

olive oil	100ml (3½fl oz), plus 1 tbsp for frying
fresh thyme sprigs	2
lemon	1, rind finely grated
garlic cloves	2, peeled and bruised
lemon juice	25ml (2 tbsp)

For the caramelised walnuts

walnuts	75g (3oz)
paprika	1 tsp
icing sugar	1 tsp
vegetable oil	3 tbsp

1. To make the dressing, place the olive oil in a small pan with the thyme sprigs, lemon rind and garlic cloves. Warm gently but do not boil. Remove from the heat and leave to infuse for 30 minutes.

2. To make the caramelised walnuts, cook the walnuts in boiling water for 5 minutes, then drain and dry on kitchen paper. Mix together the paprika and icing sugar and fold in the walnuts. Heat the vegetable oil in a frying pan and cook the walnuts for 1 to 2 minutes, or until brown. Drain and leave to cool.

3. Preheat the grill to high. To make the salad, brush all the vegetables with half the infused oil. Place the onions in the base of a grill pan, sprinkle with caster sugar and cook under the preheated grill for 5 to 10 minutes, turning them halfway through cooking. They should be soft and slightly charred at this stage. Add the chicory and chillies and cook for 5 minutes, then add the radicchio and cook for a further 1 minute. Remove the vegetables from the grill and allow to cool slightly. Roughly chop the radicchio and chicory and finely slice the chillies. Season the vegetables and place in a bowl.

4. Whisk the lemon juice into the remaining infused oil and season. Combine all the vegetables and gently toss together with the dressing, blue cheese and the caramelised walnuts. Arrange on individual plates, garnish with parsley and serve at room temperature.

Preparation time: 25 min **Cooking time:** 20 min, plus 30 min infusing **Cals per serving:** 360 **Serves:** 6

Sweet Red Onion and Gorgonzola Salad

olive oil	4 tsp
red onions	3, about 500g (1lb 2oz) total weight, cut into wedges, root intact
soft light brown sugar	2 tsp
balsamic vinegar	2 tbsp
mixed salad leaves	275g (10oz), washed and dried
gorgonzola	200g (7oz), crumbled
For the dressing	
runny honey	2 tsp
Dijon mustard	½ tsp
red wine vinegar	2 tbsp
extra-virgin olive oil	6 tbsp

1. Heat the olive oil in a large frying pan with a lid, add the onion wedges in a single layer, cover with a lid and cook over a low to moderate heat for 15 minutes, or until the onions have softened and are beginning to brown on the underside.

2. Sprinkle the sugar over the onions, cover the pan and cook for a further 10 minutes until the exposed side is beginning to caramelise. Add the balsamic vinegar and cook uncovered until most of the vinegar has evaporated and the onions are sticky.

3. To make the dressing, put the honey, mustard and red wine vinegar in a bowl, season with salt and pepper and whisk together. Whisk in the oil to form an emulsion.

4. Put the salad leaves in a bowl with the caramelised onions and the gorgonzola and toss together. Divide among six plates, then pour the dressing over to moisten.

Preparation time: 20 min, plus 15 min cooling
Cooking time: 30 min   **Cals per serving:** 324   **Serves:** 6

Marinated Herring, Potato and Dill Salad

1. Put the potatoes in cold water, bring to the boil and cook for 15 to 20 minutes, or until tender. Drain, then cut into wedges.

2. Meanwhile, make the dressing. Mix the soured cream, mayonnaise and dill together in a large bowl, then season well.

3. To assemble the salad, put the potatoes, gherkins and herrings in a bowl with the dressing and toss together. Check the seasoning and serve.

Preparation time: 15 min   **Cooking time:** 15–20 min
Cals per serving: 646   **Serves:** 4

new potatoes	1kg (2¼lb)
soured cream	2 tbsp
mayonnaise	6 tbsp
chopped fresh dill	2 tbsp
pickled gherkins	8, thinly sliced
sweet cured herrings	2 × 280g tubs, drained and sliced into 2cm (¾in) strips

Sweet Red Onion and
Gorgonzola Salad

Mixed Bean Salad with Lemon Vinaigrette

mixed beans	400g can, drained
chickpeas	420g can, drained
shallots	2, chopped
For the vinaigrette	
lemon juice	2 tbsp
runny honey	2 tsp
extra-virgin olive oil	100ml (3½fl oz)
chopped fresh mint	3 tbsp
roughly chopped fresh flat-leaf parsley	4 tbsp
fresh mint sprigs and finely grated lemon rind	to garnish

1. Put the beans, chickpeas and the shallots into a bowl. To make the vinaigrette, whisk together the lemon juice, seasoning and honey. Gradually whisk in the oil and stir in the chopped mint and parsley.

2. Toss the bean mixture in the dressing, then garnish with the mint sprigs and lemon rind and serve.

Preparation time: 15 min   **Cals per serving:** 289   **Serves:** 6

Asparagus and Quail's Egg Salad

1. Cook the quail's eggs in boiling water for 2 minutes, drain and plunge into cold water. Cook the asparagus in boiling salted water for 2 minutes, or until just tender. Drain, plunge into cold water and set aside to cool.

2. Whisk together the lemon juice and oil and season. Stir in the spring onions and set aside.

3. Peel the eggs and cut in half. Put in a large bowl with the asparagus, watercress, dill and tarragon. Pour over the dressing and lightly toss all the ingredients together. Season and serve.

Preparation time: 20 min, plus 15 min cooling
Cooking time: 4 min   **Cals per serving:** 300   **Serves:** 8

quail's eggs	4
asparagus spears	24
lemon	½, juice of
olive oil	6 tbsp
large spring onions	4, finely sliced
watercress	100g bag, chopped
fresh dill sprigs	
fresh tarragon sprigs	

Asparagus with Aïoli Sauce

garlic cloves	4, crushed
sea salt	1 tsp, plus extra for the asparagus
large egg	1
sunflower oil	300ml (10fl oz)
lemon juice	2 tbsp
boiling water	3–4 tbsp
asparagus spears	700g (1½lb)

1. Put the garlic, salt and egg into a food processor or blender and whiz for at least 30 seconds until everything is well combined. With the motor running, pour in the oil very slowly until the mixture has thickened and all the oil has been added. Spoon into a bowl, add the lemon juice and boiling water to lighten the sauce. Cover and chill.

2. Trim the woody ends of the asparagus and cook in a large pan of boiling salted water for 5 to 7 minutes or until just tender. Drain very carefully and arrange on a serving dish with the Aïoli Sauce spooned over. Serve at room temperature.

Preparation time: 20 min   **Cooking time:** 7 min
Cals per serving: 377   **Serves:** 6

Mini Yorkshires with Steak and Horseradish

1. Preheat the oven to 200°C/180°C fan oven/Gas Mark 6. Heat the oil in a frying pan and sear the steak over a medium to high heat to brown on both sides. For rare, slice into 24 pieces now; for medium rare, reduce the heat and cook for a further 3 minutes (5 minutes for well done) before slicing – these timings are a rough guide and it depends on the thickness of the steak.

2. Meanwhile, put the Yorkshires in a roasting tin and heat for 10 minutes.

3. Mix together the crème fraîche and horseradish sauce. Arrange the steak on the puddings, top with the horseradish cream. Season with black pepper and garnish each pudding with a watercress sprig.

Preparation time: 20 min   **Cooking time:** 10 min
Cals per serving: 60   **Makes:** 24

sunflower oil	1 tbsp
rump steak	300g (11oz)
mini Yorkshire puddings	2 × 120g packs
crème fraîche	6 tbsp
horseradish sauce	1 tbsp
watercress sprigs	to garnish

Lightly Curried
Mussel Soup

olive oil	4 tbsp
shallots	2, finely chopped
curry powder	½ tsp
mussels	725g (1lb 9oz), cleaned and scrubbed
dry white wine	200ml (7fl oz)
crème fraîche	100g (3½oz)
chopped fresh flat-leaf parsley	2 tbsp, optional

1. Heat the oil in a large pan, add the shallots and curry powder and cook for 5 minutes or until the shallots are softened.

2. Add the mussels, white wine and 100ml (3½fl oz) water, cover and bring slowly to the boil. Boil for a few seconds until the mussels open. Discard any that do not open. Remove from the heat and stir in the crème fraîche. Sprinkle with parsley, if using, then season with salt and black pepper to taste.

Preparation time: 25 min   **Cooking time:** 8 min
Cals per serving: 289 for 4, 578 for 2
Serves: 4 as a starter, 2 as a main course

Moroccan
Lamb Soup

1. In a large pan, heat 3 tablespoons of the olive oil and gently fry the onion for 3 minutes. Add the celery and garlic and cook for 2 minutes, then turn up the heat and add the red pepper. Fry for 2 to 3 minutes, stirring, then add the harissa paste and stir well.

2. Add the lentils and stir to coat. Pour in the passata and the stock, stir and simmer for about 10 minutes.

3. Fry the sausages in the remaining oil for a few minutes until browned. Remove from the pan, reserving a little oil, then cool. Cut on the diagonal into 2.5cm (1in) chunks and add to the soup.

4. Trim the lamb. Fry the steaks for 2 minutes on each side, then cut into 1cm (½in) slices. Serve the soup topped with the sausage chunks and lamb slices and garnish with the mint sprigs.

Preparation time: 15 min   **Cooking time:** 30 min
Cals per serving: 1022   **Serves:** 4

olive oil	4 tbsp
onions	125g (4oz), chopped
celery	125g (4oz), diced
garlic clove	1, crushed
red pepper	1, diced
harissa paste	1 tbsp
cooked green lentils	2 × 300g cans, drained and rinsed
passata	500g carton
lamb stock	600ml (1pt)
small spicy sausages, such as merguez	8
lamb steaks	4, about 125g (4oz) each
fresh mint sprigs	to garnish

Lightly Curried
Mussel Soup

Light lunch: Spicy Crab Cakes with Chilli Mayo, Roasted Oriental Salmon and Iced Pistachio and Orange Parfait

Lunch Party: Lunch shouldn't be **too heavy** a meal. Try to put together a menu of **simply cooked and light dishes**, full of **fresh fragrant flavours** for the maximum impact. This **sophisticated** menu of **lightly spiced Crab Cakes**, served with a **chilli and coriander mayo**, followed by the **Roasted Oriental Salmon**, with a wonderful **balance of flavours**, and served chilled with **wedges of lime**, is simple, but **impressive**. Nothing could be easier as the salmon is prepared well ahead of guests arriving. A light **dessert** is usually more **welcome** than a **rich, heavy pudding** and the **Iced Pistachio and Orange Parfait** makes a **refreshing finish** to a **dazzling** midday **meal**.

Twice-baked
Roquefort Soufflés

butter 50g (2oz), plus extra for greasing
plain flour 50g (2oz)
milk around 300ml (10fl oz)
roquefort 125g (4oz), crumbled
large eggs 4, separated
double cream or crème fraîche 200ml (7fl oz)
selection of salad leaves to garnish

1. Preheat the oven to 180°C/160°C fan oven/Gas Mark 4. Baseline and lightly butter six to eight 150ml (5fl oz) ramekin dishes (the volume of the mixture is sometimes enough for eight). Melt the butter in a medium-sized pan, stir in the flour and mix to a smooth paste. Add the milk gradually and bring just to the boil, stirring continuously. Cool a little, then beat in the cheese and egg yolks. Season well. Whip the egg whites to soft peaks and fold this into the cheese mixture.

2. Fill each ramekin three-quarters full with the mixture. Place the ramekins in a roasting tin and add enough hot water to come halfway up the sides of the ramekins. Cook for 20 minutes or until firm to the touch. Remove the ramekins from the roasting tin and allow the soufflés to cool for at least 2 hours.

3. Lightly butter a baking sheet. Run a round-bladed knife around the edge of the soufflés and carefully turn out on to the baking sheet. At this stage you can chill the soufflés for up to 24 hours or freeze the soufflés until ready to use.

4. Add 1 teaspoon of coarse ground pepper to the cream, then spoon 2 to 3 tablespoons on top of each soufflé. Bake at 200°C/180°C fan oven/Gas Mark 6 for 20 to 25 minutes or until golden (you can cook straight from frozen, but allow a further 10 minutes cooking time). Serve immediately, garnished with salad leaves.

Preparation time: 15 min, plus 10 min cooling
Cooking time: 40 min, plus minimum 2 hr cooling
Cals per serving: 410 for 6, 313 for 8 **Serves:** 6–8

Cod with Oriental Vegetables

thick cod fillets	4, about 175g (6oz) each
lime	1, rind grated
chilli oil	1 tbsp
sesame oil	1 tbsp
red chilli	1, deseeded and chopped
garlic cloves	2, chopped
spring onions	8, trimmed and sliced
shiitake mushrooms	125g (4oz), sliced
carrots	225g (8oz), cut into matchsticks
pak choi	300g (11oz), chopped
soy sauce	2 tbsp

1. Put the cod fillets in a shallow, non-metallic dish. Mix the lime rind with the chilli oil and rub this over the fillets. Season well, cover and leave in a cool place for 30 minutes.

2. Heat the sesame oil in a large frying pan, add the chilli, garlic, spring onions, mushrooms and carrots and stir-fry for 2 to 3 minutes, over a high heat, until the vegetables begin to soften. Add the pak choi and stir-fry for 1 to 2 minutes more. Add the soy sauce and cook for a further minute. Season and set aside. Preheat the grill.

3. Grill the cod fillets under a moderately hot grill for 2 to 3 minutes on each side or until the flesh has turned opaque and is firm to the touch.

4. Place the cod on a serving dish, pile the stir-fried vegetables on top of the cod and serve.

Preparation time: 20 min, plus 30 min marinating
Cooking time: about 6 min   **Cals per serving:** 235   **Serves:** 4

Roasted Mediterranean Fish

1. Cook the potatoes in a large pan of boiling, salted water for 20 minutes until tender. Drain and set aside. When cool, cut them in half.

2. Preheat the oven to 200°C/180°C fan oven/Gas Mark 6. Put the tomato sauce into a frying pan with the mushrooms and 4 tablespoons of water. Bring the mixture to the boil and allow to bubble for 1 to 2 minutes.

3. Transfer the mixture to an ovenproof dish, add the olives and potatoes, then arrange the fish on top. Season with pepper and sprinkle with parmesan. Cook for 10 to 15 minutes, or until the fish is cooked. Sprinkle with basil, then garnish with basil sprigs before serving.

Preparation time: 10 min   **Cooking time:** 37 min
Cals per serving: 300   **Serves:** 4

small new potatoes	350g (12oz), scrubbed
ready made tomato pasta sauce	350g jar
button mushrooms	150g (5oz), sliced
pitted black olives	50g (2oz)
cod fillets	450g (1lb), cut into chunks
freshly grated parmesan	3 tbsp
chopped fresh basil	2 tbsp, plus sprigs to garnish

Roasted
Oriental Salmon

whole salmon	2.5kg (5½lb), cleaned and descaled
lime wedges	to serve

For the marinade

dark soy sauce	175ml (6fl oz)
rice wine vinegar or dry sherry	175ml (6fl oz)
garlic cloves	6, cut into wafer thin slices
fresh root ginger	7.5cm (3in) piece
runny honey	3 tbsp
whole star anise	4, lightly crushed

1. Make three to four diagonal slashes on either side of the cleaned fish and place it in a non-metallic dish.

2. To make the marinade, combine all the ingredients in a food processor or blender. Coat the salmon well with the marinade, then cover and chill for at least 8 hours, or overnight, turning it occasionally.

3. Preheat the oven to 200°C/180°C fan oven/Gas Mark 6. Place the salmon on a large piece of foil in a roasting tin, spoon a little of the marinade over the top and loosely wrap the foil around the fish. Cook for 35 to 40 minutes or until the salmon is just cooked through.

4. Open the foil and place the fish under a hot grill for 6 to 8 minutes or until golden. Cool and chill the salmon until required.

5. Arrange the banana leaves on a serving plate and place the salmon on top. Garnish with lime wedges, then serve.

Note: The cooking time will depend on the thickness of the fish rather than its weight – a fatter-fleshed fish will take more time than a lean one, even if they weigh the same.

Preparation time: 20 min, plus at least 8 hr marinating
Cooking time: 40 min, plus as least 2 hr cooling
Cals per serving: 390   **Serves:** 8

Roasted
Oriental Salmon

Fish Tagine with Couscous

firm fish fillets such as 1.1kg (2½lb), skinned
monkfish or cod and cut into chunks
olive oil 120ml (4fl oz), plus
extra for drizzling
onions 900g (2lb), chopped
aubergines 450g (1lb), cubed
chopped plum tomatoes 400g can, chopped
passata 500g carton
fish stock 200ml (7fl oz)
pitted green olives 125g (4oz)
fresh coriander 2 tbsp, chopped
fresh flat-leaf parsley 2 tbsp, chopped
fresh coriander leaves 2 tbsp, chopped,
plus extra to garnish

For the chilli paste
large red chillies 3
large garlic cloves 2
ground coriander 1 tbsp
cumin seeds 2 tbsp
saffron threads large pinch
lemon 1, rind grated
and juice of
olive oil 2 tbsp

For the couscous
couscous 350g (12oz)
chopped fresh mint 4 tbsp

1. To make the chilli paste, preheat the oven to 200°C/180°C fan oven/ Gas Mark 6. Place the chillies on a baking sheet and roast for 10 minutes. Cool, peel and deseed the chillies. Leave the oven on. Place the chillies in a food processor with the remaining ingredients and pulse to a fine paste.

2. To make the tagine, place the fish in a bowl with 2 tablespoons of the chilli paste. Toss the fish well in the paste, then cover the bowl and chill. Leave the fish to marinate while you make the tagine sauce.

3. Heat 3 tablespoons of the olive oil in a heatproof casserole or tagine (the word 'tagine' refers to the North African clay dish in which the stew is cooked) and cook the onions for 10 minutes until deep golden brown Add the remaining chilli paste and cook for 5 minutes more.

4. Heat the remaining olive oil in a separate frying pan until hot. Add the aubergines, then mix in the tomatoes, passata and fish stock. Bring to the boil, then simmer gently for 30 minutes.

5. Add the marinated fish to the casserole with the olives, spoon some of the sauce over the fish. Season, cover and cook in the oven for a further 15 to 20 minutes. The fish should be white rather than opaque when cooked. Season to taste.

6. Place the couscous in a bowl. Pour 450ml (15fl oz) boiling water over, then cover and leave to soak according to packet instructions. Season, fork in the mint and drizzle with olive oil. Stir the coriander and parsley into the tagine, garnish with the extra coriander leaves and serve immediately with the warm couscous.

Preparation time: 30 min   **Cooking time:** 1 hr 30 min
Cals per serving: 569 for 6, 420 for 8   **Serves:** 6–8

Salmon in a Brioche Crust

sliced smoked salmon 450g (1lb), chilled
large egg white 1
double cream 3 tbsp
lemon 1, rind finely grated
lemon juice 1 tbsp
fresh chives 1 tbsp, finely chopped
skinless salmon fillet 800g (1lb 12oz), cut from the middle
spinach 225g (8oz), trimmed, blanched and dried
egg yolk 1, beaten
pink peppercorns 1 tsp

For the brioche dough
strong white bread flour 375g (13oz), sifted plus extra to dust
easy-blend yeast 2 tsp
caster sugar 1 tsp
salt ½ tsp
large eggs 2, beaten
unsalted butter 100g (3½oz), melted and cooled
oil for greasing

To garnish
lemon wedges
fresh chives
crushed pink peppercorns

1. To make the brioche dough, place the flour in a large bowl. Add the yeast, sugar and salt and mix. Make a well in the centre and mix in the eggs, butter and 100ml (3½fl oz) cold water to make a pliable dough.

2. Turn the dough out on to a lightly floured work surface and knead for about 5 minutes until smooth and elastic. (A soft dough will give a light texture; try not to add any extra flour when kneading.) Place the dough in a large greased bowl and cover with greased clingfilm. Allow to rise at room temperature for 1½ hours or until doubled in volume.

3. Meanwhile, make the filling: put 125g (4oz) of the salmon in a food processor and whiz for 10 seconds until smooth. Using the pulse button, add the egg white slowly. Transfer to a small bowl and beat in the cream gradually, then add the lemon rind, juice and chives. Season with pepper (don't add salt as smoked salmon is salty). Cover and chill for 10 minutes.

4. Halve the salmon fillet horizontally. Spread the bottom half with smoked salmon mixture and place the other half fillet on top. Place a sheet of clingfilm, three times the width of the fillet, on a clean surface. Cover two-thirds of the clingfilm with the remaining smoked salmon, season with pepper, then cover with spinach leaves. Place the stuffed fillet at the other end of the clingfilm; season. Using the clingfilm, completely wrap the fillet in the spinach and smoked salmon. Chill for 5 to 10 minutes.

5. Preheat the oven to 200°C/180°C fan oven/Gas Mark 6. Place a large baking sheet in the oven to heat. On a lightly floured work surface, roll the brioche dough to a rectangle measuring about 33cm (13in) by 40cm (16in) or large enough to wrap around the salmon easily. Place the salmon in the centre and lightly brush the edges of the dough with a little of the egg yolk, mixed with 1 tablespoon of water. Fold the brioche around the fish, sealing the edges, then trim off any excess pastry. Invert the salmon to a floured baking sheet, seam-side down.

6. Brush the surface with a little more egg wash and decorate with the brioche trimmings. Brush again with the egg wash and score the surface lightly with the back of a knife. Dot with peppercorns and leave to prove in a warm place for 20 minutes or until it feels spongy. Place the baking sheet on to the hot baking sheet in the oven and cook for 50 to 55 minutes until deep golden brown. Serve hot garnished with lemon, chives and peppercorns. If serving cold, carefully transfer to a cooling rack.

Preparation time: 45 min, plus 1 hr 30 min rising, 20 min chilling and 20 min proving **Cooking time:** 55 min
Cals per serving: 580 **Serves:** 8

Beefsteak in Mustard Sauce

oil-water spray
sirloin steaks or fillet steaks 4, about 175g (6oz) each, trimmed of all fat
large garlic cloves 2, crushed
red wine 150ml (5fl oz)
beef stock 150ml (5fl oz)
Dijon mustard 1 tbsp
green salad and roast potatoes to serve

1. Spray a non-stick pan with the oil-water spray and place over a medium heat. Season the steaks with salt and pepper.

2. Sear the steaks over a medium to high heat for 2 to 3 minutes on both sides for rare. For medium rare, reduce the heat and cook for a further 3 minutes (5 minutes for well done), then set aside.

3. Put the garlic in the pan and sizzle for 1 minute. Add the wine and stock, stirring and scraping up the brown bits on the bottom of the pan with a wooden spoon. Bring to the boil and simmer for about 2 minutes or until reduced by about half, then stir in the mustard and simmer briskly for a further 1 minute. Pour in any juices that have accumulated under the steaks.

4. Quickly cut the steaks into slices on the diagonal and stir back into the simmering mustard sauce. Serve with a salad and roast potatoes.

Preparation time: 5 min   **Cooking time:** 10 min
Cals per serving: 337   **Serves:** 4

Beefsteak in
Mustard Sauce

Medallions of Beef with
Guinness and Black Olives

light sunflower oil 2 tsp, plus extra
for brushing
shallots 2, chopped
celery stick 1, chopped
carrot 1, chopped
leek 1, chopped
garlic clove 1, crushed
Guinness 440ml can
bay leaf 1
fresh parsley sprig 1
fresh oregano sprig 1, plus extra to garnish
beef stock cube 1
tail and fillet of beef 550g (1lb 4oz),
sirloin or strip loin
butter 25g (1oz)
plain flour 40g (1½oz)
soft light brown sugar 2 tbsp
**black olives (either with
stone, or pitted)** 125g (4oz)
**Colcannon mashed
potatoes and
fresh vegetables** to serve

1. Heat the oil in a pan over a gentle heat, add the vegetables and garlic, and cook until the vegetables are just starting to turn golden. Pour the Guinness over, then add the bay leaf, parsley, oregano and stock cube. Simmer until the liquid has reduced by half.

2. Meanwhile, slice the beef into small rounds, slanting your knife against the meat. Brush each piece on both sides with a little oil. Put on a plate and set aside, or cover and return to the fridge until ready to use.

3. Melt the butter in a separate pan, add the flour and stir over a low heat until the mixture turns light brown. When the stock liquid has reduced, remove the bay leaf and pour into the butter and flour, stirring all the time until all the liquid is combined. Remove from the heat and, using a hand blender, purée the gravy until smooth. Return to the heat, add the sugar, then season with salt and pepper. If the gravy is too thick, thin it down with a little water. Add the olives and return to simmering point.

4. Heat a heavy-based frying pan until nearly smoking. Add the medallions of beef and cook for 1 minute on each side (or longer, according to how you like your meat cooked). Place on warmed plates and pour the Guinness and black olive gravy over. Garnish with oregano and serve with Colcannon (mashed potatoes with sautéed spring onions) or with plain mashed potatoes and fresh vegetables of your choice.

Preparation time: 15 min   **Cooking time:** 55 min
Cals per serving: 417   **Serves:** 4

Fillet of Beef with Roquefort Butter Sauce

roquefort	125g (4oz), crumbled
unsalted butter	125g (4oz), softened
beef fillet	900g (2lb)
vegetable oil	about 100ml (3½fl oz)
garlic cloves	2, crushed
large aubergines	2, about 400g (14oz) each, cut lengthways into 1cm (½in) slices
onions	150g (5oz), finely chopped
medium-dry sherry	150ml (5fl oz)
fresh meat stock	750ml (1¼pt)
lemon juice	to taste
fresh rosemary sprigs	to garnish

To serve
baby spinach
beetroot shavings
Soft Polenta (see side dishes, page 241)

1. Preheat the oven to 220°C/200°C fan oven/Gas Mark 7. Gently stir the cheese into the butter (don't overbeat or it will turn grey). Cover and chill.

2. Season the beef. Heat 1 tablespoon of the oil in a frying pan for 1 to 2 minutes, then brown the beef for 1 to 2 minutes on each side. Set aside to cool.

3. Spread the garlic over the beef. Brush each side of the aubergine slices with oil and fry in a non-stick frying pan for 4 to 5 minutes on each side or until golden; cool. Wrap the aubergine slices around the beef and tie at intervals with string; season and set aside.

4. Heat 2 tablespoons of the oil in the frying pan, add the onion and cook for 10 minutes or until golden, add the sherry, bring to the boil and bubble to reduce by half. Add the stock, bring to the boil again and cook for 10 to 15 minutes or until reduced by half. Set the sauce aside.

5. Roast the beef for 30 minutes for rare, 35 for medium-rare and 40 minutes for well done. Cover the meat loosely with foil and set aside in a warm place to rest for 10 minutes.

6. Reheat the sauce, whisking in the roquefort butter a little at a time. Add the lemon juice.

7. Thinly slice the beef and stir any pan juices into the sauce. Garnish with rosemary sprigs and serve with the sauce on the side, spinach, beetroot and Soft Polenta.

Preparation time: 30 min   **Cooking time:** 1 hr 10 min
Cals per serving: 585   **Serves:** 6

Fillet of Beef en Croûte

beef fillet	1–1.4kg (2¼–3lb), trimmed
butter	50g (2oz)
shallots	2, chopped
dried porcini	15g (½oz), soaked in 100ml (3½fl oz) boiling water
garlic cloves	2, chopped
flat mushrooms	225g (8oz), finely chopped
chopped fresh thyme	2 tsp
chicken liver pâté	170g pack
Parma ham slices	2 x 80g packs
flour	to dust
ready-rolled puff pastry	375g (13oz)
medium egg	1, beaten

For the rich red wine sauce

olive oil	2 tbsp
shallots	350g (12oz), finely chopped
garlic cloves	3, chopped
tomato purée	3 tbsp
balsamic vinegar	2 tbsp
red wine	200ml (7fl oz)
beef stock	600ml (1pt)

1. Put the beef on a board and season all over with salt and pepper. Melt half the butter in a large frying pan over a medium heat. When foaming, put the fillet in the pan and brown all over for 4 to 5 minutes, taking care not to burn the butter. Put the beef on a plate and leave to cool.

2. Melt the remaining butter in a separate pan, add the shallots and cook for 1 minute. Drain the porcini, reserving the liquor. Chop the porcini, then add to the pan with the garlic, the reserved liquor and the flat mushrooms. Increase the heat and cook until the mushrooms are dry in the pan, then season and add the thyme. Cool.

3. Put the pâté in a bowl and beat until smooth, add the mushroom mixture and stir well until thoroughly combined. Season to taste. Transfer the cold fillet to a board and use a palette knife to spread half the mushroom mixture evenly over one side of the beef.

4. Lay half the Parma ham on clingfilm, with the slices overlapping. Invert the mushroom-topped beef on to the ham. Spread the remaining mushroom mixture over the beef, then wrap the rest of the Parma ham, also overlapping, on top of the mushroom mixture. Wrap in clingfilm and chill. Preheat the oven to 220°C/200°C fan oven/Gas Mark 7.

5. On a lightly floured surface, cut one-third of the pastry off. Roll this out to 3mm (⅛in) thick and 2.5cm (1in) bigger than the beef. Prick well. Transfer to a baking sheet and bake for 12 to 15 minutes or until brown and crisp. Cool; trim to the size of the beef. Unwrap the beef, brush with the egg and place on the cooked pastry.

6. Roll out the remaining pastry to a rectangle, measuring 25 x 30cm (10 x 12in). Roll over with a lattice pastry cutter and gently ease the lattice open. Cover the beef with the lattice. Tuck the ends under and seal the edges. Brush with more beaten egg. Cook on a baking sheet for 40 minutes for rare to medium rare, 45 minutes for medium. Leave to stand for 10 minutes before carving.

7. Meanwhile, make the red wine sauce. Heat the olive oil in a pan, add the shallots and cook until soft. Add the garlic and tomato purée, cook for 1 minute, then add the balsamic vinegar.

8. Bubble until reduced to almost nothing, then add the red wine and reduce by half. Pour in the beef stock and bubble until reduced by one-third. Serve with the beef.

Preparation time: 1 hr, plus soaking, cooling and 10 min standing
Cooking time: 1 hr–1 hr 10 min
Cals per serving: 747 for 6, 560 for 8   **Serves:** 6–8

Lamb, Prune and Almond Tagine

coriander seeds 2 tsp
cumin seeds 2 tsp
chilli powder 2 tsp
paprika 1 tbsp
ground turmeric 1 tbsp
garlic cloves 5, chopped
olive oil 6 tbsp
lamb leg steaks 1.4kg (3lb)
ghee or clarified butter 75g (3oz)
large onions 2, finely chopped
carrot 1, roughly chopped
lamb stock 900ml (1½pt)
ready-to-eat prunes 300g (11oz)
cinnamon sticks 4
bay leaves 4
ground almonds 50g (2oz)
shallots 12
honey 1 tbsp
toasted almonds and
fresh flat-leaf parsley chopped, to garnish

1. Blend the coriander, cumin, chilli powder, paprika, turmeric, garlic and 4 tablespoons of the oil in a pestle and mortar or a blender. Coat the steaks in the paste, cover and chill for at least 5 hours, or overnight.

2. Preheat the oven to 170°C/150°C fan oven/Gas Mark 3. In a large flameproof casserole, melt 25g (1oz) of the ghee, add the onions and carrot and cook until softened, then remove and put to one side. Fry the lamb on each side in the remaining ghee.

3. Add a little of the stock to the casserole and bring to the boil, scraping up the sediment from the bottom. Return the onion and carrot to the casserole and add 100g (3½oz) of the prunes.

4. Add the remaining stock to the pan with the cinnamon sticks, bay leaves and ground almonds; season. Cover and cook in the oven for 2 hours, or until the meat is really tender.

5. Meanwhile, fry the shallots in the rest of the olive oil and the honey until they turn a deep golden brown. Add the shallots to the casserole 30 to 40 minutes before the end of cooking time.

6. Take the lamb out of the sauce and put to one side. Bring the sauce to the boil, bubble and reduce to a thick consistency. Return the lamb to the casserole, add the remaining prunes, then bubble for 3 to 4 minutes. Garnish with almonds and parsley to serve.

Clarified Butter: Melt some butter in a small pan and heat gently without allowing it to colour. Skim off the foam as it rises to the top, leaving the milk solids to sink to the bottom. Pour the clear butter into a bowl through a sieve lined with kitchen paper. Allow to settle for 10 minutes, then pour into another bowl, leaving any sediment behind. Cool, then store in a jar in the fridge for up to six months.

Preparation time: 20 min, plus at least 5 hr marinating
Cooking time: 2 hr 30 min **Cals per serving:** 630 **Serves:** 6

Roast Lamb with Harissa

For the harissa

large red peppers	2, about 400g (14oz) total weight
large red chillies	4, deseeded and roughly chopped
garlic cloves	6
ground coriander	1 tbsp
caraway seeds	1 tbsp
salt	2 tsp
olive oil	4 tbsp

For the lamb

boned leg of lamb, plus bones	1.8kg (4lb)
oil	2 tbsp
bunch fresh rosemary	1
bunch fresh thyme	1
shallots	350g (12oz), peeled, root left intact, blanched
garlic bulb	1, broken up into cloves, skin left on
dry white wine	300ml (10fl oz)
fresh lamb or chicken stock	600ml (1pt)
roasted chillies, garlic and fresh thyme sprigs	to garnish

1. To make the harissa, grill the peppers until the skins are completely blackened and the flesh is soft, then cover and leave to cool. When cool enough to handle, peel, core and deseed the peppers.

2. Place the chillies in the food processor with the garlic, coriander and caraway seeds and whiz to form a rough paste. Add the peppers, salt and olive oil and whiz again for 1 to 2 minutes, or until smooth. (Spoon any remaining harissa into a screw-top jar, cover with a thin layer of olive oil and store in a cool place for up to two weeks.)

3. Preheat the oven to 200°C/180°C fan oven/Gas Mark 6. To prepare the lamb, spread the bone cavity with about 3 tablespoons of the harissa. Roll up and secure with cocktail sticks or sew up using a large needle and thread.

4. Heat the oil in a roasting pan over a moderate heat and brown the lamb on all sides. This should take about 5 minutes. Season, then place the rosemary and thyme under the lamb and add the bones to the roasting tin. Roast for 1 hour for pink lamb or 1½ hours for well done. Baste the lamb from time to time and add the shallots and garlic to the roasting pan 45 minutes before the end of the cooking time.

5. Transfer the lamb to a carving dish with the shallots and garlic. Cover loosely with foil and leave to rest for about 10 minutes in a low oven.

6. Skim any fat off the sediment in the roasting pan. Add the wine to the pan, bring to the boil and bubble until reduced by half. Add the stock, return to the boil and bubble until reduced by half again. Adjust the seasoning and strain. Remove the cocktail sticks or thread from the lamb and garnish with roasted chillies and garlic and the thyme. Serve with the shallots, garlic and gravy.

Preparation time: 40 min   **Cooking time:** 1 hr 40 min
Cals per serving: 786   **Serves:** 4

Easy Rack of Lamb

onion	1, sliced
vegetable stock	300ml (½ pt)
butter	for greasing
potatoes	1kg (2¼lb), thinly sliced
garlic cloves	2, sliced
French trimmed	8 bone, about 315g
racks of lamb	(11oz) each
grainy French mustard	3 tbsp
fresh breadcrumbs	75g (3oz)
chopped fresh rosemary	2 tsp
fresh flat-leaf parsley	4 tbsp, chopped
olive oil	6 tbsp
long sprig fresh rosemary	1

1. Preheat the oven to 200°C/180°C fan oven/Gas Mark 6. Put the onion in a pan of cold water, bring to the boil and simmer for 2 minutes and drain. Bring the stock to the boil.

2. Butter a 1.3 litre (2¼ pint) roasting tin. Layer the potatoes, onion and garlic in the tin, starting and ending with potatoes. Season and add the stock. Cook for 1 hour, or until the potatoes are softened and browned. Baste every 20 minutes.

3. Season the lamb with salt and pepper and spread the mustard evenly over the meaty side of the lamb.

4. Put the breadcrumbs in a bowl. Add the rosemary, parsley and oil, season with salt and pepper and mix well. Press the mixture over the mustard layer. Put the lamb on a wire rack, resting on the rosemary sprig.

5. Turn the oven up to 220°C/200°C fan oven/Gas Mark 7. Sit the rack on top of the potato dish and return to the oven for 40 minutes for rare, 50 minutes for medium rare. Cover with foil and leave to rest in a warm place for 10 minutes before carving and serving with the potatoes.

Preparation time: 25 min, plus 10 min resting
Cooking time: 1 hr 40 min–1 hr 50 min
Cals per serving: 590 **Serves:** 4

Lamb Cutlets with Cannellini Beans

1. Heat the oil in a pan and fry the onion, garlic and red pepper for 5 minutes until soft. Add the spinach and stir until it wilts.

2. Add the stock, cannellini beans and the sun-dried tomato paste to the pan and season to taste.

3. Bring to the boil, simmer for 5 minutes, then add the peas and cook for a further 5 minutes.

4. Meanwhile, place the cutlets under a hot grill and cook for 3 to 4 minutes on each side or until cooked to your taste.

5. Spoon the cannellini mixture on to a plate and place the lamb cutlets on top. Serve with French beans.

Preparation time: 5 min **Cooking time:** 15 min
Cals per serving: 549 **Serves:** 2

olive oil	1 tbsp
small onion	1, chopped
garlic clove	1, crushed
red pepper	1, deseeded and roughly chopped
spinach leaves	75g (3oz), stalks removed
vegetable stock	250ml (9fl oz)
cannellini beans	400g can, drained
sun-dried tomato paste	4 tbsp
frozen peas	50g (2oz)
lamb cutlets	6, trimmed
French beans	to serve

Pork with Artichokes,
Beans and Olives

vegetable oil	2 tbsp
whole pork fillets	2, about 275g (10oz) each, cut into 1cm (½in) slices
chopped fresh thyme	2 tbsp
olive oil	100ml (3½fl oz)
artichoke hearts	400g can, drained, rinsed and quartered
flageolet beans	400g can, drained and rinsed
pitted green olives	185g jar, drained and rinsed
lemon	1, juice of

1. Heat the vegetable oil in a frying pan and fry the pork for 2 minutes on each side. Add the thyme and season with salt and pepper.

2. Meanwhile, heat the olive oil in a pan, add the artichokes and beans and cook for 3 to 4 minutes. Add the olives and lemon juice and season with black pepper.

3. Place the pork on top of the artichokes, beans and olives and serve.

Preparation time: 20 min   **Cooking time:** 10 min
Cals per serving: 623   **Serves:** 4

Pork Wrapped in Pastry
with Apricots

olive oil	3 tbsp
onions	225g (8oz), chopped
white wine vinegar	1 tbsp
white wine	150ml (5fl oz)
ready-to-eat dried apricots	250g (9oz), finely chopped
chopped fresh sage	1 tbsp
whole pork fillets	2, about 700g (1½lb) total weight
plain flour	to dust
ready-made puff pastry	350g (12oz)
medium egg	1, lightly beaten
chicken stock	300ml (10fl oz)

1. Heat 2 tablespoons of the oil in a pan, add the onions and cook, stirring, for 10 minutes or until softened. Stir in the vinegar and bubble until evaporated, then add the wine, apricots and 150ml (5fl oz) water. Bring to the boil and simmer for 20 minutes or until all the liquid has evaporated. Season well, add the sage and set aside to cool. Reserve about half the apricot mixture for the sauce. Wipe out the pan.

2. Cut each pork fillet into three pieces and season with pepper. Heat the remaining oil in the pan, brown the pork fillets for a few minutes on all sides, then set aside to cool.

3. On a lightly floured work surface, roll the pastry out to about 3mm (⅛in) thick. Cut into three rectangles about 23cm (9in) long and as wide as the length of each piece of pork. Spread some apricot mixture at one end of each piece, place the pork on top and roll up the pastry lengthways, spooning more apricot mixture on the pork as you roll. Use water to stick the edges together. Keep each side open so that they look like sausage rolls. (They will keep in the fridge for 24 hours.)

4. Brush the pastry with the egg mixed with a generous pinch of salt and use a knife to score the top. Chill the pork parcels on a baking sheet for 30 minutes.

5. Heat a baking sheet at 220°C/200°C fan oven/Gas Mark 7. Transfer the pork parcels on to the preheated baking sheet and cook for 30 minutes. Leave to rest for 10 minutes.

6. Put the reserved apricot mixture in a pan, add the stock, bring to the boil and bubble for 5 to 10 minutes. Serve with the pork.

Preparation time: 30 min, plus 30 min cooling, 30 min chilling and 10 min standing **Cooking time:** 1 hr 10 min
Cals per serving: 734 **Serves:** 6

Moroccan magic:
Hummus and Pitta
Bread, Lamb, Prune
and Almond Tagine
and Vegetable and
Chickpea Couscous

Celebratory Supper: When preparing an **evening party** for a **special occasion**, you want to put together a **really memorable menu**. A **themed dinner party** is often well-received. You can even **lay the table** and **create an ambience** in keeping with the theme. A **Moroccan-style banquet** is **impressive**. Start with **nibbles of pitta breads and hummus**. The **Lamb, Prune and Almond Tagine,** with **meltingly tender** pieces of meat **flavoured with delicate spices** and slowly cooked, makes a **wonderfully rich** main course. Serve with the **Vegetable and Chickpea Couscous** a **colourful** side dish to soak up the delicious **juices** from the **tagine**.

Honey Pork with Roast Potatoes and Apple

loin of pork, with crackling and 4 bones	1kg (2¼lb)
salt	1 tsp
olive oil	4 tbsp
butter	25g (1oz)
Charlotte potatoes	700g (1½lb), scrubbed and halved lengthways
large onion	1, cut into 8 wedges
clear honey	1 tbsp
mixed with grainy mustard	1 tbsp
Cox's apples	2, cored and each cut into 6 wedges
fresh sage leaves	12
dry cider	175ml (6fl oz)

1. Preheat the oven to 220°C/200°C fan oven/Gas Mark 7. Put the pork on a board and with a sharp knife score the skin into thin strips, cutting about halfway into the fat underneath. Rub the salt and 2 tablespoons of the oil over the skin and season well with pepper.

2. Put the meat on a rack, skin-side up over a large roasting tin (if you do not have a rack, just put the pork in the tin). Roast in the oven on a high shelf for 25 minutes. Turn the oven down to 190°C/170°C fan oven/Gas Mark 5 and continue to roast the ham for 15 minutes.

3. Add the remaining oil and the butter to the roasting tin. Scatter the potatoes and onion around the meat, season with salt and pepper and continue to roast for 45 minutes.

4. Brush the meat with the honey and mustard mixture. Add the apples and sage leaves to the tin and roast for a further 15 minutes.

5. Remove the pork from over the tin and wrap completely in foil, then leave to rest. Put the potatoes, onions and apples in a serving dish and return to the oven to keep warm.

6. Put the roasting tin, with the cooking juices in, on the hob and heat, then add the cider and stir well to make a thin gravy. Season to taste.

7. Cut the meat away from the bone and cut between each bone. Pull the crackling away from the meat and cut into strips. Carve the joint, giving each person some meat, crackling and a bone to chew. Serve with the gravy and potatoes, onions and apples.

Preparation time: 20 min   **Cooking time:** 1hr 40 min
Cals per serving: 770   **Serves:** 4

Honey Pork with
Roast Potatoes
and Apple

Ginger and Honey-glazed Ham

unsmoked gammon, on the bone	4.5–6.8kg (10–15lb)
shallots	2, peeled and halved
cloves	6
bay leaves	3
celery sticks	2, cut into 5cm (2in) pieces
English mustard	2 tbsp
fresh root ginger	5cm (2in) piece, peeled and thinly sliced

For the glaze

dark brown sugar	225g (8oz)
runny honey	2 tbsp
brandy or Madeira	100ml (3½fl oz)

For the chutney

mangoes	4, peeled, sliced and chopped into 5cm (2in) chunks
mixed spice	1 tsp
cardamom pods	4, seeds removed and crushed
cinnamon sticks	2, roughly chopped
raisins	4 tbsp

1. Put the gammon in a large pan. Add the shallots, cloves, bay leaves, celery and enough cold water to cover. Bring to the boil, cover and simmer gently for about 5 hours. Remove any scum with a slotted spoon. Lift the ham out of the pan, discard the vegetables and herbs and leave the ham to cool.

2. Preheat the oven to 200°C/180°C fan oven/Gas Mark 6. Using a sharp knife, carefully cut away the ham's thick skin to leave an even layer of fat. Score a diamond pattern in the fat with a sharp knife. Put the ham into a roasting tin. Smother evenly with the mustard and tuck the ginger into the scored fat.

3. For the glaze, put the sugar, honey and brandy in a pan and heat until the sugar has dissolved. Brush the glaze evenly over the ham.

4. In a bowl, mix together the chutney ingredients, add any remaining glaze, then spoon around the ham.

5. Cook the ham for 30 to 40 minutes, basting every 10 minutes. Remove the ham from the roasting tin and put to one side. Stir the chutney and place under a grill for 5 minutes to allow the mango to caramelise. Serve the ham, carved in thin slices, with the chutney on the side.

Preparation time: 1 hr   **Cooking time:** 5 hr 45 min
Cals per serving: 234 for 8, 174 for 10   **Serves:** 8–10

Spiced Duck with Port and Berry Sauce

small duck breasts	6, about 225g (8oz) each, well trimmed and fat scored in a diamond pattern
ground allspice	¼ tsp
ground cinnamon	½ tsp
fresh flat-leaf parsley	to garnish

For the port and berry sauce

vegetable oil	4 tsp
onion	175g (6oz), chopped
golden caster sugar	3 tbsp
red wine vinegar	3 tbsp
port	450ml (15fl oz)
red wine	450ml (15fl oz)
fresh chicken stock	450ml (15fl oz)
cinnamon stick	1
bay leaf	1
clove	1
frozen mixed berries, such as, redcurrants, blackcurrants, raspberries (not strawberries)	175g (6oz), thawed and drained

1. Preheat the oven to 220°C/200°C fan oven/Gas Mark 7.

2. To make the sauce, heat the oil in a saucepan, add the onion and cook gently for 10 to 15 minutes or until soft. Add the sugar and cook over a high heat until golden. Add the vinegar, then bubble and reduce until all the liquid has evaporated. Add the port, bubble and reduce by one-third, then add the red wine and reduce by half. Add the stock, cinnamon stick, bay leaf and clove. Bring to the boil; bubble for 25 minutes or until reduced by half. Strain and reserve the liquid.

3. To make the spiced duck, heat a heavy-based flameproof casserole until hot and add the duck, skin-side down. Cook, covered, for 10 minutes or until the skin is brown (don't cook the flesh side). Remove the duck and place in a roasting tin, skin-side up. Season with salt and pepper, allspice and cinnamon.

4. Roast the duck for 10 minutes for rare, 15 minutes for medium rare and 20 minutes for well done. Set aside.

5. Add any juices from the roasting tin to the reserved sauce, bring to the boil and add the berries. Check the seasoning. Slice the duck breasts and arrange on plates, then spoon the port and berry sauce around. Garnish with parsley and serve.

Preparation time: 10 min   **Cooking time:** 1 hr 15 min
Cals per serving: 1211   **Serves:** 6

Guinea Fowl with Madeira and Spiced Oranges

oil	1 tbsp
butter	25g (1oz)
guinea fowl joints or	6–8, about 2kg
corn-fed chicken joints	(4½lb) total weight
shallots or button onions	225g (8oz), peeled with the root end trimmed
streaky bacon	225g (8oz), cut into thin strips or lardons
tangerines	4, halved
kumquats	50g (2oz), halved
fresh root ginger	2.5cm (1in) piece, peeled and coarsely grated
garlic cloves	2, crushed
plain flour	2 tbsp
Madeira	300ml (10fl oz)
fresh chicken stock	600ml (1pt)
cinnamon stick	1
tangerine	1, juice of
redcurrant jelly	3 tbsp
vacuum-packed chestnuts	200g (7oz), optional
chopped fresh flat-leaf parsley	to garnish
couscous	to serve (see side dishes, page 230)

1. Preheat the oven to 170°C/150°C fan oven/Gas Mark 3. Heat the oil and butter in a deep flameproof casserole. Add the guinea fowl in batches and cook until browned on the skin side before turning and browning on the other side. Remove with a slotted spoon and set aside. Add the shallots, bacon, tangerine halves and kumquats to the pan and cook, stirring, until brown. Stir in the ginger and garlic and cook for 1 minute.

2. Stir in the flour, Madeira and stock. Return the joints to the casserole, then add the cinnamon stick, tangerine juice and redcurrant jelly.

3. Bring to the boil; cover and cook in the oven for 50 to 60 minutes or until tender. (The cooking time depends on the thickness of the joints, not their weight, so return it to the oven, if necessary.)

4. Discard the cinnamon stick. Lift the guinea fowl out of the sauce, cover with foil and keep warm. In a small pan, bring the sauce to the boil, add the chestnuts, if using, and bubble for 10 minutes or until reduced by half. Pour over the guinea fowl, to serve. Garnish with the parsley and serve with couscous on the side.

Preparation time: 30 min   **Cooking time:** 1 hr 15 min
Cals per serving: 600   **Serves:** 6

Guinea Fowl with Madeira
and Spiced Oranges

Italian Chicken
Cassoulet

black olive tapenade	8 tsp
chicken quarters	8, about 350g (12oz) each
garlic bulbs	4 halved vertically
fennel bulbs	4, quartered
olive oil	300ml (10fl oz)
Toulouse sausages or other spicy sausage	450g (1lb)
black peppercorns and crushed rock salt	4 tsp
fresh rosemary sprigs	8, plus extra to garnish
lemons	4 (8 tbsp juice and reserve the squeezed lemon halves)
fresh chicken stock	900ml (1½pt)
cannellini beans	3 x 396g cans, drained
Parma ham	140g pack
Salt-baked New Potatoes	to serve (see side dishes, page 234)

1. Preheat the oven to 220°C/200°C fan oven/Gas Mark 7. Tuck 1 teaspoon of tapenade under the skin of each chicken quarter. Set aside. Place the garlic and fennel in a large roasting tin with 4 tablespoons of the olive oil. Roast for 30 minutes. Leave the oven on.

2. Heat 3 tablespoons of the olive oil in a large, non-stick frying pan. Fry the chicken in batches, skin side down for about 4 minutes or until a deep chestnut brown, then turn over and fry for 1 minute on the bone side. Put the chicken, skin side up, in two large roasting tins or two wide, shallow, flameproof dishes.

3. Lower the heat under the frying pan and brown the sausages all over in the fat, then add to the chicken. Add the roasted fennel and garlic to the dish with the peppercorns, salt, rosemary, lemon juice and reserved lemon halves, cut into chunks. Pour over the remaining olive oil.

4. Roast for 45 minutes, swapping the tins around halfway through. Remove the tins from the oven, add the chicken stock and beans. Return to the oven for 15 minutes, then place the slices of Parma ham over the top and cook for a further 10 to 15 minutes, or until the ham is crisp and the chicken is cooked through. Strew with rosemary sprigs and serve with the new potatoes.

Freezing: Complete the recipe, but don't add the Parma ham.

To use: Thaw at cool room temperature overnight, place in dishes, cover and cook at 200°C/180°C fan oven/Gas Mark 6 for 20 minutes, add the Parma ham and complete the recipe.

Preparation time: 30 min   **Cooking time:** 2 hr
Cals per serving: 1274   **Serves:** 8

Chicken Breasts with Courgette and Herb Stuffing

courgettes	225g (8oz), coarsely grated
salt	1 tsp
butter	25g (1oz)
small onion	1, finely chopped
cream cheese	50g (2oz)
fresh breadcrumbs	50g (2oz)
large egg	1
parmesan	25g (1oz), grated
chopped fresh herbs, such as parsley, mint and basil	2 tbsp
chicken breasts	6
olive oil	2 tbsp
white wine	100ml (3½fl oz)
fresh chicken stock	450ml (15fl oz)
fresh thyme and rosemary sprigs	
tarragon and marjoram sprigs	to garnish
steamed broccoli florets	to serve

1. Place the courgettes in a colander and sprinkle with 1 teaspoon of salt, mix and leave to drain for 10 minutes. Rinse and pat dry. Melt the butter in a small pan, add the onion and cook until soft; cool.

2. Whiz the courgettes, onion, cream cheese, half the breadcrumbs, the egg, parmesan and herbs in a food processor. If the stuffing is a little too wet, add more breadcrumbs; season with salt and pepper.

3. Cut a pocket in each chicken breast. Spoon in the stuffing and secure with a cocktail stick.

4. Preheat the oven to 200°C/180°C fan oven/Gas Mark 6. Heat the oil in a roasting tin, large enough to hold the chicken in one layer. Brown the chicken, skin side down, over a medium heat for 3 minutes, then turn and seal the other side for 1 minute. Remove from the tin and set aside. Pour the wine into the tin, bring to the boil and scrape the sediment from the base of the tin. Add 150ml (5fl oz) of the stock, the thyme and rosemary sprigs; season and bring to the boil.

5. Return the chicken to the roasting tin, skin side up, in a single layer. Roast for 15 to 20 minutes or until the juices run clear when the chicken is pierced with a skewer.

6. Slice the chicken and keep warm. Skim the fat from the liquid in the casserole, add the remaining stock, bring to the boil and bubble for 10 minutes or until syrupy. Spoon over the chicken, garnish with tarragon and marjoram and serve with broccoli.

Preparation time: 45 min, plus 10 min standing
Cooking time: 40 min   **Cals per serving:** 395   **Serves:** 6

Spiced Poussin with Saffron and Figs and Fragrant Couscous

sunflower oil	2 tbsp
small onions	6, peeled and quartered
fresh root ginger	2.5cm (1in) piece, finely chopped
coriander seeds	1 tsp, crushed
saffron strands	large pinch
ground turmeric	1 tsp
cinnamon stick	1
poussins	2, about 350g (12oz) each
ready-to-eat dried figs	250g pack

For the couscous

reserved liquid from the poussin (see above) or chicken or vegetable stock	150ml (5fl oz)
couscous	250g (9oz)
harissa paste	1 tsp
or large red chilli	1, deseeded and left whole
blanched almonds	50g (2oz), toasted
golden raisins	50g (2oz)
chopped fresh flat-leaf parsley	2 tbsp
chopped fresh mint	3 tbsp, to garnish

1. Preheat the oven to 190°C/170°C fan oven/Gas Mark 5. Heat the oil in a flameproof casserole large enough to hold the poussins side by side and fry the onions for about 10 minutes or until soft and golden. Add the ginger and fry for 1 to 2 minutes. Stir in the coriander seeds, saffron, turmeric and cinnamon stick and fry together for a further 2 minutes.

2. Place the poussins in the casserole, breast-side down, and cook until lightly browned. Scatter the figs around and pour in 500 ml (17fl oz) of boiling water. Season with plenty of salt and pepper, cover tightly and cook for 1 hour. The flesh of the poussins should be falling off the bone.

3. Lift the poussins, figs, onion and cinnamon stick from the cooking liquid with a slotted spoon; discard the cinnamon stick. Place the poussins and figs in an ovenproof dish, then cover and keep warm in a low oven. Reserve the liquid to prepare the couscous.

4. Bring the cooking liquid from the poussins to the boil in a small pan. Take the pan off the heat and stir in the couscous, harissa and the almonds and raisins.

5. Cover with foil and leave to soak for 10 minutes. Fluff up the couscous grains with a fork and garnish with the herbs. Remember to remove the chilli, if using. Serve the poussins on a bed of couscous.

Preparation time: 15 min **Cooking time:** 1 hr 15 min
Cals per serving: 612 **Serves:** 4

Spiced Poussin with Saffron and Figs and Fragrant Couscous

Winter Venison
Stew

stewing venison	900g (2lb), cut into 4cm (1½in) cubes
crushed black peppercorns	1 tsp
juniper berries	6, optional
chopped fresh thyme	1 tbsp
onions	2
red wine	300ml (11fl oz)
olive oil	100ml (3½fl oz)
sunflower oil	4 tbsp
raw pancetta, or streaky	200g (7oz), rind
or back bacon	removed and cut
or lardons	into narrow strips
garlic clove	1, crushed
plain flour	2 tbsp
stock	300ml (11fl oz)
bay leaf	1
shallots	350g (12oz)
butter	25g (1oz)
caster sugar	1 tsp
vacuum-packed chestnuts	225g (8oz)
sweetened dried	
cranberries	75g (3oz)

1. Remove any sinew from the venison, then place the meat in a large bowl. Add the peppercorns, juniper berries, if using, thyme, and one onion, thickly sliced, plus the wine and olive oil and mix together thoroughly. Cover and chill for 24 to 48 hours.

2. Drain the venison, reserving the marinade, but discarding the onion. Pat the meat dry with kitchen paper. Heat 2 tablespoons of the sunflower oil in a flameproof casserole and brown the venison all over, in batches, over a high heat.

3. Preheat the oven to 170°C/150°C fan oven/Gas Mark 3. Add the pancetta to the casserole and fry for 5 to 10 minutes until browned, then remove the venison and pancetta and set aside. Add the remaining sunflower oil, lower the heat to a moderate setting, and fry the remaining onion, finely chopped, and the garlic for 10 minutes or until golden. Stir in the flour, then the reserved marinade. Bring to the boil and bubble for 2 to 3 minutes.

4. Return the venison, any juices and the pancetta to the casserole, with the stock and the bay leaf. Season to taste. Bring to the boil, cover and simmer for 5 minutes, then transfer to the oven and cook for 1 hour 15 minutes or until tender (venison marinated for 48 hours probably needs slightly less time). Meanwhile, place the shallots in a pan of cold water, bring to the boil and simmer for 3 to 4 minutes, then drain, leave to cool a little, then peel.

5. Heat the butter in a medium-sized frying pan, add the shallots and the sugar, then cover and cook for 15 to 20 minutes until the shallots are soft to the centre and a sticky golden brown. Add the chestnuts and cranberries, stir the mixture well and cook for a further 2 to 3 minutes.

6. Remove the venison from the oven 5 minutes before the end of cooking time. Stir the shallot mixture into the stew and return to the oven for a further 5 minutes.

Preparation time: 1 hr, plus 24–28 hr marinating
Cooking time: 2 hr 10 min   **Cals per serving:** 664   **Serves:** 6

Salmis of Pheasant with Walnuts and Mushrooms

young oven-ready pheasants or guinea fowls	2
butter	25g (1oz), softened
sherry vinegar	5 tbsp
onion	225g (8oz), chopped
carrots	175g (6oz), chopped
celery sticks	175g (6oz), diced
fresh bay leaves	3
dried porcini mushrooms	15g (½oz)
mushroom ketchup	4 tbsp
red wine or wine and port mixed	450ml (15fl oz)
fresh chicken or game stock	600ml (1pt)
wild or flat black mushrooms	175g (6oz), sliced
walnut halves	125g (4oz)
fresh thyme sprigs	to garnish

For the kneaded butter

butter	50g (2oz), softened
plain flour	40g (1½oz)

1. Preheat the oven to 230°C/210°C fan oven/Gas Mark 8. Smear the pheasants all over with the softened butter. Lay them on their sides in a large roasting tin and roast for 15 minutes (guinea fowls for 20 minutes). Turn the birds over and roast for another 15 minutes (guinea fowls for 20 minutes). Remove from the oven – they should be quite rare.

2. When cool enough to handle, remove the legs and cut the breast off the bone. Place the legs under a preheated grill and cook for 4 to 5 minutes each side. Arrange the legs in the bottom of a 2.8 litre (5 pint) shallow ovenproof dish and place the breast meat on top. Cool completely, then cover and chill for 3 hours or overnight.

3. Meanwhile, break up the carcasses and place in a large saucepan. Add the sherry vinegar to the roasting tin, scraping the bottom to dislodge any sediment, then add to the carcass stock pot with the next eight ingredients. Slowly bring to the boil, turn down the heat and simmer for 1 hour. Strain the stock into a jug, discard the vegetables and herbs and return the stock to the pan. Bring to a fast boil and reduce to 750ml (1¼ pint). Season well.

4. Make the kneaded butter by mixing the butter and flour to a smooth paste. Gradually whisk the kneaded butter into the stock, bring to the boil and bubble until syrupy. Add the mushrooms and walnuts to the sauce, then cool quickly, cover and chill until the game is ready to serve.

5. To serve, reduce the oven temperature to 180°C/160°C fan oven/Gas Mark 4. Reheat the sauce, pour it over the game and cover. Place in the oven and cook for about 1 hour or until hot to the centre. Garnish with thyme sprigs.

Preparation time: 20 min, plus at least 3 hr chilling
Cooking time: 1 hr 50 min, plus 1 hr reheating
Cals per serving: 715   **Serves:** 4

Mushroom and Chestnut Gratin

small sweet potatoes 700g (1½lb), peeled and
cut in half
butter 50g (2oz)
chestnut mushrooms 700g (1½lb), quartered
dry white wine 150ml (5fl oz)
crème fraîche 100ml (3½fl oz)
chopped fresh thyme 1 tsp
fresh white breadcrumbs 3 tbsp
grated parmesan 5 tbsp

1. Preheat the oven to 190°C/170°C fan oven/Gas Mark 5. Cook the sweet potatoes in boiling salted water until just tender. Drain and allow to cool before cutting into 5mm (¼in) slices. Set aside.

2. Melt half the butter in a large frying pan and when foaming, add half the mushrooms and fry over a high heat for about 3 minutes. Remove from the pan and set aside. Wipe out the pan and repeat the process with the remaining butter and mushrooms.

3. Add the wine to the pan, bring to the boil and allow to bubble until reduced by half. Add the crème fraîche and let bubble for a further 2 to 3 minutes. Put the mushrooms back in the pan with the thyme and season with salt and pepper.

4. Turn the mushrooms into a 1.4 litre (2½ pint) capacity ovenproof dish and arrange the potatoes around the edge, in an overlapping layer. Mix together the breadcrumbs and parmesan and sprinkle over the potatoes. Bake for 15 minutes or until hot and golden on top.

Preparation time: 15 min   **Cooking time:** 35 min
Cals per serving: 410   **Serves:** 4

Mushroom and
Chestnut Gratin

Potato and Celeriac Puffs

For the potato base

waxy potatoes 350g (12oz), peeled and sliced
butter 40–50g (1½–2oz)

For the celeriac topping

celeriac 700g (1½lb), peeled and cut into 2.5cm (1in) chunks
vegetable stock 600ml (1pt)
double cream 284ml carton
garlic cloves 2, crushed
bay leaf 1
grated nutmeg pinch of
medium eggs 3, separated
Tomato and Apple Chutney and Shallot and Mushroom Sauce to serve (see page 225)
fresh chives to garnish

1. To make the potato bases, place the potatoes in a pan of cold salted water; bring to the boil, boil for 1 minute, then drain. Heat half the butter in a non-stick frying pan and cook the potatoes in batches for 2 to 3 minutes or until golden brown on both sides, adding more butter when necessary. Cool slightly and arrange in layers in the bottom of six 6cm (2½in) metal rings placed on a baking sheet. Season between each layer and set aside. Preheat the oven to 200°C/180°C fan oven/Gas Mark 6.

2. For the celeriac topping, place the celeriac in a pan, add the stock, cream, garlic, bay leaf, nutmeg and season, bring to the boil and simmer for 15 minutes. Drain and reserve the cooking liquid. In a food processor or blender, whizz the celeriac with 2 tablespoons of the cooking liquid until smooth. Place the celeriac purée in a bowl and beat in the egg yolks. Whisk the egg whites to form soft peaks and fold into the celeriac.

3. Spoon the mixture on top of the potatoes, filling to the top of the rings. Bake for 30 minutes or until puffed and golden.

4. Remove the rings from the puffs, place a spoonful of the Tomato and Apple Chutney on top, then garnish with chives and serve with the Shallot and Mushroom Sauce.

Preparation time: 45 min   **Cooking time:** 55 min
Cals per serving: 450   **Serves:** 6

Tomato and Apple Chutney

tomatoes	700g (1½lb), peeled, deseeded and chopped
apple	1, peeled, cored and roughly chopped
onion	50g (2oz), chopped
garlic clove	1, crushed
soft light brown sugar	125g (4oz)
finely chopped fresh root ginger	1 tsp
turmeric	½ tsp
sultanas	125g (4oz)
white wine vinegar	3 tbsp

1. Mix all the ingredients together in a pan. Bring to the boil and simmer for 30 minutes or until reduced and thick. Cool and serve with the Potato and Celeriac Puffs (see page 224).

Preparation time: 15 min   **Cooking time:** 30 min
Cals per serving: 170   **Serves:** 6

Shallot and Mushroom Sauce

1. Heat the olive oil in a large pan and fry the chopped shallots until golden brown. Add the wine, bring to the boil and boil until reduced to about 2 tablespoons. Add the mushrooms and cook for 3 to 4 minutes. Add 600ml (1 pint) of water, the celery and thyme sprigs. Bring to the boil and simmer for 20 minutes.

2. Meanwhile, heat the butter in a frying pan, add the whole shallots and sprinkle over the caster sugar. Cover and cook gently for 20 to 25 minutes until caramelised.

3. Remove the thyme and celery from the sauce and pour over the shallots. Bring to the boil and boil, uncovered, until reduced by half.

4. To thicken the sauce, combine the softened butter and flour and whisk into the sauce. Simmer for 1 to 2 minutes. Season and serve with the Potato and Celeriac Puffs (see page 224).

Preparation time: 10 min   **Cooking time:** 1 hr
Cals per serving: 110   **Serves:** 6

olive oil	1 tbsp
shallots	2, finely chopped
red wine	300ml (10fl oz)
button mushrooms	225g (8oz), quartered
celery stick	1, cut in half
fresh thyme sprigs	4
butter	25g (1oz)
whole peeled shallots	350g (12oz)
caster sugar	1 tsp
butter	15g (½oz), softened
plain flour	15g (½oz)

Roasted Ratatouille

red peppers	400g (14oz), deseeded and roughly chopped
aubergines	700g (1½lb), cut into chunks
onions	450g (1lb), peeled and cut into petals
garlic cloves	4–5
olive oil	150ml (5fl oz)
fennel seeds	1 tsp
passata	200ml (7fl oz)
fresh thyme sprigs	to garnish

1. Preheat the oven to 240°C/220°C fan oven/Gas Mark 9. Place the peppers, aubergines, onions, garlic, olive oil and fennel seeds in one layer in a roasting tin, then season and toss together. Cook for 30 minutes, or until the vegetables are charred and beginning to soften, tossing frequently during cooking.

2. Stir the passata through the vegetables and return the roasting tin to the oven for 50 to 60 minutes, stirring occasionally. Garnish with thyme sprigs and serve.

Freezing: Complete step 1, then cool, wrap and freeze.

To use: Thaw at room temperature overnight. Complete recipe.

Preparation time: 15 min   **Cooking time:** 1 hr 30 min
Cals per serving: 238   **Serves:** 6

Broad Bean and Lemon Risotto

1. Cook the broad beans in a large pan of boiling salted water for 3 to 5 minutes or until just tender. Plunge into icy cold water to cool. Drain, peel off the outer skin, if you like, and set aside.

2. Melt the butter in a large pan, add the onion and cook over a medium heat for 5 minutes or until beginning to soften. Add the rice and continue to cook, stirring, for 1 to 2 minutes. Pour in a ladleful of the hot stock and simmer gently, stirring frequently until most of it is absorbed. Keep adding the stock in this way, for about 20 minutes until the rice is tender, but still has a bite to it; it should look creamy and soft.

3. Add the broad beans, lemon rind and juice and warm through. Stir in the parmesan and season to taste.

4. Serve the risotto immediately, garnished with grated parmesan and lemon rind.

frozen broad beans	350g (12oz)
butter	25g (1oz)
onion	1, finely chopped
arborio rice	200g (7oz)
hot vegetable stock	1ltr (1¾pt)
lemon	1, rind finely grated and juice of
parmesan	75g (3oz), freshly grated
grated parmesan and lemon rind	to garnish

Preparation time: 25 min   **Cooking time:** 35 min
Cals per serving: 380   **Serves:** 4

Roasted
Ratatouille

Vegetarian feast: Mushroom
and Chestnut Gratin and
Summer Pudding

Vegetarian Dinner Party: This is a great **chance to experiment** with different flavours, and foods. Try to **create a colourful and interesting mix** of dishes. A **Roasted Ratatouille with the Potato and Celeriac Puffs** makes a **spectacular meal**. The **Broad Bean and Lemon Risotto** either as a starter or main course is perfect with a **simple green salad**. The **Mushroom and Chestnut Gratin** is a **deliciously satisfying** dish, cooked in a **creamy sauce**, topped with **sweet potatoes** and a **golden crust of breadcrumbs and parmesan**. And for the finale, bring on the **Summer Pudding**, garnished with **garlands of berries**, oozing with **summer goodness**.

Vegetable and Chickpea Couscous

onions, carrots, fennel and courgettes about 350g (12oz) each, cut into large chunks
vegetable stock 1.1ltr (2pt)
bay leaves 2
large red pepper 1, cut into large chunks
chickpeas 400g can, drained
couscous 350g (12oz)
butter 25g (1oz)

1. Put the onions, carrots and fennel into a large pan, add the vegetable stock and bay leaves and season well. Bring slowly to the boil and cook for 5 to 10 minutes or until the vegetables begin to soften.

2. Take off the heat, add the courgettes, red pepper and chickpeas, return to the boil and cook for a further 3 to 4 minutes.

3. Meanwhile, soak the couscous according to packet instructions with 1 teaspoon of salt. Melt the butter in a large, deep frying pan. Add the couscous, break up the grains with a fork, heat through and season. Add the hot vegetables to the couscous and serve.

Preparation time: 15 min   **Cooking time:** 20 min
Cals per serving: 284   **Serves:** 6

Saffron Roasted
Vegetable Couscous

fennel bulbs	3, cut into wedges
red onions	3, cut into wedges
olive oil	100ml (3½fl oz)
aubergine	700g (1½lb), cut into large pieces
courgettes	700g (1½lb), cut into large pieces
red peppers	3, cut into large pieces
runny honey	2 tbsp
saffron threads	generous pinch
instant couscous	1 x 500g pack
extra-virgin olive oil	for drizzling

1. Preheat the oven to 240°C/220°C fan oven/Gas Mark 9. Place the fennel and onions into two large roasting tins. Mix 2 tablespoons of the olive oil into each batch. Cook for 15 minutes.

2. Divide the aubergine, courgettes and red peppers between the two roasting tins (containing the fennel and onions), then drizzle with 1 tablespoon of the olive oil and 1 tablespoon of the honey and season. Mix together and roast for 50 to 55 minutes or until golden brown and tender, tossing the vegetables from time to time and swapping the tins halfway through. When cooked, transfer to a bowl and leave to cool.

3. Pour 600ml (1 pint) of boiling water over the saffron threads and leave to stand for 20 minutes. Place the couscous in a bowl with 1 teaspoon of salt and the remaining oil and pour the saffron liquid over. Cover and leave to stand for 10 minutes. Fluff up with a fork to separate the grains.

4. Stir the vegetables through the couscous and check the seasoning. Drizzle with a little olive oil before serving.

Preparation time: 20 min, plus 30 min standing
Cooking time: 1 hr 10 min   **Cals per serving:** 168   **Serves:** 239

Soufflé
Potatoes

floury potatoes	700g (1½lb), peeled and cut into chunks
butter	for greasing
finely grated parmesan	6 tbsp
fresh four cheese sauce	300g carton
wholegrain mustard	1 tbsp
medium eggs	3, separated

1. Put the potatoes in a pan of cold salted water and cook for 20 minutes, or until tender. Drain, mash in the pan over a gentle heat for 2 minutes to dry a little. Put in a bowl and cool for 10 minutes.

2. Preheat the oven to 200°C/180°C fan oven/Gas Mark 6. Butter six 250ml (9fl oz) ramekins, sprinkle each with 1 tablespoon of the parmesan and put them on a baking sheet.

3. Add the cheese sauce, mustard and egg yolks to the potato, season well with salt and pepper and beat together.

4. Whisk the egg whites in a clean, grease-free bowl until stiff peaks form, then fold them into the mashed potato. Spoon into the prepared ramekins and bake for 30 minutes until well risen. Serve immediately.

Preparation time: 10–15 min   **Cooking time:** 50 min
Cals per serving: 200   **Serves:** 6

Paprika
Potatoes

1. Cook the potatoes in a pan of boiling water for 5 minutes. Drain, rinse, then toss in the olive oil, paprika and plenty of seasoning to coat.

2. Barbecue or grill under a preheated grill for 10 minutes until golden and cooked through.

Preparation time: 5 min   **Cooking time:** 15 min
Cals per serving: 200   **Serves:** 4

potatoes	550g (1lb 4oz), scrubbed and cut into wedges
olive oil	3 tbsp
paprika	2 tbsp

Roast Potatoes with Rosemary and Garlic

potatoes	1.8kg (4lb), peeled and cut into large chunks
vegetable oil	3 tbsp
unsalted butter	75g (3oz)
fresh rosemary sprigs	
garlic cloves	6, unpeeled

1. Preheat the oven to 200°C/180°C fan oven/Gas Mark 6. Put the potatoes in a pan of cold, salted water, bring to the boil and cook for 5 to 10 minutes, or until the potatoes begin to soften. Drain and return to the pan, put over a low heat and shake the pan until the potatoes are dry and a little fluffy. Put to one side.

2. Heat the vegetable oil and butter in a roasting tin. Put the warm potatoes in the tin with the rosemary and garlic and toss to cover them evenly in the oil and butter mixture. Season well. Roast for 1 hour, or until the potatoes are brown and crisp, turning the potatoes over from time to time to ensure they are cooked evenly.

Preparation time: 30 min **Cooking time:** 1 hr 10 min
Cals per serving: 109 for 8, 87 for 10 **Serves:** 8–10

Mini Baked Potatoes with Caraway Seeds

1. Preheat the oven to 220°C/200°C fan oven/Gas Mark 7. Toss the potatoes in the oil and sprinkle over the caraway seeds and salt. Season with black pepper.

2. Roast the potatoes for 35 to 45 minutes or until golden and cooked through. Serve with crispy bacon and soured cream.

Preparation time: 10 min **Cooking time:** 35–45 min
Cals per serving: 115 **Serves:** 6

small potatoes	18, scrubbed
olive oil	2 tbsp
caraway seeds	1 tbsp
sea salt	1 tbsp
crispy bacon and soured cream	to serve

Salt-baked
New Potatoes

new potatoes 550g (1lb 4oz), parboiled
olive oil 2 tbsp
sea salt flakes 1 tbsp

1. Preheat the oven to 200°C/180°C fan oven/Gas Mark 6. Toss the potatoes in the olive oil and salt. Roast for 40 minutes until golden.

Preparation time: 10 min   **Cooking time:** 40 min
Cals per serving: 157   **Serves:** 4

Jerseys in a Parcel with
Lemon and Rosemary

1. Preheat the oven to 200°C/180°C fan oven/Gas Mark 6. Place the potatoes in a bowl with the olive oil, and salt and pepper to season, then add the rosemary. Toss together, turn out on to a large sheet of oiled foil on a baking sheet and scatter over the lemon rind.

2. Fold the foil over to make a parcel and bake for 40 to 50 minutes or until tender. The potatoes can also be cooked on a barbecue – allow about 25 to 30 minutes. Unwrap the parcel at the table to serve.

Preparation time: 10 min   **Cooking time:** 40–45 min
Cals per serving: 180 for 4, 120 for 6   **Serves:** 4–6

Jersey Royals 700g (1½lb), lightly scrubbed
extra-virgin olive oil 2 tbsp
sea salt 1 tsp
roughly chopped fresh rosemary 2 tsp
small lemon 1, rind finely grated

Jerseys in a Parcel
with Lemon and
Rosemary

Jersey Royals with Mint and Petit Pois

olive oil 3 tbsp
Jersey Royals 900g (2lb), scrubbed and thickly sliced
frozen petits pois 175g (6oz)
chopped fresh mint 3 tbsp

1. Heat half the olive oil in a non-stick frying pan, add half the potatoes and cook for 5 minutes, turning, until brown on both sides. Remove the potatoes from the pan with a slotted spoon and set aside. Repeat with the remaining oil and potatoes.

2. Return all the potatoes to the pan and cook all of them together, covered loosely, for a further 10 to 15 minutes.

3. Meanwhile, cook the petits pois in a pan of boiling water for 2 minutes, then drain well. Add the petits pois to the potatoes and cook through for 2 to 3 minutes.

4. Toss the petits pois and potatoes with the mint, salt and pepper just before serving.

Preparation time: 15 min   **Cooking time:** 30 min
Cals per serving: 175   **Serves:** 6

Creamed Cumin and Turmeric Potatoes

1. Cook the potatoes in a pan of boiling salted water for about 10 to 15 minutes until tender. Drain and immediately mix with the turmeric and chilli powder.

2. Heat the oil in a heavy-based pan, add the cumin seeds and cook for 1 minute until they turn nut brown. Add the potatoes and cook for 10 minutes until lightly golden.

3. Add the yogurt, milk and ¼ tsp salt, lower the heat, cover and cook for 5 minutes. Serve immediately.

Preparation time: 10 min   **Cooking time:** about 25 min
Cals per serving: 321   **Serves:** 4

potatoes 550g (1lb 4oz), peeled and roughly cut
turmeric ½ tsp
red chilli powder ½ tsp
vegetable oil 2 tbsp
cumin seeds 1 tsp
Greek yogurt 200g (7oz)
milk 100ml (3½fl oz)

Autumn Pumpkin and Mushroom Bake

butter 50g (2oz), plus extra if needed

small onion 1, finely diced

garlic cloves 2, crushed

chopped fresh thyme ½ tsp, plus extra to garnish

pumpkin or 800g (1lb 12oz),
butternut squash peeled and chopped

field mushrooms 400g (14oz), broken into even-sized pieces

double cream 284ml carton

parmesan 100g (3½oz), freshly grated

1. Preheat the oven to 200°C/180°C fan oven/Gas Mark 6. Warm the butter in a frying pan until foaming, add the onion, garlic and thyme and stir-fry over a medium heat until the onion becomes soft, but not coloured. Add the pumpkin and continue to cook, tossing gently for 3 to 4 minutes until it starts to soften.

2. Turn up the heat, add the mushrooms, then season and cook until the mushroom juices start to flow (add extra butter if it looks too dry). Add the cream, bring to the boil, and cook for 5 to 10 minutes, or until the sauce looks syrupy.

3. Spoon the mixture into a large ovenproof dish, sprinkle with parmesan, and bake for 10 minutes. Garnish with thyme, to serve.

Preparation time: 5 min   **Cooking time:** 20–25 min
Cals per serving: 565 for 4, 364 for 6   **Serves:** 4–6

Mushrooms with Cherry Tomatoes

portabella or large
flat mushrooms 6
flavourless oil for greasing
garlic cloves 2, finely sliced
cherry tomatoes 6 sprigs, about
on the vine 125g (4oz) each
olive oil 3 tbsp

1. Preheat the oven to 200°C/180°C fan oven/Gas Mark 6. Put the mushrooms into a greased roasting tin, scatter over the garlic, arrange a sprig of cherry tomatoes – still on the vine – on top of each mushroom, then drizzle with olive oil.

2. Season well with salt and freshly ground black pepper, then cover with foil and bake for 15 minutes.

3. Take the foil off the mushrooms and continue to roast, uncovered, for a further 15 minutes.

Preparation time: 10 min   **Cooking time:** 30 min
Cals per serving: 120   **Serves:** 6

Chilli Red Onions and Goat's Cheese

1. Preheat the oven to 200°C/180°C fan oven/Gas Mark 6. Put the butter in a small bowl. Beat in the chillies and season well with salt and pepper.

2. Cut the root off one of the onions, sit it on its base, then make several deep cuts in the top to create a star shape, slicing about two-thirds of the way down the onion. Repeat with the other five onions. Divide the chilli butter equally between them, pushing it down into the cuts.

3. Put the onions in a small roasting tin, cover with foil and bake for 40 to 45 minutes or until soft. About 5 minutes before the onions are ready slice each goat's cheese into two, leaving the rind intact, then put on a baking sheet and bake for 2 to 3 minutes. Put the onion on top of the goat's cheese and serve drizzled with balsamic vinegar.

Preparation time: 10 min   **Cooking time:** 30 min
Cals per serving: 120   **Serves:** 6

unsalted butter 75g (3oz), softened
medium red chilles 2, deseeded and finely diced
crushed chillies 1 tsp
small red onions 6, peeled
Somerset goat's cheese 3 x 100g packs
balsamic vinegar to serve

Mushrooms with Cherry Tomatoes
and Chilli Red Onions and Goat's
Cheese make perfect partners
to roast chicken

Roasted Mediterranean Vegetables

plum tomatoes	2, halved
onion	1, peeled and quartered
red peppers	2, deseeded and cut into strips
courgette	1, thickly sliced
garlic cloves	2, unpeeled
olive oil	3 tbsp
chopped fresh thyme	1 tsp
hummus and toasted sesame seeds	to serve, optional

1. Preheat the oven to 220°C/200°C fan oven/Gas Mark 7. Place the tomatoes in a roasting tin with the onion, peppers, courgette and garlic cloves. Drizzle with olive oil, season with salt and pepper and sprinkle with thyme.

2. Cook for 35 to 40 minutes, or until tender, turning occasionally. Serve with hummus and a sprinkling of toasted sesame seeds, if using.

Preparation time: 15 min   **Cooking time:** 35–40 min
Cals per serving: 225   **Serves:** 2

Creamy Leeks

1. Cook the leeks in a pan of boiling salted water for 7 to 10 minutes until just tender. Drain and plunge them immediately into icy cold water. After 15 minutes, drain the leeks again and dry well with several layers of kitchen paper. Put the leeks in a food processor or blender and whiz until roughly chopped. Remove half and set aside, then whiz the remainder until smooth.

2. Heat the butter in a frying pan, add all the leeks and stir over a high heat. Add the crème fraîche and season; stir until hot and bubbling. Serve with a sprinkling of grated nutmeg.

Preparation time: 15 min, plus 15 min cooling
Cooking time: 20 min
Cals per serving: 132 for 8, 106 for 10   **Serves:** 8–10

leeks	900g (2lb), trimmed and thickly sliced
butter	25g (1oz)
crème fraîche	150ml (5fl oz)
freshly grated nutmeg	to serve

Cauliflower
Cheese

cauliflower	1, broken into florets
butter	50g (2oz)
pancetta	125g (4oz), cubed
baby button mushrooms	125g (4oz), cleaned and halved
plain flour	25g (1oz)
English mustard powder	pinch of
cayenne pepper	pinch of
milk	300ml (10fl oz)
mature cheddar	75g (3oz), grated
chopped fresh parsley	1 tbsp
natural dry white breadcrumbs	2 tbsp

1. Preheat the grill to high. Cook the cauliflower in a pan of boiling salted water for 3 to 5 minutes, or until just tender. Drain.

2. While the cauliflower is cooking, melt 25g (1oz) of the butter in a frying pan. When bubbling add the pancetta and fry for 3 minutes. Reduce the heat and add the mushrooms, then cook for a further 2 minutes. Remove and drain on kitchen paper.

3. Melt the remaining butter in a pan. Add the flour, mustard and cayenne pepper to make a roux. Stir over a medium heat for 1 minute. Remove the pan from the heat and gradually stir in the milk.

4. Return the pan to the heat and stir until boiling, then reduce the heat and simmer for a further 2 minutes. Remove the pan from the heat and stir in 25g (1oz) of the cheddar and the parsley, then season to taste.

5. Mix together the cauliflower, pancetta and mushrooms and spoon into a shallow heatproof dish. Pour the sauce over and sprinkle with the remaining cheddar and breadcrumbs. Place under the grill until golden and bubbling. Serve straight away.

Note: For a vegetarian version omit the pancetta.

Preparation time: 15 min   **Cooking time:** 20 min
Cals per serving: 364   **Serves:** 4

Soft Polenta

1. Bring the milk and a good pinch of salt to the boil in a large saucepan. Remove from the heat and add the polenta in a slow, steady stream, stirring constantly with a wooden spoon. Return the mixture to a low heat and simmer, stirring, for 5 minutes.

2. Remove from the heat and stir in the olive oil and parmesan. Season with plenty of salt and pepper. Serve immediately.

Preparation time: 5 min   **Cooking time:** 10 min
Cals per serving: 273   **Serves:** 6

milk	900ml (1½pt)
salt	pinch of
polenta	125g (4oz)
olive oil	4 tbsp
parmesan	75g (3oz), finely grated

Celeriac Mash

celeriac 900g (2lb), peeled and roughly chopped
potatoes 900g (2lb), peeled and roughly chopped
double cream 142ml carton
milk 150ml (5fl oz)

1. Place the celeriac and potatoes in a pan of cold salted water. Bring to the boil and cook for 20 to 30 minutes, or until the vegetables are tender. Drain and mash either with a potato masher or by whizzing quickly in a food processor.

2. Heat the cream and milk together and beat into the mash over a low heat. Season well with salt and pepper, to serve.

Preparation time: 30 min   **Cooking time:** 15 min
Cals per serving: 248   **Serves:** 6

Red Cabbage

1. Remove and discard the outer leaves of the red cabbage, then finely shred the rest of the cabbage, discarding the core.

2. Add the vinegar and ginger to a large pan of water and bring to the boil. Add the cabbage, season with salt and cook for 5 to 10 minutes.

3. Drain and discard the ginger. Serve in a warmed bowl, drizzled with olive oil and fresh thyme.

Preparation time: 10 min   **Cooking time:** 5–10 min
Cals per serving: 30   **Serves:** 6

red cabbage 1.4kg (3lb)
white wine vinegar 2 tbsp
fresh root ginger 2.5cm (1in) piece
olive oil and fresh thyme to serve

Celeriac Mash

Stir-fried Green
Vegetables

oil 2 tbsp
courgettes 225g (8oz), thinly sliced
mangetout 175g (6oz), trimmed
butter 25g (1oz)
frozen peas 175g (6oz), defrosted

1. Heat the oil in a large frying pan, add the courgettes and cook for 1 to 2 minutes. Add the mangetout and cook for a further minute. Add the butter and peas and cook for 1 minute more. Season and serve.

Preparation time: 10 min **Cooking time:** 4 min
Cals per serving: 107 **Serves:** 6

Minted Peas
and Beans

1. Cook the peas and beans in a pan of boiling salted water for 5 minutes, or until tender, then drain.

2. Heat the butter in a frying pan and sauté the spring onions and courgettes. Add the crème fraîche and bring to the boil, then lower the heat and simmer for 2 minutes.

3. Mix in the peas and beans, mint and sugar, then season with salt and black pepper, to serve.

Preparation time: 10 min **Cooking time:** 12 min
Cals per serving: 380 for 4, 253 for 6 **Serves:** 4–6

shelled fresh peas 450g (1lb)
French beans 225g (8oz)
butter 25g (1oz)
bunch spring onions 1, trimmed and thickly sliced
courgettes 225g (8oz), cut into wedges
crème fraîche 200ml (7fl oz)
fresh mint 3 tbsp, roughly chopped
sugar 1 tsp

Brussel Sprouts with Pancetta

pancetta or prosciutto 100g pack
Brussels sprouts 1.1kg (2½lb), trimmed
pecans 75g (3oz), roughly chopped
butter 25g (1oz)

1. Grill the pancetta until golden and crisp. Drain on kitchen paper and allow to cool. Meanwhile, cook the sprouts in a large pan of boiling salted water for 7 to 10 minutes, or until tender.

2. Drain the sprouts, then return to the pan. Toss well with the pecans, butter and seasoning. Turn into a serving dish. Break up the pancetta and sprinkle over the top.

Preparation time: 5 min   **Cooking time:** 10 min
Cals per serving: 50 for 8, 40 for 10   **Serves:** 8–10

Garlic Bruschetta

garlic cloves 3, peeled and bruised with a rolling pin
white country bread 6 thick slices
olive oil 5 tbsp

1. Heat a griddle pan until hot. Meanwhile, rub the garlic cloves on both sides of the bread, then brush the bread on both sides with the olive oil.

2. Put the bread on the hot griddle and cook until golden, pressing down on both sides. Serve with soup.

Preparation time: 5 min   **Cooking time:** 5–10 min
Cals per serving: 230   **Serves:** 6

sweet things

Sticky Banoffee
Pies

bananas	4, peeled and sliced
lemon	1, juice of
digestive biscuits	150g (5oz)
unsalted butter	75g (3oz), melted, plus extra for greasing
ground ginger	1 tsp, optional
Merchant Gourmet BanoffeeToffee Dulce de Leche (toffee sauce)	450g jar
double cream	284ml carton, lightly whipped
plain chocolate shavings	to serve

1. Toss the bananas in the lemon juice and set aside. Put the biscuits in a food processor and whiz to a crumb. Add the melted butter and ginger and process for 1 minute to combine.

2. Butter six 10cm (4in) metal rings or tartlet tins and line with grease-proof paper. Press the biscuit mixture into each ring.

3. Divide the toffee sauce equally among the rings and top with the bananas. Pipe or spoon on the cream, sprinkle with chocolate shavings and chill. Remove from the rings or tins and serve.

Preparation time: 25 min, plus 30 min chilling
Cals per serving: 740   **Serves:** 6

Sticky Banoffee
Pies

Raspberry
Cheesecakes

Madeira cake 250g (9oz)
fresh orange juice 175ml (6fl oz)
raspberries 350g (12oz)
ricotta cheese 250g (9oz)
caster sugar to taste
powdered gelatine 2 tsp
fresh strawberries
or raspberries to decorate

1. Cut the cake lengthways into six slices. Using a round cutter, stamp out six 6cm (2½in) circles of cake.

2. Make six foil collars (see note) and slip one around each cake circle and transfer to a baking sheet. Spoon 1 tablespoon of the orange juice over each cake circle.

3. Whiz 225g (8oz) of the raspberries in a food processor or blender, then push through a sieve. Mix together the purée and ricotta cheese and add sugar to taste.

4. Put 2 tablespoons of the orange juice in a small heatproof bowl, then sprinkle the gelatine over the top and leave to soak for 5 minutes. Place the bowl over a pan of simmering water and stir until melted. Allow to cool a little, then stir into the raspberry purée. Spoon the mixture over the cake circles and chill in the fridge for 2 hours, or until set.

5. Whiz the remaining raspberries in a food processor or blender with the remaining orange juice, then sieve and add sugar to taste.

6. Remove the foil collars. Decorate each cheesecake with a few strawberries or raspberries and serve with the raspberry purée.

Note: To make foil collars, take strips of foil 20 x 30cm (8 x 12in); fold twice lengthways into bands 5cm (2in) wide. Curl round in circles and secure with a paper clip.

Preparation time: 25 min, plus 5 min soaking   **Cooking time:** 3 min, plus 2 hr chilling   **Cals per serving:** 262   **Serves:** 6

Chocolate and Orange Truffle Torte

large eggs	4
caster sugar	125g (4oz)
plain flour	40g (1½oz)
cocoa powder	2 tbsp
butter	75g (3oz), melted and cooled, plus extra for greasing
Grand Marnier or brandy	4 tbsp

For the chocolate and orange truffle mixture

plain chocolate, with 70% cocoa content	450g (1lb), chopped
double cream	568ml carton
large egg yolks	4
caster sugar	50g (2oz)
large oranges	3, rind of
cocoa	to dust

For the caramelised physalis

physalis	12
caster sugar	125g (4oz)

1. Preheat the oven to 180°C/160°C fan oven/Gas Mark 4. To make the base, using a food processor, whisk the eggs and the caster sugar together on high until the mixture has doubled in volume and is very thick. (If you do not have a food mixer, place the eggs and sugar in a large heatproof bowl and whisk using an electric whisk or large balloon whisk over a pan of simmering water until thick. Remove from the heat and whisk until cool.)

2. Sift the flour with the cocoa powder and lightly fold into the eggs, then add the butter, folding until just combined. Do not over mix as the air will be knocked out of the mixture and the resulting cake will be flat.

3. Grease a 25cm (10in) loose-bottomed cake tin and baseline with non-stick baking parchment. Pour the mixture into the tin and bake for 25 to 30 minutes. Cool for 10 minutes before turning out on to a wire rack. Drizzle with Grand Marnier, then allow to cool. Return, upside down, to the clean tin and press firmly into the base.

4. For the chocolate and orange truffle mixture, melt the chocolate in a heatproof bowl with half the cream, over a pan of simmering water. When melted, stir until smooth, remove from the heat and leave to cool.

5. Whisk the remaining cream to soft peaks. Using an electric whisk, beat the egg yolks and sugar together until pale and fluffy. Beat the egg mixture into the cooled chocolate, then fold the chocolate mixture into the whipped cream with the orange rind. Immediately pour this over the cake in the cake tin and chill for at least 2 to 4 hours or until the truffle mixture is set firm. The torte is best left overnight before serving.

6. To serve, remove the torte from the tin and dust with cocoa powder. Cut into portions and decorate with caramelised physalis.

7. For the physalis, fold back the dried 'petals' of the physalis, exposing the orange fruit and set aside. Place the caster sugar in a small heavy-based pan, add 6 tablespoons of water, dissolve over a gentle heat, bring to the boil and bubble until a rich caramel colour. Dip the base of the pan in cold water, then immediately dip the physalis into the caramel. Place on an oiled baking sheet and leave to set in a dry atmosphere for 3 hours.

Freezing: Complete recipe to end of step 5, wrap and freeze.

To use: Thaw at cool room temperature overnight. Complete recipe.

Preparation time: 30 min, plus 2–4 hr or overnight chilling
Cooking time: 30 min   **Cals per serving:** 560   **Serves:** 12

Caramelised Citrus Tart with Dark Berry Ice

plain flour	250g (9oz), sifted
butter	100g (3½oz), chilled and diced
icing sugar	100g (3½oz), sifted
large egg	1, lightly beaten
large egg white	1, lightly beaten

For the filling
medium eggs	8
caster sugar	200g (7oz)
double cream	568ml carton
lemons and limes	2 lemons and 6 limes, juice of, about 175ml (6fl oz) in total
limes	4, rind grated

For the dark berry ice
caster sugar	75g (3oz)
frozen berry mix	500g (1lb 2oz)

For the candied limes
limes	2, frozen for 2 hours
granulated sugar	125g (4oz)

For the caramelised topping
icing sugar	sifted, to dust
grated lime rind	to decorate

1. To make the pastry, place the flour, butter and icing sugar in a food processor and whiz until the mixture resembles fine breadcrumbs. Add the beaten whole egg and whiz briefly, adding a few drops of chilled water if necessary for the dough to come together into a ball. Wrap the dough in clingfilm and chill for at least 30 minutes. Preheat the oven to 200°C/180°C fan oven/Gas Mark 6.

2. Roll the pastry into a 30cm (12in) diameter circle and use to line a 20cm (8in) diameter, 5cm (2in) deep, loose-bottomed tart tin. Chill for 20 minutes. Line with greaseproof paper and baking beans and bake for 15 minutes. Remove the paper and beans. Return to oven for 10 to 15 minutes, then brush with the beaten egg white; return to the oven for 2 to 3 minutes, then remove and leave to cool. Reduce the oven temperature to 150°C/130°C fan oven/Gas Mark 2.

3. To make the filling, whisk the eggs gently for 30 seconds, then add the sugar and cream and whisk until evenly combined. Finally, whisk in the lemon and lime juice and the lime rind. The mixture will thicken suddenly at this point – don't be alarmed.

4. Pour the mixture into the cooled pastry case. Bake for 1 hour, or until just set. To stop the custard cracking, cover the surface with foil cut to fit exactly. Cool in the tin for 20 minutes, then unmould. Remove the foil when the tart is completely cool.

5. To make the berry ice, dissolve the sugar and 100ml (3½fl oz) water in a small pan over a low heat. In a food processor, process the hot syrup and berries to form a purée. Freeze until needed.

6. To make the candied limes, use a sharp serrated knife to cut the limes into thin slices. Dissolve the sugar in 100ml (3½fl oz) water over a low heat, then add the lime slices. Poach for 15 minutes, then drain, reserving the syrup. Set aside until cool.

7. To caramelise the surface, cut the tart into eight pieces and place on a baking sheet. Chill for 1 hour in the freezer. Cover the pastry edges with foil to stop them burning. Dust each slice liberally with icing sugar and place the baking sheet under a preheated grill for 2 to 4 minutes until the icing sugar caramelises. Serve with the dark berry ice and lime slices, sprinkle with lime rind and drizzle with the reserved lime syrup.

Preparation time: 50 min, plus cooling, chilling and freezing
Cooking time: 1 hr 50 min   **Cals per serving:** 875   **Serves:** 8

Caramelised Citrus Tart
with Dark Berry Ice

Pears in
Malmsey Madeira

Malmsey Madeira or
dark cream sherry 300ml (10fl oz)
caster sugar 225g (8oz)
lemons 2, pared rind of
vanilla pod 1, split
firm underripe pears 6

1. Pour the Malmsey Madeira and 150ml (5fl oz) of water into a pan and add the caster sugar, lemon rind and vanilla pod. Heat gently until the sugar is dissolved and then boil for 3 minutes. Set aside.

2. Decorate the pears by using a canelle knife to etch spirals or stripes into the skin of the fruit, retaining the stalks.

3. Stand the pears in the smallest pan that will take them. Pour the syrup over the top and tuck the lemon rind and vanilla pods among them. Cover, bring to the boil and simmer gently for anything between 30 minutes to 1 hour, depending on the ripeness of the pears, until tender.

4. Lift the pears out of the syrup and set aside. Boil the syrup until reduced by half, then strain over the pears. Serve at room temperature.

Freezing: Complete the recipe, then pack and freeze.

To use: Thaw at cool room temperature overnight.

Preparation time: 15 min   **Cooking time:** 30 min –1 hr, plus 2 hr cooling   **Cals per serving:** 290   **Serves:** 6

Pear Tarte Tatin

1. Put the sugar and butter in a pan and gently heat until the sugar dissolves (do not stir as the sugar may crystallise). Increase the heat and bubble until the mixture is a deep caramel colour, then pour into a greased 20cm (8in) diameter round cake tin.

2. Add the cinnamon pieces to the tin, then arrange the pears over the caramel. Scrape out the seeds from the vanilla pod and spread over the pears. Allow the caramel to cool until it sets.

3. Preheat the oven to 200°C/180°C fan oven/Gas Mark 6. Cover the pears with a 23cm (9in) circle of pastry, tucking the edges inside the tin. Make six slashes in the pastry to let the steam out.

4. Cook for 30 to 35 minutes or until golden. Leave the tart to stand for 10 minutes before carefully inverting it on to a deep plate before serving.

Preparation time: 15 min, plus cooling and 10 min standing
Cooking time: 45 min   **Cals per serving:** 427   **Serves:** 4

caster sugar 100g (3½oz)
butter 50g (2oz)
cinnamon stick 1, broken in half
ripe pears 2, peeled, quartered and cored
vanilla pod ½, split lengthways
ready-rolled puff pastry 200g (7oz)

Plum Tarte Tatin

plain flour 175g (6oz), sifted, plus extra to dust
butter 200g (7oz), chilled and cubed
caster sugar 150g (5oz)
plums 700g (1½lb), halved and stoned

1. To make the pastry, put the flour in a food processor with 125g (4oz) of the butter and 25g (1oz) of the caster sugar. Pulse until the mixture resembles fine breadcrumbs, then add 2 to 3 tablespoons of cold water and pulse until it begins to form a ball. Wrap and chill for 30 minutes.

2. Melt the remaining butter and sugar in a flameproof, heavy-based frying pan. Cook, stirring, for 2 to 3 minutes until the sugar begins to turn light brown. Add the plums and cook for 5 minutes or the juices begin to run and the plums soften. During this time stir the plum juices into the sugar mixture. Increase the heat and bubble until the juices are syrupy. Lift the plums out of the pan into a greased 23cm (9in) diameter, shallow oven-proof dish or cake tin, cut-side up, and pour the juice over. Allow to cool.

3. Preheat the oven to 220°C/200°C fan oven/Gas Mark 7. On a lightly floured work surface, roll the pastry into a circle slightly larger than the dish and about 5mm (¼in) thick. Lay the pastry over the plums, tuck the edges down into the dish and make a few slits through the pastry with a knife to let the steam out. Chill for 20 minutes.

4. Bake for 20 minutes or until the pastry is golden. Leave to stand for 5 minutes before carefully inverting on to a plate before serving.

Preparation time: 30 min, plus 50 min chilling and 5 min standing
Cooking time: 30 min   **Cals per serving:** 485   **Serves:** 6

Apple Bananas with Rum Mascarpone

1. Spoon the mascarpone into a bowl and stir in the sugar and rum. Cover and set aside in a cool place.

2. Barbecue the unpeeled bananas over medium hot coals, or grill for 8 to 10 minutes, turning frequently until tender and blackened.

3. Split the bananas open, sprinkle a little chocolate inside each and top with the mascarpone. Sprinkle over the remaining chocolate before serving.

Preparation time: 10 min   **Cooking time:** 8–10 min
Cals per serving: 360   **Serves:** 6

mascarpone 250g pot, chilled
light muscovado sugar 2–3 tsp
dark rum 2–3 tbsp
apple bananas 12
dark chocolate 75g (3oz), chopped

Pear Galettes with Chocolate Sauce

**ready-to-bake pain
chocolat dough with
chocolate pieces** 1 tube
plain flour to dust
firm ripe pears 2, cored and cut into
thick slices
ground cinnamon
dark soft brown sugar 6 tsp
semi-skimmed milk 4 tbsp
cinnamon and icing sugar to dust

1. Place a baking sheet in the oven at 200°C/180°C fan oven/Gas Mark 6 to heat. Unroll the dough on to a lightly floured work surface; set aside the chocolate pieces. Using a cup or saucer, cut out six circles, about 10cm (4in) in diameter, and place on a second baking sheet.

2. Arrange the pears on top of the dough and sprinkle each one with a little cinnamon and 1 teaspoon of sugar.

3. Place the second baking sheet in the oven on top of the hot baking sheet and cook for 6 to 8 minutes or until the galettes are golden brown.

4. Meanwhile, to make the chocolate sauce, bring the milk to the boil, then whisk in the reserved chocolate pieces. Bubble for about 3 minutes, or until the sauce is syrupy. Dust the galettes with a little cinnamon and icing sugar. Serve with the warm chocolate sauce.

Note: If you cannot find the ready-made dough, use 350g (12oz) puff pastry and 40g (1½oz) plain chocolate, broken into small pieces. Roll out the pastry and complete the recipe, cooking for 20 minutes.

Preparation time: 15 min   **Cooking time:** 10 min
Cals per serving: 220   **Makes:** 6

Roast Apples with Butterscotch Sauce

1. Preheat the oven to 220°C/200°C fan oven/Gas Mark 7. Soak the sultanas in the brandy and set aside for 10 minutes, then stuff each apple with equal amounts of sultanas.

2. Place the apples in a roasting tin, sprinkle over the light muscovado sugar and apple juice. Cook for 15 to 20 minutes, or until soft.

3. Meanwhile, make the sauce. Melt the butter, light muscovado sugar, golden syrup and treacle in a heavy-based pan, stirring continuously. When the sugar has dissolved and the mixture is bubbling, stir in the brandy and cream. Bring back to the boil and set aside.

4. Remove the apples from the oven. Serve with the sauce, hazelnuts and a dollop of ricotta cheese.

Preparation time: 5 min, plus 10 min soaking
Cooking time: 15–20 min   **Cals per serving:** 822   **Serves:** 6

sultanas 125g (4oz)
brandy 2 tbsp
large Bramley apples 6, whole, but cored
light muscovado sugar 4 tbsp
apple juice 2 tbsp

For the butterscotch sauce
butter 125g (4oz)
soft brown sugar 125g (4oz)
golden syrup 2 tbsp
black treacle 2 tbsp
brandy 4 tbsp
double cream 284ml carton
hazelnuts 125g (4oz), chopped
and toasted
ricotta cheese to serve

Pear Galettes with
Chocolate Sauce

Foil-baked Figs with Honey and Marsala

large ripe figs 12
melted butter for brushing
cinnamon stick 1, roughly broken
runny Greek honey 6 tbsp
marsala 6 tbsp
crème fraîche to serve

1. Preheat the oven to 200°C/180°C fan oven/Gas Mark 6. Make a small slit three-quarters of the way through each fig. Take two sheets of foil big enough to hold the figs in one layer. With the shiny side up, lay one piece on top of the other and brush the top piece all over with melted butter.

2. Stand the figs in the middle of the foil and scatter over the pieces of broken cinnamon stick. Bring the sides of the foil together loosely, leaving a gap at the top, and pour in the runny honey and marsala. Finally, scrunch the edges of the foil together so that the figs are loosely enclosed.

3. Put the foil parcel in the oven or on a barbecue, over medium hot coals, and cook for about 10 to 15 minutes, depending on how ripe the figs are, until they are very tender.

4. Just before serving, open up the foil slightly at the top and cook for 2 to 3 minutes more, to allow the juices to reduce and become syrupy.

5. Serve the figs immediately with a large dollop of crème fraîche and the syrupy juice spooned over.

Preparation time: 10 min   **Cooking time:** 13–18 min
Cals per serving: 140   **Serves:** 6

Chilled Chocolate Biscuit Cake

butter 125g (4oz), chopped plus extra for greasing
plain chocolate 150g (5oz), broken into pieces
paneforte 250g (9oz), finely chopped
cantuccini biscuits or RichTea biscuits 100g (3½oz), finely chopped
Amaretto, rum or brandy 2–3 tbsp
ice cream to serve

1. Grease and baseline an 18cm (7in) square cake tin. Place the butter and chocolate in a heatproof bowl over a pan of simmering water. Stir until melted, then set aside.

2. In a large bowl, mix together the paneforte, cantuccini biscuits and liqueur. Add the chocolate mixture and stir to coat the cake and biscuits well. Pour the mixture into the cake tin and chill for at least 2 hours. Cut into wedges and serve with ice cream.

Freezing: Complete the recipe but do not cut. Wrap and freeze.

To use: Thaw at cool room temperature for 4 hours. Cut into wedges to serve.

Preparation time: 15 min, plus 2 hr chilling
Cooking time: 5 min   **Cals per serving:** 464   **Serves:** 6

Winter Cinnamon and Orange Stack

Earl Grey tea leaves 1 tbsp
ready-to-eat dried apricots 200g (7oz), cut into chunks
ready-to-eat dried prunes 150g (5oz), cut into chunks
ready-to-eat dried figs and dates 50g (2oz), cut into chunks
Grand Marnier 3 tbsp
lemon 1, rind and juice of
orange 1, juice of
vanilla pod 1, split
star anise 1

For the cinnamon cream
double cream 142ml carton
mascarpone 250g (9oz)
ground cinnamon ½ tsp
lemon 1, rind grated
orange 1, rind grated
caster sugar 1 tsp

For the filo stack
filo pastry 8 sheets, about 125g (4oz) total weight
butter 50g (2oz), melted
small bananas 2, peeled and sliced
icing sugar 25g (1oz), sifted, to dust
ground cinnamon 1 tsp, to dust

For the honey and orange syrup
runny honey 4 tbsp
oranges 2, rind finely shredded, and juice of
cinnamon stick 1
fresh rosemary sprig 1

1. Pour 450ml (15fl oz) of boiling water over the tea leaves and leave to stand for 5 minutes. Place the dried fruits in a bowl, pour the strained tea over and add the Grand Marnier. Leave to macerate overnight.

2. Place the dried fruits and liquid in a pan with the lemon juice and rind, orange juice, vanilla and star anise. Bring slowly to the boil and simmer for 20 minutes. Remove and discard the lemon rind and star anise and set the fruits aside to cool. Scrape the seeds out of the vanilla pod, cover and reserve for the cinnamon cream.

3. Preheat the oven to 200°C/180°C fan oven/Gas Mark 6. To make the cinnamon cream, whip the cream until it just holds its shape, then whisk in the mascarpone. Mix in the ground cinnamon, lemon and orange rind, caster sugar and reserved vanilla seeds. Cover and chill.

4. Cut the filo into nine 10 x 25cm (4 x 10in) rectangles, then brush each sheet with the melted butter. Create three stacks, each made of three sheets placed one on top of the other. On one of the stacks, score the filo lightly into six equal portions. Bake all the pastry for 8 to 10 minutes. Remove from the oven and leave to cool.

5. To assemble, drain the fruit and mix with the bananas. Place an unmarked filo stack on a large serving dish, cover with half the dried fruit mixture and top with half the cinnamon cream. Place a second unmarked filo stack on top and repeat the layering, finishing with the marked filo stack. Dust with icing sugar and ground cinnamon and serve with the warm honey and orange syrup.

6. To make the orange syrup, place all the ingredients in a pan, then bring to the boil and bubble for 8 to 10 minutes, or until the mixture is syrupy.

Preparation time: 35 min, plus macerating and chilling
Cooking time: 8–40 min   **Cals per serving:** 689   **Serves:** 6

Gooey Chocolate Soufflés

caster sugar	125g (4oz)
cocoa powder	50g (2oz)
egg whites	9, at room temperature
cream of tartar	pinch of
dark chocolate	15g (½oz), finely chopped or grated
dark rum	2 tsp
natural vanilla extract	1 tsp

1. Preheat the oven to 180°C/160°C fan oven/Gas Mark 4. Sift together 100g (3½oz) of the caster sugar with the cocoa. Put to one side.

2. Using an electric whisk, whisk the egg whites with the cream of tartar until foamy. Continue whisking at a high speed, adding the remaining sugar, until forming stiff peaks.

3. With a large metal spoon, fold the sugar and cocoa mixture into the egg whites with the chocolate, rum and vanilla. The mixture should be combined, but still stiff.

4. Divide the mixture between eight 175ml (6fl oz) ovenproof tea or coffee cups or ramekins. Put them in a large roasting tin and add enough boiling water to come halfway up the sides. Bake for 12 to 15 minutes or until puffed and set round the edges, but still soft in the centre.

Preparation time: 10 min **Cooking time:** 15 min
Cals per serving: 204 **Serves:** 8

Prune and Armagnac Soufflés

1. Preheat the oven to 190°C/170°C fan oven/Gas Mark 5. Soak the prunes overnight in the Armagnac. Grease six 150ml (5fl oz) capacity ramekins. Mix the hazelnuts with the brioche crumbs, if using, and dust the ramekins with this mixture.

2. Melt 25g (1oz) butter in a pan, add the flour and mix to a smooth paste. Pour in the milk, stirring continuously, and bring to the boil. Cool the mixture a little, beat in the egg yolks, then stir in the prunes and Armagnac. Whisk the whites to soft peaks, add the caster sugar and whisk until stiff peaks. Fold the egg whites into the mixture with a few drops of vanilla extract.

3. Fill the ramekins with the prune mixture and place in a roasting tin. Add enough hot water to come halfway up the sides of the ramekins.

4. Cook for 20 to 25 minutes, or until firm to the touch in the centre. Dust with icing sugar and serve with vanilla ice cream.

Preparation time: 30 min, plus soaking overnight
Cooking time: 35 min **Cals per serving:** 210 **Serves:** 6

ready-to-eat dried prunes	125g (4oz) stoned and chopped
Armagnac or brandy	3 tbsp
butter	25g (1oz), plus extra for greasing
hazelnuts	1 tbsp, toasted and chopped
brioche crumbs	1 tbsp, optional
plain flour	25g (1oz)
milk	200ml (7fl oz)
large eggs	3, separated
caster sugar	50g (2oz)
vanilla extract	few drops
icing sugar	to dust
vanilla ice cream	to serve

Gooey Chocolate Soufflés

Peaches in Marsala

marsala	100ml (3½fl oz)
caster sugar	75g (3oz)
cinnamon stick	1, broken
vanilla pods	2, split
oranges	2, pared rind and juice of
fresh mint leaves	handful
ripe peaches	8

1. Place all the ingredients, except the peaches, in a large wide pan with 900ml (1½ pints) of water. Bring to the boil and bubble for 5 minutes. Add the peaches (in a single layer), return to the boil, cover and simmer for 5 to 10 minutes, or until the peaches are almost soft (the cooking time will depend on their ripeness). Allow to cool in the syrup.

2. Lift the peaches out with a slotted spoon and place in a glass serving bowl. Strain the liquid, reserving the flavourings. Bring the syrup back to the boil and bubble for 20 minutes or until reduced by half and turned syrupy. Cool and pour over the peaches in the serving bowl and decorate with the reserved flavourings.

Preparation time: 10 min   **Cooking time:** 35–40 min
Cals per serving: 90   **Serves:** 8

Ginger and Mint Fruit Salad

1. Place the wine, sugar and ginger in a pan with 600ml (1 pint) of water and heat gently until the sugar has dissolved. Increase the heat and bring to the boil, then turn down and simmer gently for 20 to 30 minutes. Remove from the heat and leave to cool.

2. Put all the fruit in a large serving bowl and strain the cooled syrup over. Chill for at least 2 hours.

3. To serve, chop the mint leaves and add to the fruit salad. Decorate with extra mint sprigs.

Preparation time: 50 min, plus 30 min cooling and minimum
2 hr chilling   **Cooking time:** 30 min
Cals per serving: 143   **Serves:** 24

ginger wine	70cl bottle
caster sugar	225g (8oz)
fresh root ginger	25g (1oz)
large mangoes	3, peeled and roughly chopped
large papayas	3, peeled and roughly chopped
Charentais melons	2, halved, deseeded, peeled and chopped
seedless red grapes	450g (1lb), stalk removed
fresh mint sprigs	2, plus extra to decorate

Mini Chocolate and Cherry Puddings

unsalted butter	125g (4oz), melted and cooled, plus extra for greasing
Bournville chocolate	125g (4oz), chopped
large eggs	4
golden caster sugar	125g (4oz)
self-raising flour	50g (2oz), sifted
cocoa powder	1 tbsp, sifted
hazelnuts	75g (3oz), chopped and toasted, plus extra to decorate
morello cherries	75g (3oz), drained, plus extra to decorate

For the chocolate sauce

Bournville chocolate	75g (3oz)
Kirsch or brandy	2 tbsp, plus extra for drizzling, optional
double cream	142ml carton, plus extra to serve

1. Preheat the oven to 180°C/160°C fan oven/Gas Mark 4. Grease and baseline eight 150ml (5fl oz) dariole moulds.

2. Put the chocolate in a heatproof bowl and set over a pan of simmering water to melt. Stir until smooth, then leave to cool.

3. Beat the eggs and sugar together until they are pale and light and have doubled in volume.

4. Fold in the flour, cocoa and melted butter, then stir in the melted chocolate, hazelnuts and cherries.

5. Spoon the mixture into the prepared moulds and place on a baking sheet. Bake for 25 to 30 minutes. Cover with foil during cooking, if they brown too quickly.

6. To make the sauce, put the chocolate, Kirsch, and cream in a pan and heat gently until smooth.

7. Turn out the puddings and spoon 1 teaspoon of Kirsch over each, if using. Spoon over the sauce and decorate with the extra cherries and hazelnuts. Serve with a little double cream.

Preparation time: 35 min   **Cooking time:** 25–30 min
Cals per serving: 510   **Serves:** 8

Sweet endings: Burnt Honey and Thyme Ice Cream, Pears in Malmsey Madeira and special cheeses for a spectacular finish

The Sweet Trolley: When choosing **desserts**, try to **complement** the **starter and main course**. If the main meal is **rich and heavy** go for a **lighter, fresher** dessert. Or, if the **first course is light**, you can choose something **more indulgent**. These **Pears in Malmsey Madeira** are **elegantly simple**, poached whole and **bathed in a rich Madeira sauce**. **Homemade ice cream** is also a fine end to a meal. The **Burnt Honey and Thyme Ice Cream** is delicious: **thick and creamy**, with a **hint of thyme and honey**. A cheeseboard is also **a great way to finish** a meal and **a bowl of fresh fruit** with a few **beautiful exotic fruits** can make a **wonderful centrepiece**.

Summer
Pudding

red and blackcurrants	175g (6oz) each, stripped from their stalks
blackberries	275g (10oz)
orange	½, rind finely grated
caster sugar	175g (6oz)
raspberries	350g (12oz)
thin slices two-day-old white bread or brioche	9–10, crusts removed
cassis	2 tbsp, optional
crème fraîche or cream	to serve

1. Put the redcurrants, blackcurrants and blackberries in a large pan with the orange rind and caster sugar and gently mix together. Cover and cook for 4 to 5 minutes, stirring from time to time. Next, add the raspberries and cook for a further 2 to 3 minutes. Remove the fruit mixture from the heat and cool for 30 minutes.

2. Cut a round from one slice of bread to line the base of a 1.1 litre (2 pint) pudding basin. Place four slices of bread equally spaced around the sides of the pudding basin. Use triangles cut out of one or two slices of bread to fill in the gaps between the slices – make sure you cover the sides of the bowl completely.

3. Add the cassis, if using, to the fruit. Reserve about 3 tablespoons of the fruit juice, then spoon half the fruit and juice into the basin. Put another slice of bread on top and add the remaining fruit and juice. Cover the fruit with more slices of bread and fold over any slices that stick out around the edge of the basin.

4. Put the basin on a large plate. Place a small plate on top of the basin and place a heavy weight on top. Chill overnight. To serve, loosen the sides of the pudding with a palette knife and invert on to a serving plate. Use the reserved juices to pour over the pudding, ensuring any white parts of the bread are covered. Serve with crème fraîche or cream.

Preparation time: 20 min, plus 30 min cooling and overnight chilling
Cooking time: 8 min   **Cals per serving:** 224   **Serves:** 8

Summer Pudding

Port and Orange Jellies

ruby port 450ml (15fl oz)
powdered gelatine 6 tsp
golden granulated sugar 125g (4oz)
oranges 8, segmented
double cream for pouring

1. Splash cold water into eight 150ml (5fl oz) fluted moulds and chill the moulds in the freezer.

2. Pour the port into a bowl and sprinkle over the gelatine. Set aside.

3. Put the sugar in a large pan with 600ml (1 pint) of cold water. Heat gently to dissolve, then bring to the boil and bubble for about 15 minutes, until the liquid has reduced by half.

4. Stir in the soaked gelatine until the gelatine is completely dissolved.

5. Put the orange segments in the flutes of the moulds so they stand up and rest against the edge of the mould. Fill each mould halfway up with the liquid. Chill to set, then pour in the rest of the liquid and chill again.

6. To serve, dip each mould briefly in a bowl of hot water to loosen. Upturn on to a plate and pour the cream over.

Preparation time: 25 min, plus chilling and setting
Cooking time: 15 min   **Cals per serving:** 200   **Serves:** 8

Crème Anglaise Trifle

1. Place the milk in a pan with the split vanilla pod and bring slowly to the boil. Remove from the heat, then cover and infuse for 20 minutes.

2. Whisk the egg, yolks and caster sugar together and add the milk. Return to a clean pan and cook gently without boiling, stirring, until the custard thickens. Strain into a bowl and cool for 1 hour, then chill for 3 hours. To prevent a skin forming, sprinkle the surface with caster sugar.

3. Lightly whip the cream until just stiff, then whisk in the chilled custard. Pour 1 tablespoon of Cassis into the bottom of four tall glasses. Place a sponge cake in each, then build up the layers starting with custard, then cherries and Cassis, finishing with the custard. Decorate with cherries, to serve.

Preparation time: 20 min, plus 20 min infusing, 1 hr cooling and 3 hr chilling   **Cooking time:** 6 min   **Cals per serving:** 770   **Serves:** 4

whole milk 450ml (15fl oz)
vanilla pod 1, split
large egg 1
large egg yolks 2
caster sugar 4 tbsp, plus extra for sprinkling
double cream 200ml (7fl oz)
crème de Cassis or sweet sherry 200ml (7fl oz)
trifle sponges, Madeira sponge or madeleines 8
cherries 450g (1lb), stoned, plus extra to decorate

White Chocolate and Red Fruit Trifle

frozen mixed berries 3 x 500g packs
caster sugar 125g (4oz), plus 1 tsp
biscotti or
cantuccini biscuits 250g (9oz)
dessert wine or fruit juice 5 tbsp

For the white chocolate topping
double cream 450ml (15fl oz)
good quality white 200g (7oz),
chocolate such as Lindt broken into pieces
fresh custard 500g carton, remove from fridge 20 min before using
crème fraîche 500ml carton

1. Put the berries in a large pan with the sugar and heat gently for about 5 minutes until the sugar has dissolved and the berries have thawed.

2. Drain the berry mixture through a sieve with a bowl underneath to catch the juices. Return the juices to the pan and bring to the boil; simmer for about 10 minutes, or until reduced to about 150ml (5fl oz). Mix with the berries and leave to cool in the bowl.

3. Lay the biscotti in the bottom of a 3.1 litre (5½ pint) trifle dish and spoon the dessert wine or fruit juice on top, then the cooled berries.

4. Lightly whip the cream, place half in the fridge and leave the remainder at room temperature. Put the chocolate in a bowl over a pan of gently simmering water and stir until melted. Pour into a cold bowl, gradually fold in the custard a little at a time, then fold in the room temperature cream. Doing it in this order stops the chocolate from separating.

5. Cover the fruit evenly with the custard mixture. Beat the crème fraîche until smooth, fold in the reserved chilled whipped cream and extra sugar, then spoon over the custard. Chill for 2 hours. Remove from the fridge 20 minutes before serving.

Preparation time: 45 min, plus 20 min standing and 2 hr chilling
Cooking time: 15 min
Cals per serving: 814 for 8, 612 for 10   **Serves:** 8–10

Iced Pistachio and Orange Parfait

flavourless oil, such as safflower for greasing
shelled, unsalted pistachio nuts 75g (3oz), lightly toasted and chopped
double cream 200ml (7fl oz)
large egg whites 4
icing sugar 75g (3oz), sifted
orange-flavoured liqueur, such as Grand Marnier 2 tbsp
white chocolate 75g (3oz)
pistachio nuts toasted and chopped, to decorate

For the white chocolate caraque
white chocolate 25g (1oz), to serve

1. Lightly oil and baseline six 150ml (5fl oz) ramekins with greaseproof paper. Sprinkle the base lightly with chopped pistachio nuts. Cut six strips of greaseproof paper, each measuring 5 x 25cm (2 x 10in). Lightly oil one side of the paper and sprinkle with a few nuts. Reserve the remaining nuts. With the nut side facing inwards, curl the paper around the insides of the ramekins.

2. Lightly whip the cream. Whisk the egg whites until stiff, then gradually whisk in the icing sugar. Fold in the remaining nuts, liqueur and cream. Do not over-mix. Divide the mixture between the ramekins and freeze for 4 hours, preferably overnight.

3. Melt the chocolate in a heatproof bowl over a pan of simmering water. Cut six more strips of non-stick baking parchment, each measuring 5 x 25cm (2 x 10in). Spread the chocolate thinly over each strip. Leave to firm slightly. Unmould the parfaits and remove the lining papers. Lift the chocolate-covered strips and carefully wrap them around the parfaits, chocolate side inside. Freeze until set (about 30 minutes).

4. To make the caraque, melt the white chocolate in a heatproof bowl over a pan of simmering water. Pour it out on to a marble slab or work surface, spread it out evenly and leave to set until no longer sticky to the touch. Holding a large knife at a slight angle to the surface, push the blade across the chocolate, towards you, to shave off long, thin curls. Adjust the angle of the blade to obtain the best curls. Store in an airtight container for up to one week.

5. Peel away the parchment from the parfaits. Decorate with pistachio nuts and white chocolate caraque and serve.

Freezing: Complete the recipe to the end of step 3. Pack the parfaits and freeze for up to four weeks. Complete step 4 up to one day in advance.

Preparation time: 1 hr, plus 4–6 hr or overnight freezing
Cals per serving: 364   **Serves:** 6

Iced Pistachio and
Orange Parfait

Iced Plum
Creams

dark-skinned plums 450g (1lb)
sloe gin 200ml (7fl oz)
caster sugar 75g (3oz)
large eggs 2
mascarpone 150ml tub
light sunflower oil for greasing
redcurrants to decorate
Cranberry Biscuits to serve (see below)

1. Wash the plums and split in half. Put them in a pan with the sloe gin and 40g (1½oz) of the caster sugar; cover with a tight-fitting lid and bring to the boil. Simmer for about 20 minutes until the plums are tender. Cool and drain, reserving the juice. Remove the stones from the cooled plums and whiz the plums in a food processor until smooth; put to one side.

2. Separate the eggs and reserve one white. Whisk the yolks with the remaining caster sugar and the reserved plum juice for 2 to 3 minutes until pale and lightly thickened. Whisk the plum purée and mascarpone together, then carefully fold in the egg yolk mixture. Whisk the reserved egg white until stiff and carefully fold into the mixture.

3. Divide the plum mixture between six or eight 150ml (5fl oz), lightly oiled dariole moulds or ramekins. Cover and place in the freezer for 4 hours to set.

4. To serve, invert the creams on to plates and unmould. (You can eat the creams straight from the freezer, but it's better to leave them for 5 to 10 minutes in the fridge before serving.) Decorate with redcurrants and serve with Cranberry Biscuits.

Preparation time: 40 min, plus 4 hr freezing   **Cooking time:** 20 min
Cals per serving: 231 for 6, 173 for 8   **Serves:** 6–8

Cranberry
Biscuits

1. Preheat the oven to 200°C/180°C fan oven/Gas Mark 6. Whiz the butter and caster sugar in a food processor. Add the cranberries, flour and ground rice and pulse until the mixture comes together.

2. Turn on to a floured work surface and shape into an oblong, about 13x 7.5 x 2cm (5 x 3 x ¾in). Wrap and chill for 30 minutes, then slice into about 24 biscuits, about 3mm (⅛in) thick. Place on a non-stick baking sheet and bake for 8 to 10 minutes or until golden. Leave to cool before removing the biscuits from the sheet.

Preparation time: 5 min   **Cooking time:** 8–10 min
Cals per serving: 76   **Makes:** 24 biscuits

butter 125g (4oz), chilled
caster sugar 50g (2oz)
dried cranberries 25g (1oz)
plain flour 125g (4oz)
ground rice 75g (3oz)

Burnt Honey and Thyme Ice Cream

milk	600ml (1pt)
double cream	568ml carton
fresh thyme sprigs	8
dark runny honey	150ml (5fl oz), plus
such as Mexican	extra for drizzling
large egg yolks	6
Orange Tuile Biscuits	to serve (see below)

1. Place the milk, double cream and thyme sprigs in a pan and bring to the boil. Remove from the heat and set aside for 20 to 30 minutes to infuse. Strain the milk and discard the thyme sprigs.

2. Place the honey in a small pan and heat gently. Bring to the boil and bubble for 4 to 5 minutes, or until it has a slightly burnt caramel smell. Remove from the heat and immediately place the pan in a bowl of cold water to stop the cooking process. Set aside.

3. Place the egg yolks in a bowl and whisk in the infused milk slowly until thoroughly combined. Return the mixture to the clean pan and cook over a gentle heat, stirring until thickened, but do not boil. Strain it into the honey and stir until well combined. (It may be necessary to warm the mixture gently.) Allow to cool, then cover and chill for 30 minutes.

4. Place the chilled mixture in an ice cream machine and freeze according to the manufacturer's instructions. If you do not have an ice cream machine, place the custard mixture in a clean enamelled or stainless steel roasting tin and freeze for about 1 hour. Stir the ice cream as it begins to set around the edges and return to the freezer. Repeat until the ice cream is completely frozen (this will take 4 to 6 hours), then transfer to a freezerproof container and return to the freezer. Serve the ice cream drizzled with honey and accompanied by the Orange Tuile Biscuits.

Preparation time: 5 min, plus 30 min infusing, 30 min chilling and 6 hr freezing   **Cooking time:** 20 min   **Cals per serving:** 630   **Serves:** 6

Orange Tuile Biscuits

1. Preheat the oven to 200°C/180°C fan oven/Gas Mark 6. In a large bowl, lightly whisk the egg whites with the icing sugar. Lightly stir in the flour, orange rind and butter. Cover and chill for 30 minutes.

2. Line two baking sheets with non-stick baking parchment. Place 3 teaspoonfuls of the mixture in mounds, spaced well apart, on the baking sheet and spread them out to 9cm (3½in) circles. Bake for 12 minutes until just brown around the edges.

3. While still warm, quickly shape each biscuit over a rolling pin, to curl. Repeat with the remaining mixture.

Preparation time: 20 min, plus 30 min chilling
Cooking time: 6–12 min   **Cals per serving:** 55   **Makes:** about 24

large egg whites	3
icing sugar	100g (3½oz), sifted
plain flour	100g (3½oz), sifted
orange	1, rind grated
unsalted butter	75g (3oz), melted

Turkish Delight
Crème Brûlée

double cream 750ml (1¼pt)
vanilla pod 1, split, seeds removed and reserved
Turkish delight 6 pieces
large egg yolks 8
caster sugar 75g (3oz)
rosewater 2 tbsp
demerara sugar for sprinkling

1. Put the cream in a heavy-based pan with the vanilla pod seeds. Slowly bring to the boil and set aside for 20 minutes. Cut the pieces of Turkish delight into small pieces and place into the base of six 150ml (5fl oz) capacity earthenware dishes.

2. In a separate bowl, beat together the egg yolks, caster sugar and the rosewater. Pour the vanilla-flavoured cream on to the egg mixture and mix together until thoroughly combined.

3. Return the cream and egg mixture to the pan and cook, stirring constantly, over a low to moderate heat until bubbles start to appear on the surface, but do not allow the custard to boil. Pour immediately into the earthenware dishes. Set aside to cool, then chill overnight. Do not cover the dishes as you want a skin to form on the top of the custard.

4. Liberally sprinkle the custards with demerara sugar. Preheat the grill and, when hot, put the dishes underneath until the sugar has melted and is a deeper brown. Allow the dissolved sugar to set hard for 10 minutes before serving.

Preparation time: 15 min, plus 20 min infusion and overnight chilling
Cooking time: 10 min   **Cals per serving:** 818   **Serves:** 6

Turkish Delight
Crème Brûlée

Chocolate Terrine with Vanilla Bean Sauce

plain chocolate with 70% cocoa solids	350g (12oz), broken into small pieces
cocoa powder	40g (1½oz), plus extra to dust
large eggs	6, beaten
soft light brown sugar	125g (4oz)
double cream	284ml carton
brandy	5 tbsp, optional
oil	for greasing

For the vanilla bean sauce

single cream	568ml carton
vanilla pod	1, split, seeds removed and reserved
large egg yolks	4
caster sugar	75g (3oz)
cornflour	½ tsp

1. Put the chocolate and cocoa in a heatproof bowl over a pan of just simmering water and stir occasionally until melted and glossy. Cool.

2. Preheat the oven to 150°C/130°C fan oven/Gas Mark 2. Whisk together the eggs and sugar, then whisk the cream until soft peaks form. Gradually combine the egg mixture, chocolate and cream. Add brandy, if using. Grease and baseline a 900g (2lb) loaf tin and pour in the mixture; tap the base on a work surface to level the mixture.

3. Stand the tin in a roasting tray, filled with enough hot water to come halfway up the sides of the tin, then cover with non-stick baking parchment. Bake for 1¼ hours or until just set in the centre. Leave in the tin for 30 minutes, lift out and chill overnight.

4. To make the sauce, gently heat the cream and vanilla seeds in a heavy-based pan until the cream just comes to the boil. Put to one side to cool and infuse for 15 minutes.

5. Whisk together the egg yolks, sugar and cornflour, add a little of the cooled cream and whisk until smooth. Add the remaining cream and stir well. Pour back into the cleaned pan and stir over a moderate heat for 5 minutes, or until thickened (it should coat the back of a spoon). Strain, cool, cover and chill.

6. Serve the terrine in slices with the vanilla bean sauce poured around and dusted with cocoa powder.

Preparation time: 45 min, plus 1 hr cooling and overnight chilling
Cooking time: 1 hr 45 min   **Cals per serving:** 777   **Serves:** 12

Mango and Lime
Mousse

very ripe mangoes 2, stones removed
lime juice 3 tbsp
gelatine 10g sachet
large eggs 3
large egg yolks 2
caster sugar 50g (2oz)
double cream 100ml (3½fl oz), lightly whipped, plus extra to decorate
limes 2, rind finely grated, plus extra to decorate

1. Purée the mango flesh to give about 300ml (10fl oz). Put the lime juice into a small heatproof bowl, then sprinkle over the gelatine and leave to soak for 1 minute.

2. In a large bowl, whisk together the eggs and the egg yolks with the caster sugar for 4 to 5 minutes until thick and mousse-like. Gently fold the mango purée, whipped cream and lime rind into the mousse mixture.

3. Dissolve the gelatine and lime juice mixture in the bowl over a pan of boiling water, then carefully and lightly fold into the mango mixture, making sure everything is evenly combined. Pour the mousse into glasses, put in the freezer for 20 minutes, then transfer to the fridge for at least 1 hour. Decorate with whipped cream and curls of lime rind.

Preparation time: 15 min, plus 1 hr 20 min freezing and chilling
Cals per serving: 175   **Serves:** 6

Queen of Puddings

milk	568ml carton
butter	25g (1oz)
large lemon	1, rind grated
large eggs	3, separated
caster sugar	175g (6oz)
fine fresh breadcrumbs	100g (3½oz)
lemon curd	4 tbsp

1. Put the milk, butter and lemon rind in a pan and heat gently until the butter melts. Set to one side until lukewarm. Mix the egg yolks and 25g (1oz) of the sugar together in a bowl until thoroughly combined, then blend in the warm milk. Add the breadcrumbs and pour into a 1.1 litre (2 pint) ovenproof dish. Leave to stand for 20 minutes.

2. Preheat the oven to 180°C/160°C fan oven/Gas Mark 4. Put the dish in a roasting tin, filled with enough hot water to come halfway up the sides of the dish. Cook for 25 to 30 minutes or until just set to the centre. Allow to cool for about 20 minutes, then spread the lemon curd over the top.

3. Whisk the egg whites to stiff peaks, then whisk in 3 tablespoons of caster sugar, a spoonful at a time, until stiff and glossy. Carefully fold in the rest of the sugar with a large spoon. Spoon the egg whites on top of the lemon curd and bake at 170°C/150°C fan oven/Gas Mark 3 for 10 to 15 minutes or until golden and crisp. Serve warm or at room temperature.

Preparation time: 10 min, plus 20 min standing and 20 min cooling
Cooking time: 50 min   **Cals per serving:** 316   **Serves:** 6

Apricot and Cardamom Crumble

1. Preheat the oven to 190°C/170°C fan oven/Gas Mark 5. Mix the apricots with the caster sugar and place in a 1.3 litre (2¼ pint) capacity ovenproof dish or divide between six individual dishes.

2. Place the cardamom seeds, flour, oats and light brown sugar in a large bowl, then rub in the butter until well combined. Mix in the hazelnuts.

3. Spoon the crumble mixture evenly over the fruit and bake for 25 to 30 minutes or until the topping is golden brown. Serve warm with a little thick Greek yogurt, if you like.

Preparation time: 15 min   **Cooking time:** 25 min
Cals per serving: 230   **Serves:** 4

fresh apricots	700g (1½lb), stoned and quartered
caster sugar	2–3 tbsp
green cardamom pods	3–4, split, seeds removed and crushed
plain flour	50g (2oz)
jumbo rolled oats	50g (2oz)
light brown sugar	50g (2oz)
butter	50g (2oz), cubed
hazelnuts	25g (1oz), browned and roughly chopped
thick Greek yogurt	to serve, optional

Queen of Puddings

Baked Honey and Orange Custard

orange	1, rind grated
milk	450ml (15fl oz)
double cream	142ml carton
runny honey	75g (3oz)
large eggs	2
large egg yolks	4
caster sugar	25g (1oz)
slivers of orange rind	to decorate
Kirsch Cherry Compote	to serve
	(see below)

1. Place the orange rind, milk and cream in a pan, then bring to the boil. Set aside for 30 minutes to infuse.

2. Place a 1.7 litre (3 pint) soufflé dish or six 150ml (5fl oz) coffee cups or ramekins in the oven at 150°C/130°C fan oven/Gas Mark 2 to warm. Bring the honey to the boil in a small heavy-based pan. Bubble for 2 to 3 minutes, until it begins to caramelise. Pour the caramel into the warmed dish or ramekins and rotate it to coat the base evenly. Leave to cool and harden.

3. Place the eggs, yolks and sugar in a bowl and beat together until smooth. Add the infused milk mixture and stir until well combined, then strain into the dish(es).

4. Place the dish, coffee cups or ramekins in a roasting tin, filled with enough hot water to come halfway up the side(s) of the dish(es). Bake at 150°C/130° fan oven/Gas Mark 2 for 1 hour 10 minutes for the soufflé dish, 45 to 50 minutes for the coffee cups or ramekins or until just set in the middle. Cool and chill for at least 6 hours or overnight. Decorate with orange rind; serve with Kirsch Cherry Compote.

Preparation time: 10 min, plus 30 min infusing and 15 min cooling
Cooking time: 50 min or 1 hr 10 min, plus at least 6 hr chilling
Cals per serving: 290   **Serves:** 8

Kirsch Cherry Compote

1. Place the stoned cherries in a pan with the caster sugar and 1 tablespoon of water. Slowly bring to the boil, then cover and simmer for 5 to 10 minutes or until tender.

2. Drain, reserving the syrup. Process the syrup and half the cherries in a food processor or blender until smooth (sieve if necessary). Stir in the Kirsch and the reserved cherries. Chill for 2 to 3 hours before serving.

Preparation time: 30 min, plus 2–3 hr chilling
Cooking time: 10 min   **Cals per serving:** 155   **Serves:** 6

stoned cherries	900g (2lb)
caster sugar	125g (4oz)
Kirsch	1 tbsp

Rhubarb and Apple Cobbler

1. Preheat the oven to 220°C/200°C fan oven/Gas Mark 7. Mix the rhubarb and apple with the caster sugar, flour, cornflour, ground ginger, butter and orange rind. Put into a 25cm (10in) shallow ovenproof dish and set aside.

2. To make the cobbler dough, sift the flour, baking powder and salt into a bowl. Rub in the butter until the mixture resembles fine breadcrumbs. Stir in the caster sugar and buttermilk (or 120ml/4fl oz milk with a generous squeeze of lemon juice). Spoon the dough on to the rhubarb in clumps, making sure it doesn't completely cover the fruit. Mix the double cream and demerara sugar together and drizzle over the top.

3. Put the dish on a baking tray and bake for 10 minutes, then lower the heat to 190°C/170°C fan oven/Gas Mark 5 and bake for a further 20 to 30 minutes or until puffed and brown and the fruit is just soft. Remove from the oven and leave to stand for 10 minutes. Serve warm with cream poured over the top.

Preparation time: 25 min, plus 10 min standing
Cooking time: 30–40 min **Cals per serving:** 449 **Serves:** 6

rhubarb	900g (2lb), cut into 2.5cm (1in) lengths
cooking apples	450g (1lb), peeled, cored and sliced
caster sugar	6 tbsp
plain flour	4 tbsp
cornflour	1 tbsp
ground ginger	½ tsp
butter	1 knob
orange	1, rind grated
cream	to serve

For the cobbler dough

plain flour	150g (5oz)
baking powder	2 tsp
salt	pinch of
butter	50g (2oz), softened
caster sugar	3 tbsp
buttermilk	120ml (4fl oz)
double cream	2 tbsp
demerara sugar	1 tsp

liquid
refreshments

Gin Fizz

gin 4 tbsp
lemon juice 2 tbsp
sugar syrup ½ tsp (see page 285)
ice cubes and soda water to serve

1. Shake the gin, lemon juice and sugar syrup vigorously in a cocktail shaker, with four ice cubes for about 1 minute.

2. Strain into a Collins glass or other tall glass and top up with soda water. Drink while still fizzing.

Variations
Silver Fizz: add 1 egg white to the basic recipe.
Mint Fizz: add 1 tbsp crème de menthe, to the basic recipe.

Whiskey Sour

1. Shake all the ingredients together in a shaker with plenty of ice and strain into a whisky glass over ice. Decorate with a cherry.

bourbon or rye whiskey 4 tbsp
lemon juice 2 tbsp
sugar syrup 1 tbsp
(see page 285)
ice cubes
cherry to decorate

Singapore Sling

ice cubes
gin 4 tbsp
cherry brandy 2 tbsp
lemon juice 2 tbsp
orange juice 2 tbsp
triple sec (eg Cointreau) 1 tbsp
Angostura bitters 1–2 dashes
soda water
slices of orange, cherries
and strawberries to decorate

1. Place two ice cubes in a highball glass. Add the gin, cherry brandy, lemon and orange juices, triple sec and Angostura bitters and stir well.

2. Top up with soda water. Place the fruit of your choice on a cocktail stick to decorate the glass.

Manhattan

1. Sir all the ingredients together with some ice cubes and strain into a cocktail glass. Decorate with a maraschino cherry, to serve.

rye 6 tbsp
Italian sweet vermouth 2 tbsp
Angostura bitters 2–3 dashes
ice cubes
maraschino cherry 1, to decorate

Classic Champagne Cocktail

1. Rub the sugar lump over the skin of the orange and place the sugar in a champagne flute. Drop the bitters on to the sugar lump, then add the Cognac and triple sec.

2. Leave for as long as possible – at least 45 minutes – for the flavours to blend. To serve, pour in the champagne and serve at once.

sugar	1 lump
orange	1
Angostura bitters	2–3 dashes
Cognac	½ tsp
triple sec (eg Cointreau)	½ tsp
or apricot brandy	
champagne	100ml (3½fl oz), chilled

Dry Martini

gin	4 tbsp
dry vermouth	1 tbsp
ice cubes	
green olive or lemon peel	thin strip, to decorate

1. Pour the gin and vermouth over ice in a mixing glass, stir well, then strain into a chilled cocktail glass.

2. Either decorate with a green olive or squeeze and twist the lemon peel over the glass, then drop it in.

Bellini

1. Purée the peach in a food processor or blender, then stir the champagne and peach together gently in a jug until blended. Pour into a champagne flute or other tall elegant glass. Sprinkle with sugar to serve.

peach	1
champagne	100ml (3½fl oz), chilled
sugar	for sprinkling

Long Island Iced Tea

gin 1 tbsp
vodka 1 tbsp
white rum 1 tbsp
tequila 1 tbsp
triple sec (eg Cointreau) 1 tbsp
lemon juice 2 tbsp
sugar syrup ½ tsp (see page 285)
ice cubes
cola to serve
lemon slices and
fresh mint sprigs to decorate

1. Stir the first seven ingredients together in a jug with ice, then strain into a long glass almost filled to the top with ice cubes.

2. Top up with cola and decorate with lemon slices and mint sprigs.

Bloody Mary

1. Shake all the ingredients together in a cocktail shaker with ice and strain into a tumbler or balloon wine glass. Decorate with a slice of lemon or other decoration of your choice.

Variations
Bloody Maria: use tequila, instead of vodka.
Virgin Mary: omit the vodka.

vodka 2 tbsp
tomato juice 120ml (4fl oz)
Worcestershire sauce 2 dashes
lemon juice a good squeeze of
Tabasco sauce a dash
salt and black pepper
ice cubes
lemon slice
or celery stick 1, to decorate

Classic Daiquiri

white rum 3 tbsp
fresh lime juice 1 tbsp
sugar syrup ½ tsp (see page 285)
strip of lemon or lime peel to decorate

1. Shake all the ingredients together in a cocktail shaker or blend in a blender, with ice and strain into a chilled cocktail glass. Decorate with a strip of lemon or lime peel.

Margarita

1. Dip the rim of a cocktail glass in lemon juice and then in salt, then place to chill in the fridge.

2. Shake all the ingredients together thoroughly with ice, then strain into the salt-rimmed cocktail glass.

lemon juice good squeeze of
salt to decorate
tequila 3 tbsp
fresh lime juice 2 tbsp
triple sec (eg Cointreau) 1 tbsp
ice cubes

Long Island
Iced Tea

Fruit Lassi

natural yogurt 575g (1lb 5oz)
fresh or frozen raspberries 200g (7oz)
honey 2 tbsp
fresh mint leaves 10–12
ice cubes crushed

1. Put all the ingredients in a blender. Whiz together, then, when smooth, pour into four tall glasses and serve immediately.

Preparation time: 5 min   **Cals per serving:** 125   **Serves:** 4

Melon Fizz

1. Place the melon flesh in a food processor and whiz until puréed. Add the orange cordial and whiz again. Pour into four tall glasses and top up with the mineral water.

Variation:

Use water melon and blackcurrant cordial.

Preparation time: 10 min   **Cals per serving:** 57   **Serves:** 4

honeydew or galia melon 350g (12oz), peeled and roughly chopped
orange cordial 100ml (3½fl oz)
sparkling mineral water 750ml (1¼pt), chilled

Raspberry and Apple Sparkle

raspberry and apple juice 525ml (18fl oz)
fresh or frozen raspberries 50g (2oz)
dessert apple 1, cored and sliced
ice cubes
tonic water 525ml (18fl oz)

1. Place the raspberry and apple juice in a jug and add the fruit and plenty of ice. Top up with tonic water to taste.

Variation: Also try apple and mango or orange and raspberry crush instead of the raspberry and apple juice.

Preparation time: 5 min   **Cals per serving:** 70   **Serves:** 5

Lime and Passion Fruit Cooler

lime	1, rind grated and juice of
passion fruit	4
natural yogurt	200g (7oz)
sparkling lemonade	600ml (1pt)

1. Place the lime rind and juice in a jug. Cut the passion fruit in half and scoop out the seeds and flesh. Strain through a nylon sieve or piece of muslin into the jug, pushing out as much juice as possible.

2. Using a fork whisk in the yogurt. Divide between four glasses and top up with lemonade. Stir and serve.

Preparation time: 5 min   **Cals per serving:** 80   **Serves:** 4

Homemade Lemonade

1. Place the lemon peel in a pan with 900ml (1½ pints) of water. Heat gently to simmering point and simmer for 5 minutes. Remove from the heat and stir in the sugar until dissolved. Squeeze the juice from the lemons and stir into the pan. Cool, then strain through a piece of muslin or a nylon sieve and chill until needed. Serve over ice with lemon slices.

unwaxed lemons	3, scrubbed and peeled, excluding the white pith
caster sugar	175g (6oz)
ice cubes and	
lemon slices	to serve

Variation:
Lemon barley water: Add 65g (2½oz) pearl barley in step 1. Cover and simmer for 25 minutes. Complete as above, straining through muslin.

Preparation time: 5 min, plus chilling   **Cooking time:** 5 min
Cals per serving: 120   **Serves:** 6

Iced Tea

Ceylon or Darjeeling tea bags	4
boiling water	900ml (1½pt)
granulated sugar	4 tsp
lemon, lime or orange juice	1 tbsp
ice	
lemon, lime or orange slices	to serve, optional

1. Place the tea bags in a pot and add the boiling water, leave to infuse for 5 minutes. Pour into a heatproof jug and discard the tea bags.

2. Add the sugar and stir until it dissolves, then stir in the lemon juice. Cool, cover and chill for at least 3 hours. Serve with ice and a slice of lemon, lime or orange, if liked.

Note: Use the quantities of tea, sugar and fruit juice as a guide and adjust to your own taste.

Preparation time: 10 min, plus chilling
Cals per serving: 25   **Serves:** 4

Tropical Yog Nog

banana 1, sliced
ripe mango 1, peeled, stoned and roughly chopped
Greek style yogurt 275g (10oz)
pineapple juice 300ml (10fl oz)

1. Place the banana and mango in a food processor and whiz to form a smooth purée. Add the yogurt and pineapple juice and whiz again to blend well. Pour into four chilled glasses and serve immediately.

Preparation time: 10 min   **Cals per serving:** 155   **Serves:** 4

The Best Fruit
Milk Shakes

1. Place the fruit and jam in a food processor or blender and whiz until a smooth purée. (Use strawberry jam for the soft summer fruits or apricot with the apricot and banana.)

2. Add two scoops of ice cream. With the motor running, gradually add the milk and whiz until frothy. Pour into two glasses. Add another scoop of ice cream to each glass and serve immediately.

Preparation time: 10 min   **Cals per serving:** 300–500   **Serves:** 2

raspberries, blackberries, strawberries, blueberries or other mixture of soft summer fruits 125g (4oz)
or apricots 125g (4oz) canned (drained weight)
large ripe banana 1
strawberry or apricot jam 2 tbsp
quality vanilla ice-cream 4 scoops
ice cold milk 300ml (10fl oz)

Ginger Apple
Punch

apple juice 525ml (18fl oz)
dessert apple 1, cored and sliced
ice
dry ginger ale 525ml (18fl oz)

1. Place the apple juice and apple slices in a jug or punch bowl. Add plenty of ice and top up with ginger ale.

Preparation time: 5 min   **Cals per serving:** 90   **Serves:** 5

Ginger Apple
Punch

Party time: Dry Martini, James Bond style, summery Bellini, sweet and sour Margarita and hot and spicy – the ultimate Bloody Mary

The Cocktail Hour: Drinks are an **important part of any party**, so to make sure your drinks party **goes with a swing** serve a few **classic cocktails,** such as the **sophisticated Dry Martini**, with a **twist of lemon** and an **olive**; or the more **summery cocktail – Bellini**, made with **puréed peaches** and **champagne**. Everyone loves a **Margarita** – **deliciously** refreshing; and there is nothing like a **Bloody Mary** to **whet the appetite**, served **hot and spicy** in a **big tumbler** over ice. Don't forget the **mixers and shakers**, plenty of ice and a few **clever garnishes** to decorate the cocktails. Glasses can be **frosted and chilled** in the freezer for a few hours before the party.

The Ultimate Hot Chocolate

plain chocolate, with 125g (4oz)
70% cocoa solids
semi-skimmed or
full fat milk 600ml (1pt)
sugar to taste
whipped cream optional

1. Chop the chocolate into small pieces. Heat the milk in a pan, then add the chocolate, continue to heat, stirring constantly, until the chocolate has melted and blended with the milk.

2. Pour into mugs, sweeten to taste and top with whipped cream, if liked.

Variation:

Add a slug of whisky, rum or brandy, if liked

Preparation time: 5 min   **Cals per serving:** 400   **Serves:** 2

Hot Chocolate and Orange Cup

1. Chop the chocolate into small pieces. Heat the milk in a pan then add the chocolate, continue to heat stirring constantly until the chocolate has melted and blended with the milk.

2. Pour into mugs to serve. Top with whipped cream, if liked.

Preparation time: 5 min   **Cals per serving:** 360   **Serves:** 2

orange flavoured dark
or milk chocolate 75g (3oz)
semi-skimmed or
full fat milk 600ml (1pt)
whipped cream to serve, optional

Warming Ginger Tea Punch

Assam or English
breakfast tea bags 4
boiling water 1.7ltr (3pt)
fresh root ginger 2.5cm (1in) piece, grated
cinnamon stick 1
unwaxed lemon 1, sliced
orange 1, sliced
caster sugar 125g (4oz)
orange and lemon slices to serve, optional

1. Place all the ingredients together in a large heatproof jug, stir and allow to infuse for 5 minutes. Remove the tea bags and strain into glasses. Serve immediately with orange and lemon slices, if using.

Preparation time: 8 min   **Cals per serving:** 50   **Serves:** 8

Mulled Wine

full-bodied red wine	75cl bottle
lemons	2
cloves	6
cinnamon stick	1
grated nutmeg	½ tsp
caster sugar	6 tbsp
brandy	3 tbsp
orange	1, sliced

1. Place the wine in a pan with 300ml (10fl oz) of water. Grate the rind and squeeze the juice from one lemon and add to the pan, with the spices. Slice the remaining lemon.

2. Add the sugar and heat gently, stirring until the sugar dissolves, bring to simmering point, then remove from the heat. Leave to stand for 10 minutes.

3. Strain into a clean pan, through a nylon sieve or piece of muslin, or remove the whole spices with a slotted spoon. Stir in the brandy and add the orange and lemon slices. Heat again, then serve in heatproof glasses.

Preparation time: 15 min   **Cals per serving:** 110   **Serves:** 8

Tea and Rum Toddy

1. Place the tea bags in a pot and add the boiling water, leave to infuse for 5 minutes.

2. Place a teaspoon of sugar and tablespoon of rum each into two heatproof glasses or mugs. Pour the tea in, stirring until the sugar dissolves. Serve immediately with a slice of lemon.

Preparation time: 7 min   **Cals per serving:** 50   **Serves:** 2

Assam or English breakfast tea bags	2
boiling water	525ml (18floz)
caster sugar	2 tsp
rum	2 tbsp
lemon slices	2

Hot Fruit Punch

light muscovado sugar	2 tbsp
cloves	8
cinnamon stick	1
grated nutmeg	¼ tsp
summer fruit juice cordial	6 tbsp
orange juice	300ml (10fl oz)
apple juice	150ml (5fl oz)
orange	1, sliced
lemon	1, sliced
apple	1, sliced

1. Place the sugar and spices in a large pan and add 1.1 litre (2 pints) of water, bring gently to the boil and boil for 1 minute then remove from the heat and allow to stand for 10 minutes.

2. Place the remaining ingredients into a large jug or punch bowl. Strain the spice syrup into the jug and discard the spices. Serve immediately.

Preparation time: 15 min   **Cals per serving:** 60   **Serves:** 8

Irish Coffee

strong hot coffee 400ml (14fl oz)
Irish whiskey 2–3 tbsp
granulated sugar 2 tsp
double cream 2 tbsp

1. Stir the coffee, whiskey and sugar together and pour into heatproof glasses. Pour the cream over the back of a spoon, in a steady stream on to the coffee so that it floats on top.

Preparation time: 5 min   **Cals per serving:** 124   **Serves:** 2

Spiced Coffee

1. Place the sugar, orange and lemon rind, cinnamon stick, cloves and brandy in a small pan with 30ml (2 tablespoons) of water. Heat gently until just steaming, then remove from the heat and allow to infuse for 10 minutes.

2. Add the coffee, then strain into heatproof glasses. Pour the cream over the back of a spoon so that it floats on top. Serve with cinnamon sticks for stirring, if liked.

Preparation time: 15 min   **Cals per serving:** 134   **Serves:** 2

demerara sugar 1 tbsp
orange 1, rind peeled in strips
lemon 1, rind peeled in strips
cinnamon stick 1
cloves 3
brandy 2 tbsp
strong hot coffee 400ml (14fl oz)
double cream 2 tbsp, to serve
cinnamon sticks 2, to serve, optional

Fresh Hot Mocha

cocoa powder 2 tbsp
instant coffee granules 2 tsp
granulated sugar 2 tsp
semi-skimmed milk 350ml (12fl oz)
mini marshmallows 15g (½oz)

1. Place the cocoa, coffee and sugar in a small pan. Stir in enough cold milk to form a smooth paste, then whisk in the remaining milk.

2. Place over a medium heat and heat gently, whisking occasionally. When bubbles appear around the edge, whisk quickly to froth the milk. Serve in mugs and top with the marshmallows.

Preparation time: 10 min   **Cals per serving:** 170   **Serves:** 2

Spiced Coffee

Index

Page numbers in italics indicate recipe photographs.

Picture Credits and Acknowledgements

Picture Credits

Page references for the dishes appearing on the chapter openers are given below. All special photography is by Frank Wieder with the exception of the following pictures from Good Housekeeping/National Magazine Company Limited:

Wake-up Calls

Buttermilk Pancakes p.41
Mike O'Toole p.17; Roger Stowell p.25

Midweek Meals

Cheat's Courgette and Goat's Cheese Pizza p.101
Steve Baxter pp.117, 121 and 131; Jean Cazals pp.95, 99 and 135; William Lingwood p.125; James Murphy p.113; Elizabeth Zeschin pp.85, 103 and 107

Main Events

Easy Rack of Lamb p.204
Steve Baxter pp.201 and 211; Martin Brigdale p.183; Jean Cazals pp.205 and 239; William Lingwood p.197; David Munns p.243; James Murphy p.175; Philip Webb pp.179 and 187; Elizabeth Zeschin p.235

Liquid Refreshments

The Best Fruit Milk Shakes p.290

Snack Attacks

Cherry Chip Cookies p.56
David Munns pp.49 and 61; Philip Webb pp.65 and 69

Packed to Go

Sushi p.149
Steve Baxter p.141; Jean Cazals pp.147 and 151; Philip Webb p.169

Sweet Things

Plum Tarte Tatin p.255
Jean Cazals pp.249 and 275; Laurie Evans p.253; Philip Webb pp.257 and 279

Acknowledgements

All recipes are taken from the GHI Archives with the exception of those appearing on pp. 164-68 and 288-96, developed by Jacqueline Bellefontaine. Special thanks to Sarah Collins and Sausage for their assistance on shoots.

Recipe Selector and Editor	Jo Younger
Assistant Editor	Victoria Webb
Index	Sue Bosanko
Typesetting	Michelle Pickering
Layout Designer	Liz Brown
Special Photography	Frank Wieder
Styling	Susan Downing
Home Economist	Jacqueline Bellefontaine